Social Forces in the Making of the New Europe

International Political Economy Series

General Editor: **Timothy M. Shaw**, Professor of Political Science and International Development Studies, Dalhousie University, Halifax, Nova Scotia

Titles include:

Andreas Bieler and Adam David Morton (*editors*)
SOCIAL FORCES IN THE MAKING OF THE NEW EUROPE
The Restructuring of European Social Relations in the Global Political Economy

Steve Chan and A. Cooper Drury (*editors*)
SANCTIONS AS ECONOMIC STATECRAFT
Theory and Practice

Aldo Chircop, André Gerolymatos and John O. Iatrides
THE AEGEAN SEA AFTER THE COLD WAR
Security and Law of the Sea Issues

Diane Ethier
ECONOMIC ADJUSTMENT IN NEW DEMOCRACIES
Lessons from Southern Europe

Jeffrey Henderson (*editor*)
INDUSTRIAL TRANSFORMATION IN EASTERN EUROPE IN THE LIGHT OF
THE EAST ASIAN EXPERIENCE

Jacques Hersh and Johannes Dragsbaek Schmidt (*editors*)
THE AFTERMATH OF 'REAL EXISTING SOCIALISM' IN EASTERN EUROPE
Volume 1: Between Western Europe and East Asia

Anne Lorentzen and Marianne Rostgaard (*editors*)
THE AFTERMATH OF 'REAL EXISTING SOCIALISM' IN EASTERN EUROPE
Volume 2: People and Technology in the Process of Transition

Gary McMahon (*editor*)
LESSONS IN ECONOMIC POLICY FOR EASTERN EUROPE FROM
LATIN AMERICA

Árni Sverrison and Meine Pieter van Dijk (*editors*)
LOCAL ECONOMIES IN TURMOIL
The Effect of Deregulation and Globalization

International Political Economy Series
Series Standing Order ISBN 0–333–71708–2 hardcover
Series Standing Order ISBN 0–333–71110–6 paperback
(*outside North America only*)

You can receive future titles in this series as they are published by placing a standing order. Please contact your bookseller or, in case of difficulty, write to us at the address below with your name and address, the title of the series and one of the ISBNs quoted above.

Customer Services Department, Macmillan Distribution Ltd, Houndmills, Basingstoke, Hampshire RG21 6XS, England

Social Forces in the Making of the New Europe

The Restructuring of European Social Relations in the Global Political Economy

Edited by

Andreas Bieler
Lecturer in the School of Politics
University of Nottingham

and

Adam David Morton
Department of International Politics
The University of Wales
Aberystwyth

Foreword by Robert W. Cox

First published 2001 by
PALGRAVE
Houndmills, Basingstoke, Hampshire RG21 6XS and
175 Fifth Avenue, New York, N. Y. 10010
Companies and representatives throughout the world

PALGRAVE is the new global academic imprint of
St. Martin's Press LLC Scholarly and Reference Division and
Palgrave Publishers Ltd (formerly Macmillan Press Ltd).

ISBN 0–333–91321–3 hardback
ISBN 0–333–92067–8 paperback

This book is printed on paper suitable for recycling and
made from fully managed and sustained forest sources.

A catalogue record for this book is available
from the British Library.

Library of Congress Cataloging-in-Publication Data
Social forces in the making of the new Europe : the restructuring
of European social relations in the global political economy / edited
by Andreas Bieler and Adam David Morton.
     p. cm. — (International political economy)
     Includes bibliographical references and index.
     ISBN 0–333–91321–3 (cloth)
     1. Social change—Europe. 2. Europe—Economic integration–
     –Social aspects. 3. Capitalism—Social aspects—Europe.
     4. Globalization. I. Bieler, Andreas, 1967– II. Morton, Adam David,
     1971– III. Series in international political economy.
     HN377 .S63 2001
     303.4′094—dc21
                                                         2001027369

10   9   8   7   6   5   4   3   2   1
10   09 08 07 06 05 04 03 02 01

Printed in Great Britain by Antony Rowe Ltd, Chippenham, Wiltshire

One cannot expect an individual or a book to change reality but only to interpret and to indicate the possible lines of action

Antonio Gramsci

Contents

Foreword

The purpose of this book is to analyse the balance of social forces in Europe in order both to identify the prevailing structure of power at the beginning of the twenty-first century and the possibilities of transforming that structure so as to enhance social equity and democratic control.

The different authors of the chapters which follow approach their task free of any determinism in a conviction that history is open ended, made by people in conditions not of their own choosing. There is no preordained 'end of history'; but change in socially desirable directions is constrained by powerful forces, forces which themselves are in constant mutation. The key to desirable change is to understand the contradictions and movements among existing social and political forces as a basis for a strategy of action.

The contributors are inspired by the thinking of Antonio Gramsci who, in his prison confinement, analysed the social and political context of his own time and place with a view to constructing a coherent bloc of emancipatory social forces. They in no sense appeal dogmatically to Gramsci's text as a model to be rigorously followed. Their tribute to Gramsci is to insert themselves, as he did in his own circumstances, into the flow of history to see how they might act upon it.

The initial conclusions of their exploration demonstrate that there are very considerable obstacles to the effective pursuit of their goals of social equity and democratic control. The Europe of the original Community was shaped by the corporatist institutions and Keynesian policies characteristic of the post-Second World War period. One might have imagined a social Europe with increasingly democratic institutions growing out of this foundation. By the mid-1970s, however, a rift emerged in the capitalism of the Atlantic world, as a more radical neo-liberal economic doctrine of a markedly expansionary kind became dominant in American and British policy. Michel Albert published his *Capitalisme contre capitalisme* in 1991 (Paris: Seuil), in which he portrayed Europe as the site of a duel between an aggressive Anglo–American globally competitive capitalism and a 'Rhineland' and 'Alpine' form of capitalism more socially oriented and managed through corporatist institutions.

By the end of the century, the Anglo–American form seemed to have become the principal form in Europe. In June 2000, the president of the Deutsche Bank, pre-eminent among the forces of European capitalism, proclaimed the demise of the 'Rhineland model', in a rather more regretful than triumphal tone. The cause of death, he said, was globalisation which imposed on all national structures the need to change in order to become more competitive. With reference to the Anglo-Saxon model, he added: 'We have a different history, culture, ways of living together, and of employer–employee relations. We have to invent a different model' (*Le Monde*, 1 June 2000).

The studies in this book underline the social consequences of neo-liberal globalisation: an increasing gap between rich and poor, unemployment, and underfunding of social services as governments strive to balance their budgets. Most insidious in the long run is what Stephen Gill calls the 'new constitutionalism' whereby international and regional enactments, conceived in the neo-liberal vision of a self-regulating world economy, remove economic processes from political (and hence from social) control.

The mobility of capital has top priority. The mobility of people is subordinated to the needs of capital through 'ordered mobility' (see Chapter 7, by Hélène Pellerin and Henk Overbeek). The demands of competitiveness trump those of social need.

Nevertheless, despite the individualist competitive view of the world propagated in neo-liberal ideology, a sense of social solidarity and social justice remains entrenched in the minds of European people; and this puts a limit on the excesses of the currently dominant tendency. This limit was manifested in the social movement in France of December 1995 which brought about a reversal of government policy; and again in the election of left-leaning governments in France, Germany and Italy some three years later. These demonstrations of public opinion may constitute a kind of popular veto on socially punitive consequences of economic policy. However, a coherent and consistent means of articulating an alternative has been lacking.

So hegemonic have neo-liberal ideas of economic management become that leaders of the left have basically accepted them. They have come forward with a compromise which attempts to maintain a certain level of social services while endorsing measures to encourage flexibility in the labour market consistent with neo-liberal principles. Trade unions of the more established workers, hoping to benefit from the competitiveness of European exports in the world market, have supported this policy, which has been called variously the 'Third Way' or the 'New Middle'. It seems to be the trend in Europe at the beginning of the twenty-first century.

The social market tradition remains firmly embedded in the 'common sense' of European people, but their political leaders attempt to reconcile it with the blandishments of neo-liberal economic theory and the power and influence of globalising capital. In the words of Bastiaan van Apeldoorn, this is 'the emerging hegemonic project of Europe's transnational capitalist class', a project for which the leaders of major European political parties of the (former) left have been the ideological messengers.

This new hegemonic project leaves space for social content; but as Hans-Jürgen Bieling argues, 'social Europe' remains largely symbolic. The divisions among workers cut across the smaller European countries as well. Those in the export sectors tend to support the trend, while those depending upon the domestic markets are more reluctant (see Chapter 6, by Andreas Bieler and Stina Torjesen). Established workers may be co-opted into the new 'historical bloc' (note the editors' definition of this term) while other workers, the unemployed and the social movements are left out. But even the established workers do not have effective participation in decision making. The 'democratic deficit' remains great and is not limited to electoral politics. The editors conclude in the final chapter that only when European trade unions reject neo-liberalism and combine with social movements can a true alternative emerge.

Europe's future will be shaped through the interaction of external and internal forces. The force of globalisation – which is both external and internal – is present in the analyses of all the contributors. Kees van der Pijl draws attention also to the geopolitical context and the dilemmas it raises for Europe. This has to do primarily with America's position in Europe and in the world. Will Europe be an adjunct to American global power, the military power that underwrites global capital? Or will Europe become an independent force in the world, claiming the space to evolve its own social project and economic organisation in co-existence with America and with the evolving societies in other parts of the world? The Kosovo war put these questions to the test; but the answer has been equivocal. The North Atlantic Treaty Organisation (NATO) observed its fiftieth anniversary not by recognising that its purpose in the Cold War had been accomplished but, with the support of major European powers, by extending its geographical sphere and implicitly its role as protector of global capital. On the other hand, the experience of Kosovo can be seen as a stimulus to Europe to develop its own independent military capability so as not to remain dependent on American air power which, in the Kosovo case, proved not to be a very effective weapon. NATO expansion into Eastern Europe and its influence in the Ukraine and the oil-rich Caucasus region pre-empts the European project of integrating Eastern Europe into the EU (see Chapter 8 by Otto Holman).

All this points to a situation in which Europe faces serious odds in reaffirming its identity as a civilisation. There is a universal top-down force of global capital supported by military power and the diffusion of popular culture through communications media which is creating a single homogeneous business-dominated civilisation. Against that is the vision of a pluralistic world of co-existing civilisations, each autonomously pursuing its own internally empowered social and economic trajectory. Europe is the key actor in this drama. The forces for homogeneity on the American model seem to be dominant; however, as the editors write in Chapter 10, historical blocs are never static but always fluid. One cannot discount a reversal of the relative strength of the forces which shape society. A first condition for reversal is that the challengers become fully conscious of their opportunities. The best chance for a pluralistic world and for freeing up the creative forces in other civilisations – in Russia, China, Japan, South and South-East Asia, Africa and Latin America, and even deep in the heart of America – lies now in Europe, in the struggle to be fought for independence and for an alternative vision of society. Europeans are not the only people who will be affected by the outcome.

ROBERT W. COX
Toronto

Acknowledgements

This book is as much a focus on collective social forces in the making of the 'New Europe' as it is a product of collective effort and struggle.

Along the way we have benefited greatly from the advice and comments given by various people. In particular we would like to thank Pinar Bilgin, Pauline Ewan, Stephen Gill, Steve Hobden and Anne Showstack Sassoon for reading and commenting on parts of the manuscript and thus playing a crucial role in formulating our ideas and approach. We also greatly appreciated, in the very early stages, some initial comments about the project from Steve Smith.

Further thanks are due to Nicola Viinikka and her team at Palgrave, to Timothy Straw for his ongoing encouragement as series editor, and to Keith Povey for his astute and detailed work as copy-editor. We are also indebted to Renzo Galeotti, artist of the book cover, for providing a wide range of his paintings for selection.

Permission to reprint and edit the original version of Chapter 3 was gratefully received from Tony Payne, Managing Editor of *New Political Economy*. This was originally published as Stephen Gill, 'European Governance and New Constitutionalism: Economic and Monetary Union and Alternatives to Disciplinary Neoliberalism in Europe', *New Political Economy*, 3:1 (1998), 5–26.

Adam David Morton acknowledges financial assistance from the Economic and Social Research Council and we would both like to thank Selwyn and Newnham Colleges, Cambridge, and the University of Wales, Aberystwyth, for institutional support.

Special thanks are due to Robert Cox for not only agreeing to contribute a foreword to the volume and commenting on previous versions of the editors' joint chapters, but also for instilling a greater degree of invigorated social engagement in and beyond many of the debates addressed in this book. We feel we are not alone in acknowledging a debt to Cox whilst at the same time trying to consider new questions and push critical analysis into additional avenues.

Finally, we would like to thank all the contributors to this volume as well as Cecilia and Julie for their patience and support in helping us to see this project to fruition.

ANDREAS BIELER (*Cambridge*)
ADAM DAVID MORTON (*Aberystwyth*)

Notes on the Contributors

Bastiaan van Apeldoorn is Lecturer in International Relations, Vrije Universiteit, Amsterdam (Netherlands). His main research interests are the political economy of European integration, processes of transnational capitalist class formation and the globalisation of capital. His work has been published in the *Journal of European Public Policy* (with Martin Rhodes), the *International Journal of Political Economy* and in an edited book by Richard Stubbs and Geoffrey Underhill, *Political Economy and the Changing Global Order* (2000).

Andreas Bieler was formerly Lecturer and Director of Studies in Social and Political Sciences at Newnham and Selwyn College, University of Cambridge, and is now Lecturer in the School of Politics at the University of Nottingham. He is author of *Globalisation and Enlargement of the European Union* (2000), and co-editor (with Richard Higgott and Geoffrey Underhill) of *Non-State Actors and Authority in the Global System* (2000).

Hans-Jürgen Bieling is Research Fellow in the Political Science Department at the Philipps University in Marburg. He is currently completing a research project on the dynamics of regime competition in the area of industrial relations within the European Union, which is sponsored by the DFG (German Research Community). He is co-editor (with Frank Deppe) of *Arbeitslosigkeit und Wohlfahrtsstaat in Westeuropa. Neun Länder im Vergleich* (1997) and author of *Dynamiken Sozialer Spaltung und Ausgrenzung: Gesellschaftstheorien und Zeitdiagnosen* (2000).

Robert W. Cox is Professor Emeritus of Political Science at York University, Toronto. His early career was in the International Labour Office from which he resigned as an Assistant Director-General in 1972. Before joining the York faculty, he was Professor of International Organisation at Columbia University, New York (1972–7). His best known books are *Production, Power and World Order: Social Forces in the Making of History* (1987) and (with Timothy Sinclair) *Approaches to World Order* (1996). Latterly he has been interested in civilisations and gave the plenary lecture to the December 1999 conference of the British International Studies Association on 'Thinking About Civilisations'.

Stephen Gill is Professor of Political Science at York University, Toronto, Canada, specialising in international political economy and international relations. Amongst others his publications include *The Global Political Economy* (co-authored with David Law, 1988); *Atlantic Relations: Beyond the Reagan Era* (ed., 1989); *American Hegemony and the Trilateral Commission* (1990); *Gramsci, Historical Materialism and International Relations* (ed., 1993); *Restructuring Global Politics* (1996, in Japanese, translated by Seiji Endo); *Globalisation, Democratisation and Multilateralism* (ed., 1997); and *Innovation and Transformation in International Studies* (co-edited with James Mittelman, 1997). He is now completing a new book entitled *The Constitution of Global Capitalism.*

Otto Holman is Senior Lecturer in International Relations at the University of Amsterdam. His publications in English include *Integrating Southern Europe* (1996) and two special issues of the *International Journal of Political Economy* (co-edited with Henk Overbeek and Magnus Ryner, 1998). He is co-editor of the *Review of International Political Economy* series in Global Political Economy (Routledge).

Adam David Morton was recently awarded his PhD as a graduate within the Department of International Politics at the University of Wales, Aberystwyth. His thesis focuses on the construction and contestation of hegemony in Mexico and the global political economy. He has published in the *European Journal of International Relations* (with Andreas Bieler), the journal *Politics* and in an edited volume by Barry K. Gills, *Globalisation and the Politics of Resistance* (2000).

Henk Overbeek is Senior Lecturer in International Relations, Vrije Universiteit, Amsterdam (Netherlands). His interests are in international political economy and European integration. His publications include *Global Capitalism and National Decline* (1990), *Restructuring Hegemony in the Global Political Economy* (ed., 1993) and two special issues of the *International Journal of Political Economy* (co-edited with Otto Holman and Magnus Ryner, 1998). He is co-editor of the *Review of International Political Economy* series in Global Political Economy (Routledge).

Hélène Pellerin is Assistant Professor in Political Science at Ottawa University. She works on questions of international migration and international political economy, with a particular focus on the regulatory mechanisms at the regional and international level of migration flows and policies. She has published in *Third World Quarterly* and *Review of International Political Economy.*

Kees van der Pijl is Professor of International Relations at the University of Sussex. His work deals with transnational classes and world politics and with the history of international relations theory. He is the author of *The Making of an Atlantic Ruling Class* (1984) and *Transnational Classes and International Relations* (1998).

Stina Torjesen recently completed her undergraduate degree in Social and Political Sciences at Trinity College, University of Cambridge (June 2000). Her dissertation focused on Norwegian trade unions in the global political economy. She continues her studies with an MPhil in International Relations at the University of Oxford starting in October 2001.

List of Abbreviations

AF	Federation of Norwegian Professional Associations
AK	Chamber of Labour (Austria)
AMUE	Association for Monetary Union in Europe
APEC	Asia and Pacific Economic Co-operation
BEC	Business Enlargement Council
BIS	Bank for International Settlements
CAG	Competitiveness Advisory Group
CDU	Christian Democrat Union (Germany)
CEE	Central and Eastern Europe
CEO	Chief Executive Officer
CFSP	Common Foreign and Security Policy
EC	European Commission
ECB	European Central Bank
ECJ	European Court of Justice
ECLAC	Economic Commission for Latin America and the Caribbean
EEA	European Economic Area
EEG	European Enterprise Group
EFTA	European Free Trade Area
EMF	European Metalworkers' Federation
EMS	European Monetary System
EMU	Economic and Monetary Union
ERT	European Round Table of Industrialists
ETUC	European Trade Union Congress
EU	European Union
FDI	Foreign Direct Investment
FF	*Fellesforbundet* (Norway)
FPÖ	Austrian Freedom Party
FTAA	Free Trade Area of the Americas
GATT	General Agreement on Tariffs and Trade
GPA	White Collar Workers' Union (Austria)
GUUAM	Georgia, Ukraine, Uzbekistan, Azerbaijan and Moldova
G-7	Group of Seven
HK	*Handel og Kontor* (Norway)
ICMPD	International Centre for Migration Policy Development
IGC	Intergovernmental Conference

IMF	International Monetary Fund
IOM	International Organisation for Migration
IPE	International Political Economy
IR	International Relations
KF	*Kommuneforbundet* (Norway)
LI	Liberal Intergovernmentalism
LO-N	Norwegian Confederation of Trade Unions
LO-S	Swedish Trade Union Confederation
NAALC	North American Agreement on Labour Co-operation
NAFTA	North American Free Trade Agreement
NATO	North Atlantic Treaty Organisation
NIDL	New International Division of Labour
NNN	*Norsk Nearings og Nytelsesmiddelarberiderforbund* (Norway)
NOPF	*Norsk Olje og Petrokjemisk Fagforbund* (Norway)
NTF	*Norsk Transportarbeiderforbund* (Norway)
OECD	Organisation for Economic Co-operation and Development
ÖGB	Austrian Federation of Trade Unions
OSCE	Organisation for Security and Co-operation in Europe
R&D	Research and Development
RCM	Regional Conference on Migration
SACO	Swedish Confederation of Professional Associations
SDI	Strategic Defence Initiative
SEA	Single European Act
SPD	Social Democratic Party (Germany)
TCO	Swedish Confederation of Professional Employees
TEU	Treaty of European Union
TINA	there is no alternative
TNCs	Transnational Corporations
UNCTAD	United Nations Conference on Trade and Development
UNHCR	United Nations High Commissioner for Refugees
UNICE	Union of Industrial and Employers' Confederations of Europe
WTO	World Trade Organisation
YS	Confederations of Vocational Unions (Norway)

Part I

Theoretical Concepts and Methodological Issues

1
Introduction: Neo-Gramscian Perspectives in International Political Economy and the Relevance to European Integration

Andreas Bieler and Adam David Morton

Introduction

After two decades of relative stagnation, European integration experienced a dramatic revival in the mid-1980s. In 1985, the Commission published its famous White Paper, *Completing the Internal Market*, which proposed 300 (later reduced to 279) measures designed to facilitate progress towards the completion of the Internal Market by 1992 through the abolition of non-tariff barriers. The Single European Act (SEA) of 1987 not only spelt out the goals of the Internal Market – that is, the four freedoms of goods, services, capital and labour – but it also strengthened the supranational institutions. The European Court of Justice (ECJ), for example, became the arbiter of the Internal Market, while the European Parliament gained a second reading and the chance to influence legislation through amendments with the introduction of the co-operation procedure. In addition, the Treaty of Maastricht was signed in 1991. Amongst other changes, it laid out the plan for Economic and Monetary Union (EMU), including a single currency to be administered by a supranational and independent European Central Bank (ECB). In other words, member states decided to give up monetary sovereignty. In January 1999, 11 member states carried out this step when they irrevocably fixed their exchange rates. At Maastricht, further steps were also taken towards a Common Foreign and Security Policy (CFSP) which, although it is still mainly organised along intergovernmental lines, could imply further future pooling and transfer of sovereignty related to defence. Finally, in the 1995 enlargement, the

European Union (EU) was extended to include Austria, Sweden and Finland and further enlargements are currently under negotiation with Central and Eastern European, and also Mediterranean, countries. In short, since 1985 the deepening and widening of integration has gone hand in hand with consolidating and expanding the EU's reach within and beyond Europe.

The main argument of this book is that the revival of European integration in the mid-1980s and the emergence of a 'New Europe' have to be analysed against the background of globalisation and the transnational restructuring of social forces since the early 1970s. Briefly, globalisation can be defined as the transnationalisation of production and finance at the material level and the shift from Keynesianism to neo-liberalism at the ideological level (Cox, 1993: 259–60, 266–7). First, the rise of financial offshore markets since the 1960s, expanding significantly between 1973 and 1984 (Strange, 1994: 107), in combination with the deregulation of national financial markets in the late 1970s but especially in the 1980s (Helleiner, 1994), led to the emergence of an integrated global financial market. Second, the growth of transnational corporations (TNCs), in numbers and size, has driven the transnational organisation of production. Their increasing importance is expressed in the rise of foreign direct investment (FDI). Outflows of FDI rose from $88 billion to $225 billion between 1986 and 1990, which is an annual increase of 26 per cent (United Nations Conference on Trade and Development, or UNCTAD, 1992: 14). There was a downturn in FDI in 1991 and 1992, mainly due to recessions in the biggest economies, but it picked up again from 1993 onwards and reached $424 billion in 1997 (UNCTAD, 1998: 2). A study of TNCs by the UN concluded, in 1992, that 'the growth of cross-national production networks of goods and services of some 35,000 transnational corporations and their more than 150,000 foreign affiliates is beginning to give rise to a [transnational] production system, organised and managed by transnational corporations' (UNCTAD, 1992: 5). These figures further increased to 53,607 parent corporations and 448,917 foreign affiliates by 1997 (UNCTAD, 1998: 4). Finally, a neo-liberal, monetarist policy replaced Keynesianism from the mid-1970s onwards, when it had become clear that the latter's expansionary response to the economic crisis of the early 1970s had failed. Efficiency and price stability are the new priorities. This includes advocacy, at the national level, of the privatisation of state-controlled enterprises and the liberalisation and deregulation of the economy; the imposition of social order rather than negotiation; and little or no commitment to redistribution or social reform.[1]

Global in its nature, this structural change has not left the EU unaffected. As elsewhere, globalisation has led to a transnational restructuring of social relations. The deregulation of national financial markets was institutionalised in the Internal Market programme, which stated that all remaining capital controls of member states had to be abolished by 1 July 1990. Only Greece and Portugal were given an extended period (until the end of 1995). Moreover, the significance of Euro-companies has increased drastically in economic and employment terms since the 1980s. The transnationalisation of production has not only affected countries such as the UK and the Netherlands, which were always characterised by the presence of TNCs, but also France and Germany (Marginson and Sisson, 1994: 18–23). Finally, the shift towards neo-liberalism was expressed by the very nature of the Internal Market programme and its drive for liberalisation and deregulation and the neo-liberal convergence criteria of EMU, focusing on low inflation and price stability (see Chapter 5 below; for the link between EMU and globalistion, see Chapter 3 below). Gill infers that 'an assessment of the recomposition of social structures and political arrangements during the 1960s, 1970s and 1980s is crucial to understanding the complexities of the "new" Europe' (Gill, 1992: 159; see also Holman and van der Pijl, 1996: 65–6; Rosamond, 1995).

We will argue that established theories of integration – neofunctionalism and intergovernmentalism – are unable to explain such instances of structural change, because they are deterministic and take existing power structures as given. Although there is a vast range of literature on the emergence of the 'New Europe' (*inter alia* George, 1996; Hoffmann and Keohane, 1991; Nugent, 1999; Richardson, 1996; Sbragia, 1992), it rarely goes beyond these mainstream approaches. Consequently, the first aim of this book is to introduce an alternative approach in order to analyse the revival of European integration. This alternative approach will involve drawing upon and developing what we refer to as a neo-Gramscian perspective, which was first introduced within the field of International Political Economy (IPE) by Robert Cox in the early 1980s (Cox, 1981, 1983).

By advancing upon the general conceptual framework of the Italian Marxist Antonio Gramsci, Cox attempted to explain the operation of hegemony at the international level as well as to consider change and transformation in world order. Since then, a host of related perspectives have emerged to focus on aspects of the global political economy and the rise of neo-liberalism (*inter alia* Augelli and Murphy, 1988; Cox, 1987; Cox with Sinclair, 1996; Davies, 1999; Gill, 1990, 1993;

Morton, 2000; Murphy, 1994; Robinson, 1996; Rupert, 1995; Stienstra, 1994; Whitworth, 1994). Moreover, initial attempts have also been made to explain aspects of European integration with the help of neo-Gramscian perspectives (*inter alia* van Apeldoorn, 1999; Bieler, 2000; Cox, 1993; Gill, 1998; Holman, 1992, 1996; Holman, Overbeek and Ryner, 1998; Holman and van der Pijl, 1996; Ryner, 1999). Such neo-Gramscian perspectives focus on social forces, engendered by the production process, as the most important collective actors. This, first, makes structural changes such as globalisation accessible, since the emergence of new social forces engendered by the transnationalisation of production and finance can be incorporated. Second, neo-Gramscian perspectives focus on class struggle as the heuristic model for the understanding of structural change. It is therefore realised that there are no inevitable developments in history. Instances of European integration are as much the outcome of an open-ended struggle as are other political developments.

Recent scholarship has focused on the relation of these perspectives to the work of Antonio Gramsci (Germain and Kenny, 1998), and elsewhere some have criticised the lack of historical materialist rigour (*inter alia* Burnham, 1991, 1994, 1997, 1999; H. Smith, 1996). Nevertheless, the similarities and differences between the various perspectives have hardly been discussed. The second aim of this book is, therefore, to focus in more detail on the way these perspectives theoretically and empirically engage with issues linked to European integration in similar, yet diverse, ways. We propose that those works commonly recognised as neo-Gramscian should avoid either accepting imposed labels or self-styling themselves as a discrete methodological 'school' claiming to overcome the failures of orthodox IPE. Hence, instead, the stress on a modest alternative which places emphasis on divergent neo-Gramscian *perspectives*, representing a plurality of approaches with numerous differences. Elsewhere, attention will be drawn to the inadequacies of other labels and, in particular, the political consequences surrounding the formation of intellectual 'schools' (see Chapter 2, by Adam David Morton).

For the present discussion, however, we will concentrate on three interrelated issues linked to the development of such neo-Gramscian perspectives in IPE. First, we place an emphasis on developing a particular 'reading' of Gramsci rather than a representative interpretation. Within this discussion, following Stuart Hall (1986, 1988a, 1991, 1997), the importance of thinking in a Gramscian way about similar problems in our own time is discussed. We will also sketch what might be historically *limited* in any undertaking that attempts to realise the practical and theoretical importance of a Gramscian way of thinking about present circumstances (Showstack Sassoon, 1995). Next, we develop criticisms of established theories of European integration before moving on to argue how a Gramscian way of thinking can provide an alternative, more comprehensive, route to considering contemporary processes of European integration and the restructuring of social relations within the global context of structural change.

Reading Gramsci on a historicist sense of thought and action

The writings of Gramsci have garnered a great deal of interest across debates in political theory and IPE. Yet, despite the diversity of issues raised by such debates, similar arguments have been made concerning the demand to return Gramsci and his ideas to the historical context which he occupied, to historicise Gramsci, before discerning any contemporary relevance (see respectively Bellamy, 1987, 1990, 1992, 1994; Bellamy and Schecter, 1993; Germain and Kenny, 1998; Martin, 1998). Such demands result in what has been recognised as an 'austere historicism' that gives the impression of preventing any appreciation of the contemporary strategic relevance of Gramsci's work (Morton, 1999).[2] This term aims to encapsulate the reductionist tendency of dissolving Gramsci's writings into the past without appreciating or developing a contemporary resonance that may transcend socio-historical context. As Joseph Femia has stated, 'an insistence on historicity is one thing; an a priori determination to fossilise all past quite another' (Femia, 1981a: 17; cf. Femia, 1998). Yet how is it possible to develop an approach to understanding the practical and theoretical context of Gramsci's work whilst remaining attentive to issues and problems of contemporary importance? On such matters inspiration can be drawn directly from Gramsci himself, which is the necessary first step towards thinking in a Gramscian way. However, as we will develop a particular reading from his writings, a few comments about how we proceed to 'read' a text will be developed first.

Any explication of Gramsci's method and philosophy cannot objectively reveal a 'true' or 'real' Gramsci and hence no 'correct' reading or 'authentic' version can be produced. After all, the understanding developed here is reliant on a translation of Gramsci's writings. Moreover, it is also circumscribed by specific interests and particular purposes, as indeed are all social science approaches. Yet does this mean that

each interpretation is as provisional and acceptable as the next interpretation? Put another way, whilst a level of impartiality cannot be
claimed, is an interpreter justified in arbitrarily shaping the text to suit
preconceptions?

The task incumbent upon any of us when interpreting writings from
the past is to maximise the significance of the historical experiences
through which concepts have been formed, and to recognise the
importance of historical context, whilst also appreciating that past
ideas may still have a bearing on the present. Therefore, in accord with
Joseph Femia, a historicist approach needs to be developed that prevents exegetical mistakes, or the outright distortion or disregard for
historical conditions and exigencies, whilst also enabling the interpreter to treat texts as vehicles for the exercise of certain preoccupa-
tions (Femia, 1981b: 130). This position can be developed further by
examining some of the methodological criteria Gramsci himself
regarded as important when developing interpretive readings of texts.

In bringing his own interpretation to particular texts, notably
Dante's *Inferno*, Gramsci displayed a clear awareness that any interpretation develops observations that are 'unexpressed' or lie inert in the
text. The active process of interpretation develops certain positions
that are non-existent within the structure of a text. Objections against
this interpretative method are certainly possible and Gramsci recognised that they would have a 'semblance of truth'. Such objections
would be especially warranted as a 'richness of expression', producing
equivocal or ambiguous assertions in a text, can become 'mutilated by
a lack of understanding'. Yet, despite these possible objections, Gramsci
still posed the question of whether a text is reconstructed and criticised
in any other way than in the historical moment in which it is received,
in the 'world of concrete expression' (Gramsci, 1985: 153–4, 267–9).

However, by moving away from the notion that the interpretation of
a text is limitless, that no one reading is better than any other, Gramsci
also condemned attempts to go 'beyond what is conveyed by the letter
of the text', making 'bizarre additions' that glide over the text. Instead,
the recommendation is to re-read the text and ascertain its meaning
(ibid.: 119–21, 372, 375). Hence Gramsci strongly warned against the
prose of commentators altering the meaning of the text (ibid.: 156–61).
These extreme positions of interpretive method notably come together
in Gramsci's writings when dealing with issues of theatre criticism.
A Shakespearean tragedy, argued Gramsci, can be given various theatrical interpretations, leading to varying forms of originality, but there is
nevertheless the 'printed' book form which exists independently from

the theatrical performance (ibid.: 140). Therefore, different readers according to changing circumstances can generate alternative readings of a text, but the text itself – the 'printed' book form – has an independent existence separate from its readership. These points are interestingly brought together in exactly this manner by the arguments of Edward Said on the worldliness of a text or the relationship between text and history (Said, 1983a).

All texts have a certain 'worldliness', a situation placed in the world, that restrains what can be done with them interpretively. The example of Shakespeare is also invoked by Said when he states:

> Each age ... re-interprets Shakespeare, not because Shakespeare changes, but because, despite the existence of numerous reliable editions of Shakespeare, there is no such fixed and non-trivial object as Shakespeare independent of his editors, ... the translators who put him in other languages, [and] the hundreds of millions who have read him. (Said, 1985: 3)

However, despite this emphasis, Said goes on to lend credence to Gramsci's position by stating, 'on the other hand, it is too much to say that Shakespeare has no independent existence at all, and that he is completely reconstituted every time someone reads ... or writes about him'. Instead, 'even so relatively inert an object as a literary text is commonly supposed to gain some of its identity from its historical moment interacting with the attentions, judgements, scholarship and performances of its readers' (ibid.: 3–4). This is a more prudent and historicist approach to issues of interpretation that both shares common assumptions with Gramsci's own criteria of interpretive method and is also useful in developing an understanding of his own writings. It is also consistent with the *absolute historicism* of Gramsci, an approach to the history of ideas and concrete political activity that conceived the historical process as a synthesis of past and present.

One of the hallmarks of the thinking of Gramsci has been his expression of a dialectical understanding of absolute historicism (Gramsci, 1971: 380). Yet to pluck one floating citation as an example of this understanding precludes an appropriate appreciation of the complexity of Gramsci's articulation of absolute historicism. For instance, in one of the few direct citations on this area, Gramsci stated (ibid.: 465): 'The philosophy of praxis is absolute "historicism", the absolute secularisation of thought, an absolute humanism of history. It is along this line that one must trace the thread of the new conception of the world.'

Yet, as Esteve Morera has noted, Gramsci's absolute historicism is not so absolute (Morera, 1990: 130): for instance, in his prison letters he argued – 'in a realistic and historicist sense' – that there was a 'certain lucidity' to the position that the soul has an immortal essence, 'as a necessary survival of our useful and necessary actions and their becoming incorporated, beyond our will, with the universal historical process' (Gramsci, 1994: 314). This kind of emphasis becomes apparent when a wider reading of a more integral text of the *Prison Notebooks* is conducted, therefore following, in a sense, Gramsci's own recommendation to return and re-read a text to ascertain its meaning.

One of the impressions throughout a reading of the *Prison Notebooks* is that the writings are suffused with sub-titled references to '*Past and Present*', for example:

How the present is a *criticism* of the past, besides [and because of] 'surpassing' it. But should the past be discarded for this reason? What should be discarded is that which the present 'intrinsically' criticised and that part of ourselves which corresponds to it. What does this mean? That we must have an exact consciousness of this real criticism and express it not only theoretically but *politically*. In other words, we must stick closer to the present, which we ourselves have helped create, while conscious of the past and its continuation (and revival) (Gramsci, 1992: 234; original emphasis).

Already a more nuanced position is established which is borne out by closer scrutiny – or a re-reading – of the text. It is therefore possible to acknowledge a historicist approach that combines the old and new within the social relations of a particular situation to the extent that in every historical phase there is a recurrence of certain questions from previous phases.

To make the point more explicit, a historicist approach to philosophical activity based on critical reflection was conceived by Gramsci which acknowledged the role played by past and existing forms of thought linked to the actual relations in the world which produced them *and* in which they were received. Such reflection is therefore not simply abstract and intellectual but concrete social activity in which ideas become a material force (ibid.: 165; Gramsci, 1996: 52–3). According to Gramsci, 'the philosophy of praxis is realised through the concrete study of past history through present activity to construct new history' (Gramsci, 1971: 427). As a result the appropriateness of the position that past ideas, questions, philosophies still have a bearing on the present, and may thus transcend social context and 'speak' to us, *can* be established but only by empirical investigation. The chapters to follow in the subsequent parts of this book will draw attention to the importance of empirical analysis, or what Gramsci called the concrete 'earthliness of thought' (ibid.: 465).

To return to the arguments of Femia, a theory is linked to the social relations of a particular epoch but some problems are perennial because underlying thoughts about certain features do recur. Accordingly, although the 'social' element of a work of philosophy is rooted in the original epoch, there may remain elements that cannot be explained by the historical context (Femia, 1981b: 124). Therefore, although we need to reaffirm a historicity in our outlook this does not mean confining such outlook to an historical straitjacket (ibid.: 127). Incidentally, this is the overriding position shared by many other scholars who think and act in a Gramscian way (e.g. Buci-Glucksmann, 1980: 11–12; Buttigieg, 1982: 22; Dombroski, 1982–3: 44; Holub, 1992: 160; Mouffe, 1979: 4; Showstack Sassoon, 1987: x, 16). In sum, analysis is considered to be grounded in determinate social relations, whilst also embodying principles that transcend such relations leaving itself open to changing circumstances. Or, as Lynne Lawner has put it, one needs to be aware of the specifically national context but as part of the historical process because Gramsci developed out of the Italian situation a theory transcending the 'here and now' of contemporary events (Lawner, 1979: 6).

One implication of thinking in a Gramscian way and working through an understanding of absolute historicism is that the meaning of Gramsci's work is established not necessarily by what he thought was significant or what he directed most attention to, thus vitiating the search for a 'real' Gramsci. Hence, whilst the integrity and historical specificity of the 'letter of the text' should not be annulled by the readings Gramsci is submitted to, the significance of his thought and practice should be related to what our *present* practical intentions and understandings of transformative politics renders significant in his work (Davidson, 1974: 142). As ever, one has to bear an attentiveness to the peculiarities of history, but Gramsci's insights and concepts can still be adapted as he indeed adapted and enriched his own concepts to changing circumstances and new conditions (Forgacs, 1989: 87–8).

Overall, then, we have to do our own work to make Gramsci work (Hall, 1997). Rather than a slavish adoption of Gramsci's work, a critical appreciation has to be developed that embraces Gramsci as an intellectual and practical inspiration rather than a prophet. That is why we place an important emphasis on Stuart Hall's call to think problems through in a Gramscian way, rather than simplistically believing that Gramsci has the answers or holds the key to our present problems (Hall, 1988a: 161). As a result, an awareness also has to be displayed of the shortcomings involved in the task of theoretically and practically translating Gramsci's work as a framework for contemporary analysis. This might involve considering a number of the following factors that could be critically scrutinised in an effort to circumscribe some of the possible anachronisms in Gramsci's approach to thought and action relevant to the present.

1. Whether a faith in the guiding role of the 'Modern Prince' – the Communist Party – is fundamentally misplaced in the light of present political realities (Holub, 1992: 160). This could include considering to what extent a more nuanced theory of the party as a 'collective intellectual' might be developed which is relevant to transnational forms of organisation within the global political economy (Augelli and Murphy, 1997: 31–2; Cox, 1999: 15; Murphy, 1999).
2. Whether there is a predetermined essentialist perception of human nature underpinning Gramsci's analysis that overrides the variety of identities that form in the consciousness of individual and collective actors (Martin, 1998; Nimni, 1991: 98).
3. Whether one needs to be reticent about the primary role attributed by Gramsci to social classes as the agents of political change (Bellamy and Schecter, 1993: 166), or whether the concept of class identity, linked to the logic of exploitation, suitably captures a broad array of social forces and identities within transnational and historical processes of class formation (van der Pijl, 1997b, 1998).
4. Whether Gramsci's analysis remains trapped within a Leninist bias towards statism (Nimni, 1991: 193) or whether he favoured more dynamic and democratic grassroots forms of social change (Femia, 1998: 107–13).
5. Or, finally, whether Gramsci was preoccupied with forms of modernity that have little contemporary relevance (Martin, 1998: 169–71).

Whilst these issues will not be developed within the confines of the present argument, the important point to make is that any analysis of present social conditions, based on a Gramscian way of thinking, should retain an active engagement both with and *against* Gramsci (Nield and Seed, 1981: 226).

It is by ultimately remaining engaged with strategic sites of political struggle, however, that analysis must proceed. The fabric of hegemony cannot be analysed at the level of theory but only by a concrete analysis of the social formation and specific changes in the relations of production. This will involve an understanding of changes in the social relations of production within particular social formations but as instances of transnational processes. History, after all, is never strictly defined by national boundaries: 'history is always "world history" and ... particular histories exist only within the frame of world history' (Gramsci, 1985: 181). The following will, therefore, begin to outline how a Gramscian way of thinking is suitably disposed to analysing the restructuring of social relations within the context of European integration. First, though, we will articulate some of the limitations of integration theories before turning to discuss the more comprehensive alternative offered by neo-Gramscian perspectives.

Some limitations of integration theories

Neo-functionalist and intergovernmentalist approaches have dominated the explanation of European integration. The former assume that integration starts when it is realised that certain economic problems yield higher welfare gains, if they are dealt with at the supranational level. The notion of spill-over is crucial for the neo-functionalist explanation of the process of integration. It can be divided into three different processes (Tranhom-Mikkelsen, 1991: 4–6). First, *functional* spill-over occurs in the economic sphere. Because of the interdependence between industrial sectors, the integration of one sector makes the integration of another necessary to reap the full welfare benefits of the first integration. This is accompanied, secondly, by *political* spill-over. Interest groups of an integrated sector are expected to shift their focus to the new decision-making centre in order to influence the decisions important to them and to press for further integration of related sectors. Finally, *cultivated* spill-over refers to the independent capacity of the supranational institutions to push for further integration. Overall, the 'main thesis was that sectoral integration was inherently expansive' (ibid.: 6). Once transnational co-operation has successfully started in one sector, the logic of spill-over automatically leads to integration in other sectors (Haas, 1958: 297; Lindberg, 1963: 294).

Neo-functionalism, however, contains two main problems. First, based on an ahistorical understanding of human beings as rational, utility-maximising individuals, the notion of spill-over implies an inevitable, teleological process of further integration along a line of objective economic rationality. The contributions in this book demonstrate, however, that instances of integration are anything but inevitable. Rather, they are the result of open-ended struggles, which could also have resulted in alternative outcomes. Second, neo-functionalism explains European integration through an emphasis on the internal dynamics of European politics. The wider structure, within which European integration is situated, is completely neglected. It is, therefore, impossible to take into account structural changes such as globalisation and the end of the Cold War.

During the two decades of relative stagnation between 1965 and 1985, neo-functionalism lost a great deal of attraction as an explanation of European integration. Only since the revival of European integration in the mid-1980s has neo-functionalism regained the attention of scholars. Burley and Mattli analyse the role of the ECJ and argue that 'the legal integration of the community corresponds remarkably closely to the original neofunctionalist model developed by Ernst Haas in the late 1950s' (Burley and Mattli, 1993: 43). Mutimer and Tranholm-Mikkelsen point out that the SEA created functional spill-over towards EMU following the free movement of capital; towards a common immigration policy resulting from the removal of border controls; towards a strengthened common regional policy due to the harmonisation of technical regulations; and towards a common social policy as a result of the free movement of labour (Mutimer, 1989: 85–92; Tranholm-Mikkelsen, 1991: 12–13). Nevertheless, the claims are more modest than in the original formulations by Haas and Lindberg. Acknowledging that nationalism and the socio-economic diversity of EU members may restrict further integration, Tranholm-Mikkelsen concluded that 'we cannot return to the automaticity of spill-over' (Tranholm-Mikkelsen, 1991: 18). The notion of spill-over is still seen as a useful tool of analysis, although only as part of an eclectic and less ambitious theoretical framework (George, 1996: 275–83). A neofunctionalist explanation of entire instances of European integration is neither attempted nor deemed to be possible.

In contrast to neo-functionalism, which emphasises the importance of non-governmental interest groups in the process of European integration, intergovernmentalism considers the international structure to be an anarchic system in which states are the only significant actors. This approach, closely related to neo-realism in International Relations (IR), argues that states pursue rationalist policies of power maximisation and security enhancement in order to ensure their survival. The most important explanatory variable is the distribution of capabilities between states. Changes in this distribution lead to actions by states to counter possible losses (Waltz, 1979). With reference to European integration, Hoffmann concludes that a convergence of national preferences is the precondition for European integration. Europe 'has to wait until the separate states decide that their peoples are close enough to justify the setting up of a European state' (Hoffmann, 1966: 910). Thus, states are seen as 'gate-keepers' between their people and Europe. They carefully guard their sovereignty, which is ensured by the principle of unanimity voting in the Council of Ministers.

Unlike neo-functionalism, intergovernmentalism takes the international setting of integration into account. Nevertheless, its exclusive focus on states in the international arena limits change to changes in the state structure. Structural changes such as globalisation, which go beyond the state structure, cannot be accounted for. By the same token, the explanation is still deterministic, since states as the main actors can only adapt to structural change. Intergovernmentalism cannot explain the particular choices made by states in response to structural change.

In order to tackle these shortcomings, Moravcsik developed the so far most sophisticated state-centric approach, which he labelled 'liberal intergovernmentalism' (LI). He first connects a liberal theory of national preference formation (see Bulmer, 1983) with an intergovernmentalist analysis of inter-state negotiations. European integration is perceived as a two-level game, in which governments are the crucial link between the national and international level (see Putnam, 1988). Finally, he adds a regime theory component. States as rational decision-makers use EU institutions and are prepared to transfer parts of their sovereignty to increase the efficiency of inter-state co-operation, and they also accept the restriction of their external sovereignty, because these 'institutions strengthen the autonomy of national political leaders *vis-à-vis* particularistic social groups within their domestic polity' (Moravcsik, 1993: 507; see also Moravcsik, 1998).

The convergence of national interests around a neo-liberal, deregulatory programme with the focus on low inflation was a precondition for the revival of European integration in the mid-1980s. In relation to the EU and the neo-liberal Internal Market programme, Cameron points to the changes in the partisan composition of national governments in the early 1980s to explain the shift from Keynesianism to neo-liberalism. Most notably, Margaret Thatcher took office in Britain in 1979, but changes also took place in Belgium, the Netherlands, Denmark and

Germany, and they 'shared one feature in common: they all represented a shift toward a more conservative position' (Cameron, 1992: 57). Nevertheless, this does not explain why François Mitterrand and the French Socialist Party decided in 1983 to remain in the Economic and Monetary System (EMS) whilst pursuing an economic austerity policy, and neither does it account for the shift of other social democratic parties from Keynesianism to economic neo-liberalism. The European left changed during the 1980s and this cannot be explained by pointing to structural and domestic events alone. Instead, the impact of neo-liberalism as a set of economic ideas has to be investigated to explain the general turn to neo-liberalism by parties of the right and left.

LI is further limited because the lobbying of interest groups is only considered to take place within the domestic realm of a country. Thereby, the significance of transnational actors (for example, TNCs) is neglected. Their level of action is European if not world-wide, maintaining production sites in several countries at the same time. This allows them, first, to develop initiatives with the Commission and to lobby several governments at the same time, and second, they can put pressure on national governments by either threatening to transfer production units to other countries or actually carrying out this threat, if certain conditions are not met. State-centric approaches can only account for TNCs by regarding them as several, unconnected actors in their individual domestic sphere, not as transnational actors transgressing the line of separation between international and domestic politics. In short, the predominant emphasis on states as the main actors in international relations prevents LI from dealing with ideas and transnational actors as independent forces behind integration. The behaviour of TNCs, such as in the investment boom of the 1980s in the EU, is interpreted as rational adaptation to credible intergovernmental commitments, while policy ideas are viewed as the result of intergovernmental demands, but not as an independent force (Moravcsik, 1995: 618). (For further criticism of LI, see Chapter 8 below.)

Finally, the exclusive state-centric focus makes all types of intergovernmentalism concentrate on inter-state negotiations as the crucial event of further integration. However, Wincott points out that instances of integration are not so much the result of intergovernmental negotiations, but emerge from the 'everyday grind of the Community' (Wincott, 1995). In other words, the process leading to negotiations and agenda-setting should be seen as more important than the negotiations themselves, as should the sites of social struggle related to the ratification of negotiation agreements.

In order to overcome the shortcomings of the neo-functionalist and intergovernmental integration theories, several scholars suggest combining intergovernmentalism with neo-functionalism as a remedy in respect of European integration (e.g. Cameron, 1992: 30). Nevertheless, this is misleading. As Puchala had already observed in 1972, 'attempts to juxtapose or combine the conventional frameworks for analytical purposes by and large yield no more than artificial, untidy results' (Puchala, 1972: 276–7). Neo-functionalist approaches cannot be combined with state-centric approaches, as their basic assumptions diametrically oppose each other. While the former speak about the supersession of states, the latter consider sovereignty to be unchangeable; hence an alternative neo-Gramscian perspective is suggested in the next section. As stated earlier, it is not possible to speak about one specific neo-Gramscian approach representing a cohesive 'school' (see Chapter 2 below). We merely attempt here to introduce some core neo-Gramscian concepts and to demonstrate how they can help to overcome the shortcomings of the established approaches of European integration.

An alternative: neo-Gramscian perspectives

Most importantly, neo-Gramscian perspectives focus on social forces, engendered by the production process, as the most important collective actors. Consequently, various fractions of labour and capital may be identified in relation to their place in the production system. This makes structural changes such as globalisation accessible, since the emergence of new social forces engendered by the transnationalisation of production and finance can be incorporated. These forces are located in the wider structure of the social relations of production, which *do not determine but shape* their interests and identity. A basic distinction can be drawn between national social forces of capital and labour stemming from national production sectors and transnational capital and labour, engendered by those production sectors, which are organised on a transnational scale. The first group can be further sub-divided into nationally-oriented capital and labour, which stem from domestic production sectors which produce for the national market, and internationally-oriented capital and labour, engendered by domestic production sectors, which produce for the international market. In Chapter 6, Bieler and Torjesen demonstrate how the Austrian,

Norwegian and Swedish labour movements were split over EU membership along these lines of division. Transnational and internationally-oriented unions supported membership, since their industrial sectors depended on access to the Internal Market, while nationally-oriented labour feared the consequences of losing state protectionism, and therefore opposed accession to the EU. In Chapter 4, van Apeldoorn distinguishes two different fractions within transnational capital. Those forces of capital which stem from globally integrated production networks and support a complete neo-liberal outlook of the EU are opposed to the transnational capital fraction, which is dependent on the European 'home market' and favours a more regionalist outlook for the EU including protectionist measures at the European level. In Chapter 9, van der Pijl further sub-divides globally integrated capital into capital fractions competing on the world market (Global capital) and internationally assertive capital operating from a secure European base (Euro-Global capital). In short, social forces as collective actors are identified by first looking at the level on which production is organised and, second, by analysing the level of trade they are involved in (also see Holman, 1992, for a similar distinction of capital fractions).

Second, neo-Gramscian perspectives reject 'the notion of objective laws of history and focus upon class struggle … [be they inter-class or intra-class] … as the heuristic model for the understanding of structural change' (Cox with Sinclair, 1996: 57–8). It is thus realised that there are no inevitable developments in history. Instances of European integration are as much the outcome of open-ended struggle as are other political developments.

Third, while the state is still considered to be an important analytical category, it is regarded as a structure within which and through which social forces operate rather than as an actor in its own right. There are several forms of state and the national interest, the *raison d'état*, cannot be separated from society, as it depends on the configuration of social forces at the state level. Gramsci's concept of the integral state is analytically useful for the conceptualisation of the relation between state and society (Gramsci, 1971: 257–64). On the one hand, the integral state consists of 'political society': that is, the coercive apparatus of the state more narrowly understood including ministries and other state institutions. On the other, it includes 'civil society', made up of political parties, unions, employers' associations, churches and so on, which 'represents the realm of cultural institutions and practices in which the hegemony of a class may be constructed or challenged' (Rupert, 1995: 27).

What we can do … is to fix two major … 'levels': the one that can be called 'civil society', that is the ensemble of organisms commonly called 'private', and that of 'political society' or 'the state'. These two levels correspond on the one hand to the function of 'hegemony' which the dominant group exercises throughout society and on the other hand to that of 'direct domination' or command through the state and 'juridical' government (Gramsci, 1971: 12).

The concept of the integral state implies, first, that the focus on social forces does not exclude an analysis of state institutions (i.e., political society). Due to the internationalisation of the state in the process of globalisation, those state institutions which are linked to the global economy (e.g., finance ministries, central banks) are given priority within a country's governmental set-up over those institutions which deal with predominantly national problems (e.g., labour ministries) (Cox, 1981: 146). This does not, however, imply that these institutions merely adjust national policies to the requirements of the global political economy (*pace* Baker, 1999; Ling, 1996; Moran, 1998). An emphasis is also placed on the role state institutions play in bringing about changes from the national to the global level resulting in globalisation (Panitch, 1994: 64; cf. Radice, 1999). As Cox has argued, though, this phenomenon needs more study (Cox, 1992: 31). This volume aims to make a contribution in this respect by introducing a series of empirical arguments analysing the restructuring of European social relations linked to the reactive and active interplay of global and national forces. Similarly, the emphasis on social forces as the main actors does not imply that political parties and interest associations – that is, civil society – are considered to be unimportant. Nevertheless, in contrast to pluralist, corporatist and policy network approaches (e.g., Lehmbruch and Schmitter, 1982; Marsh and Rhodes, 1992), they are not considered to be rationalistic, unitary actors. Rather, they are regarded as institutional frameworks within and through which different class fractions of capital and labour attempt to establish their particular interests and ideas as the generally accepted, or 'common sense', view.

Finally, neo-Gramscian perspectives take into account the independent role of ideas. On the one hand, they are considered to be part of the overall structure in the form of 'intersubjective meanings'. Hence ideas establish the wider frameworks of thought, 'which condition the way individuals and groups are able to understand their social situation, and the possibilities of social change' (Gill and Law, 1988: 74).

On the other hand, ideas may be used by actors as 'weapons' in order to legitimise particular policies and are important in that they form part of a hegemonic project organised by 'organic intellectuals' (see below, and Bieler, 2001). After all, to paraphrase Gramsci, ideas are anything but arbitrary; they are real historical facts which must be combated and their nature as instruments of domination revealed (Gramsci, 1995: 395). Hence the endeavour to examine how certain ideas are sustained and transformed in the global political economy within institutions across forms of state and civil society as moments of the overall process of European integration.

Various social forces may attempt to do this by forming an historical bloc to establish preferable forms of governance at the national, European and/or international level.[3] 'The historic[al] bloc is the term applied to the particular configuration of social classes and ideology that gives content to a historical state' (Cox, 1987: 409), and thus consists of structure and superstructure. It forms a complex, politically contestable and dynamic ensemble of social relations which includes economic, political and cultural aspects. The relationship between structure and superstructure is reciprocal. 'Superstructures of ideology and political organisation shape the development of both aspects of production ... [i.e., the social relations and the physical means of production] ... and are shaped by them' (Cox, 1983: 168).

Another important neo-Gramscian concept is hegemony. Unlike the neo-realist notion of hegemony, in which a hegemonic state controls and dominates other states and the international order thanks to its superior degree of economic and military capability (Gilpin, 1981: 29; Keohane, 1984: 32–3), it describes a type of rule which predominantly relies on consent alongside coercion. Hegemony 'is based on a coherent conjunction or fit between a configuration of material power, the prevalent collective image of world order ... and a set of institutions which administer the order with a certain semblance of universality' (Cox, 1981: 139). A fundamental class exercises a hegemonic function when it transcends particular economic-corporate interests and is capable of binding and cohering diverse aspirations, interests and identities into an historical bloc. An historical bloc therefore implies the constitution of a radical and novel reconstruction of the relational nature and identity of different interests. Following Gramsci, Cox argues that the construction of an historical bloc cannot exist without a hegemonic social class and, moreover, that the national context remains the only place where an historical bloc can be founded (Cox, 1983: 168, 174). Yet the hegemony of a fundamental class can manifest itself as a transnational phenomenon insofar as it represents the outward development of a particular mode of production. Once social hegemony has been consolidated domestically it may expand beyond this social order to move outward on a world scale (Cox, 1987: 149–50; Davies, 1999: 13).

Elsewhere, Gill has argued that the relationship between hegemony and historical bloc is not necessarily coterminous, thus distinguishing between the two concepts. For Gill, first, a historical bloc 'may at times have the potential to become hegemonic' (Gill, 1993: 40), but it also may not. Second, he argues that a historical bloc can emerge transnationally, forging links between inter- and intra-class fractions to create the conditions for a hegemony of transnational capital (Gill and Law, 1993: 110). Such a bloc comprises a transnational managerial class (e.g., located in big corporations and international financial management), their employees, and smaller firms linked to TNCs as contractors or suppliers. Additionally, the interests of a transnational historical bloc are secured through the institutions of the global political economy, such as the World Bank, the International Monetary Fund (IMF), the Trilateral Commission, the Group of Seven (G-7) industrialised countries, the Organisation for Economic Co-operation and Development (OECD), or the Bank for International Settlements (BIS) (see Gill, 1990). These mechanisms of surveillance, generically recognised as a 'G-7 nexus' (Gill, 1995b), have promoted a certain notion of market civilisation based on capitalist progress (Gill, 1995a). In the case of Europe the emergence of a transnational historical bloc, represented by large-scale finance and productive capital of global reach, has been crucial in promoting neo-liberal restructuring and support for Economic and Monetary Union (see Chapter 3 below). Overall, though, the position adopted on the relationship between hegemony and historical bloc may differ from one neo-Gramscian perspective to another and is usually driven by the purpose and empirical context of the research.

'Organic intellectuals' also play a crucial role in achieving hegemony. According to Gramsci (1971: 5):

> every social group, coming into existence on the original terrain of an essential function in the world of economic production, creates together with itself, organically, one or more strata of intellectuals which give it homogeneity and an awareness of its own function not only in the economic but also in the social and political fields.

They do not simply produce ideas, but it is their task to organise the social forces they stem from and to develop a 'hegemonic project' which is able to transcend the particular interests of this group so that other social forces are able to give their consent. Such a hegemonic project must be based on 'organic' ideas, which stem from the economic sphere. It must, however, also go beyond economics into the political and social sphere, incorporating ideas related to issues such as social reform or moral regeneration, to result in a stable hegemonic political system. It 'brings the interests of the leading class into harmony with those of subordinate classes and incorporates these other interests into an ideology expressed in universal terms' (Cox, 1983: 168). A hegemonic project is sometimes also referred to as a 'comprehensive concept of control'. Both terms are defined in the same way and often used interchangeably (Holman, 1996; Overbeek, 1990: 26; Overbeek and van der Pijl, 1993).

The argument of the book takes four steps. In the next chapter, Adam David Morton will round up the theoretical considerations of the introduction by highlighting the dangers of 'school' formation in IPE whilst further asserting the need to think contemporary problems through in a Gramscian way. In Part II, we will then turn to the role fractions of capital play in the revival of European integration. Stephen Gill outlines how transnational capital has attempted to make governments more responsive to the discipline of market forces by removing neo-liberal economic policies from democratic accountability and subordinating them to the control of technocratic and independent central bankers in the ECB. Bastiaan van Apeldoorn outlines how the struggle between different projects and fractions of transnational capital led to 'embedded neo-liberalism' at the European level, which is neo-liberal at its core and reflects the outlook of the most globalised sections of European capital, while at the same time seeking to accommodate the orientations of other social forces. Part III of the book then deals with labour and its role in the integration process. Hans-Jürgen Bieling analyses why trade unions continue to support European integration, driven by transnational capital along neo-liberal lines, although it is doubtful whether they can achieve their objectives of embedded social relations through this strategy. Andreas Bieler and Stina Torjesen then analyse splits within the Austrian, Norwegian and Swedish labour movements over EU membership. Importantly, while internationally-oriented and transnational labour supported accession to the EU in these countries, this did not imply that they were in favour of neo-liberalism; rather, they perceived the EU as a possibility to regain some control over capital lost at the national level. Finally, Hélène Pellerin and Henk Overbeek illustrate the tight connection between emerging migration control frameworks and measures for labour market restructuring and the logic of capital expansion that characterises neo-liberal regional integration processes through a comparison of the relationship between the EU members with countries of Central and Eastern Europe (CEE) and the North American countries with Central America. Then, in Part IV, Otto Holman analyses the way European integration is extended to CEE, while Kees van der Pijl makes clear that this is part of an 'Americanisation' of the whole of Europe at the expense of a solution for CEE along 'European' lines.

As diverse as the various neo-Gramscian perspectives in this volume are, they commonly share a similar social purpose concerned with developing a 'critical theory' of European integration. This implies the following three closely related points. First, 'critical theory' is capable of explaining structural changes, such as globalisation, because it 'does not take institutions and social and power relations for granted but calls them into question by concerning itself with their origins and how and whether they might be in the process of changing' (Cox, 1981: 129). In contrast to state-centric and neo-functionalist approaches, human nature, the state and the international system are not treated as unchanging substances, but as a continuing creation of new forms (Cox, 1981: 132). Second, 'critical theory' realises that 'theory is always *for* someone and *for* some purpose' (Cox, 1981: 128; original emphasis). Hence, it not only identifies the purpose behind established integration theories – further integration in the case of neo-functionalism, the preservation of modern state power and national sovereignty in the case of intergovernmentalism – but it is also capable of comprehending the social purpose behind a particular phase of European integration (van Apeldoorn, 1997b). As a result, neo-Gramscian perspectives analyse which hegemonic project has been successful, which projects lost out, and which projects may become the platform for future contestation. Finally, as a result of the first two points, an analysis of empirical events is not an end in itself for 'critical theory'; rather, it is a 'useful way of understanding the social and political world in order to change it' (Cox, 1987: 393). Ultimately, neo-Gramscian perspectives, as 'critical theory', have the goal of transforming the current dominance of the neo-liberal project and highlighting its neglect of social equality by promoting questions of social justice and increasing the general possibility for wider participation in decision making. What follows, therefore, is a study of politics, 'understood as a body of practical rules and research and of detailed observations useful for awakening an interest in effective reality and for stimulating more rigorous and more vigorous political insights' (Gramsci, 1971: 175–6), or so we hope. The conclusion (Chapter 10) will return to these issues and draw together the insights of the various contributions.

Notes

1. Globalisation as an actual phenomenon is heavily contested by authors such as Hirst and Thompson (1996). For a critical engagement with their argument, see Bieler (2000: 20–2). For an overview of the literature on globalisation, see Clark (1999) and Higgott and Reich (1998).

2. Some of the arguments from this article are drawn upon in the following discussion with further elaboration. We would also like to acknowledge and thank Richard Bellamy for his comments on this earlier article. Whilst welcoming criticisms about the historicity of ideas, he has argued that his position is not necessarily one of 'austere historicism' but merely an emphasis on the importance of context in any attempt to understand a thinker (personal correspondence, 2 January 1999).

3. Whilst noting that Gramsci's concept of historical bloc (*blocco storico*) can be referred to as 'historic bloc' we do not follow this convention. As Derek Boothman has argued (1995: xi–xii), rendering the concept as 'historic bloc' can be misleading because too much emphasis is placed on the momentous, one-off, or literally 'historic' formation of such a bloc. This can give a static or 'snapshot-like' depiction. Instead, an emphasis on historical bloc draws attention to dynamic processes that unfold, through the aspect of hegemony, within the *historical process* and thus through the making of history. As Fritz Haug (1999: 111) puts it, 'to grasp Gramsci's meaning, one has to start from his differentiation between actual history in the making [i.e., historical] and the historical past [i.e. historic]. The *blocco storico* is certainly a phenomenon of the present, which aims at a socio-political aggregated agency and potency to shape this ongoing process.'

2
The Sociology of Theorising and Neo-Gramscian Perspectives: The Problems of 'School' Formation in IPE[1]

Adam David Morton

'As there is no single school of Marxism … so too there is no single Gramscian or "Italian" school. Nor is there any consensual interpretation of Gramsci's fragmentary and often contradictory thoughts concerning social theory.'

Stephen Gill (1993: 2)

Introduction

Over a number of years an alternative theoretical approach has developed within International Political Economy (IPE) that has advanced upon the general conceptual framework of Antonio Gramsci to explain the operation of hegemony at the international level as well as to consider change and transformation in world order. This alternative framework was outlined in Chapter 1. It is the intention of this chapter to reflect more broadly on the diverse literature that has been generated by this theoretical approach, which also informs the range of different arguments contained within the book. This chapter should therefore be read as a counterpart to the introduction of the volume. As a whole, the two chapters address a series of theoretical and methodological issues germane to the chapters that follow. The objective of this chapter is to draw attention to the way such literature has been commonly represented. Although the contributions of this literature go beyond solely adopting and adapting the writings of Gramsci, there has nevertheless been a tendency to impose a cohesive label upon such work to the extent that reference is often made to a neo-Gramscian 'school'. Additionally, even a cursory examination of the literature reveals ambivalent and somewhat awkward attempts by the alleged adherents to develop an appropriate label to encompass the analyses.

Clearly the very act of developing labels, and thus the process of labelling, is inherently political. The act of labelling can have the effect of rendering issues and commitments a certain way, limiting options and restricting viewpoints. My contention is that the label of a 'school' can entail the danger of flattening out, simplifying and misrepresenting nuances, internal tensions and contradictions: the very stuff of meaningful theoretical and practical debate. As a result the label of a 'school' should be avoided due to a series of negative connotations.

To be sure, one may refer to examples of some 'schools' that have developed in broader and more positive ways; for example, the Frankfurt School or the French *Annales* School. Even so, in the case of the latter, Peter Burke (1990: 2) has suggested that it is better to speak of the *Annales* movement rather than a monolithic 'school'. Additionally, one might also think of the example of the 'English' School in International Relations (IR) within which, it is argued, there is a marked lack of consensus about a range of issues (Dunne, 1998). Yet, even in this case, whilst the notion of a school is conceived in broad terms and careful attention has been paid to insiders and outsiders, a question still remains about whether allocating the terms of debate within a particular school sets certain limits. Elsewhere in IR, with reference to developments in Security Studies, there has also been a recent attempt to develop the notion of a school as part of a creative development (Huysmans, 1998). Yet, once again, it is open to debate whether there remains an exclusionary tendency at the heart of such school formation: for instance, whether there is a marginalisation of other perspectives that are also engaged with broadening and deepening the thinking and practice of security (i.e., Bilgin, Booth and Jones, 1998).

With these differences in mind, the aim in this chapter is to raise awareness about some of the problems associated with 'school' formation in IPE. In particular, with a focus on the practices of labelling within IPE, a series of problems can be discerned connected with the labelling of a neo-Gramscian 'school'. As a consequence, it is suggested that works commonly recognised as neo-Gramscian need to avoid the imposed label of a school as well as self-styling themselves as a discrete methodological 'school' able to simply overcome the failures of 'orthodox' approaches in IPE. To commit the latter error might lend credence to the accusation that such analyses are merely 'searching for gems' in the *Prison Notebooks*, and other Gramscian sources, to 'save' IPE from a pervasive 'economism' (Gareau, 1993: 301). On the basis of recognising either the political implications of imposed labels or the inadequacy of present labels, this chapter asks how those works recognised as neo-Gramscian can be represented.

In a move to avoid representing a uniform consensus, or portraying the commonalities of neo-Gramscians as a stultifying '-ism', the argument offers a modest alternative. Emphasis is thus placed on divergent neo-Gramscian *perspectives* which represent a plurality of approaches riven with differences. This more straightforward and sensitive act of labelling offers the potential of openness by providing the scope not only to broaden the horizons of such perspectives but also to leave space for future consideration and debate rather than the possible closure of a *single* 'school'. As a result, by focusing on the meaning attached to labels and the need to contest certain labels, it is possible to reflect on the way IPE is conceived and practised. By beginning with critique and offering the alternative conceptualisation of neo-Gramscian *perspectives*, the possibility also emerges to transcend disciplinary boundaries. The plural emphasis on neo-Gramscian *perspectives* provides the chance to intersect with similar as well as diverse forms of thought and action across different disciplines, whilst engaging with concrete agents and sites of change (Bieler and Morton, 2001). It will become clear how the chapter contests the 'common sense' implications of labelling both in theory and practice, and how the endeavour to be self-reflexive about theorising invites a regular renewal of neo-Gramscian *perspectives* as times and material circumstances change. First, though, a few comments about the nature, or sociology, of theorising.

The practice of theorising

The role of theory can be explained as the task of questioning what passes as the accepted view, to show how the construction of issues is far from obvious and to question certain 'common sense' interpretations. The notion of 'common sense' is especially important here. Possibly derived from the writings of Giambattista Vico, an eighteenth-century philosopher-philologist who described 'common sense' as judgement without reflection (Vico, 1744/1984: §142, 63; §149, 64; §350, 105; §772, 293; §1406, 428), the notion was given particular prominence within the thought and action of Antonio Gramsci. So, for example, 'common sense' for Gramsci referred to the uncritical and largely unconscious way of perceiving the world that became 'common' in a specific time and place (Gramsci, 1971: 322). Put simply, it expresses the taken-for-granted. Frequently this notion of 'common sense' was used by Gramsci to refer to the pressures of social conformism – the standardisation of thought and action – manifested in the lives of everyday people, or what he referred to as popular knowledge (ibid.: 199, 242 n.42, 321–2, 326 n.5, 330n.*, 419). Yet a close reading of the *Prison Notebooks* advances beyond this notion, especially if we consult a more complete version of such writings.

To be sure, Gramsci still makes reference within the *Prison Notebooks* to the 'everyday experience' of 'real people in specific historical relations' that reflect a popular 'common sense' conception of the world (Gramsci, 1996: 48–52). Yet, crucially, 'common sense' was not just limited to a specific social stratum; it was continually transformed, in theory and in practice, so that *every* person was subject to a taken-for-granted 'common sense' of some kind:

> Every social stratum has its own 'common sense' which is ultimately the most widespread conception of life and morals. Every philosophical current leaves a sedimentation of 'common sense': this is the document of its historical reality. 'Common sense' is not something rigid and static; rather, it changes continuously, enriched by scientific notions and philosophical opinions which have entered into common usage. 'Common sense' is the folklore (that is, as it is understood) and the philosophy, the science, the economics of the scholars. 'Common sense' creates the folklore of the future, that is a more or less rigidified phase of a certain time and place (Gramsci, 1992: 173).

Clearly, then, the point here is that 'common sense' has to be contested in the practical lives of everyday people which also means contesting the historical and material reality of ideas propounded by intellectuals that construct social reality. After all, 'ideologies are anything but arbitrary, they are real historical facts which must be combated and their nature as instruments of domination exposed... precisely for reasons of political struggle' (Gramsci, 1995: 395). By extension, therefore, theory is a form of practice: by calling into question certain 'common sense' assumptions in theory it might be possible to approach practice through self-understanding and self-transformation in an effort to transcend the existing order. The emphasis is shifted towards conceiving theory as a *verb*, or something done through every-day action, rather than as a noun, or something akin to a tool that can be picked up and put down independently of action (Zalewski, 1996: 346). Therefore, although theorising can never suffice on its own and it is important to avoid collapsing practice into theory, leaving self-enclosed debates merely at the realm of ideas, it is also worth appreciating that:

> International theory underpins and informs international practice, even if there is a lengthy lag between the high-point of theories and their gradual absorption into political debate. Once established as common sense, theories become incredibly powerful since they delineate not simply what can be known but also what it is sensible to talk about or suggest. (S. Smith, 1996: 13)

Essential to the endeavour of contesting 'common sense' in IPE, therefore, is the necessity of critical self-reflection or, in Edward Said's serviceable phrase, the importance of all intellectuals representing themselves to themselves (Said, 1994: xiii). This is why the work of neo-Gramscian scholars in IPE matters and why, therefore, such analysis cannot be left uncritically examined. It also becomes impera-tive to question the 'common sense' or the taken-for-granted of neo-Gramscian work in IPE. After all, the very self-reflexivity of such work invites regular critique and renewal, as times and material cir-cumstances change, which is one indicator of the merits of such theory.

Rather than unquestioningly assuming that knowledge is an unchanging ahistorical essence, referred to by Vico (1744/1984: §127, 61) as the 'conceit of scholars', the stress, instead, is on an historicist sense of knowledge. This means that theory reflects upon the process of theorising itself in a historically specific manner to understand how meaning becomes embedded in intellectual and practical activity. As a result, by connecting knowledge and human practice in a specific social and political time and place it is possible to reflect on the expres-sion of particular perspectives. Hence the need, following Robert Cox, to become clearly aware of the perspective which gives rise to theoris-ing, to lay bare its assumptions and reflect upon its relation to other perspectives, in order to achieve a perspective on perspectives that may broaden enquiry beyond the conventional problematic (Cox, 1981: 128). This is the objective behind contesting some of the 'common sense' labels surrounding neo-Gramscian analyses whilst also focusing on the more appropriate label of neo-Gramscian *perspectives* in an attempt to maintain an openness to insights and perspectives in and beyond the confines of IPE. But before elaborating upon such an alternative we shall consider the significance and consequence of the politics surrounding labels and the act of labelling in an attempt to become aware of certain tensions and complexities.

The politics of labels and labelling

Since the seminal and on-going contributions of Robert Cox there have been a number of similar but distinct interventions within and beyond debates in IPE. These interventions, embedded in historically specific and sometimes separate social relations, have reflected particular and yet collective interests generated by and implicated in changes in the nature of capitalism towards the end of the twentieth century (see Chapter 1). Whilst these interventions go beyond solely adopting and adapting the writings of Antonio Gramsci, there is still a strong Gramscian lineage in many of the works to the degree that it has become usual practice to refer to such contributions as a neo-Gramscian 'school' or, even more curiously, as an 'Italian school'. Yet who constitutes such a 'school', on what basis are members included or excluded, and where do the labels come from?

Similar to the ire raised elsewhere about the politics of naming, it is important to note that enforced labels, in this case 'school', are usually used by critics rather than alleged adherents, or opponents rather than proponents (Campbell, 1998). Consequently, following the demarcation of an 'Italian School' by an anonymous reviewer of a collection of essays edited by Stephen Gill (1993: 21), similar references with essentialising and exclusionary connotations have gained currency. So, for example, it is possible to find presumptions about a cohesive neo-Gramscian 'school' in a variety of otherwise welcome critiques (e.g., Burnham, 1991; Cammack, 1999; Ling, 1996; Moran, 1998; H. Smith, 1996; Woods, 1995), whilst elsewhere, uncharacteristically imprecise references to a 'Canadian–Italian' school or 'Cox–Gramsci' approach can also be found (S. Smith, 1995). Several implications result from the imposition of the label 'school' and the coherence that it implies, as well as what can be recognised as a certain awkwardness of self-recognition by those supposed proponents of neo-Gramscian analyses.

First, a 'school' can imply the construction of inclusions and, as a corollary, exclusions, or even evictions, of those analyses that do not seem to comply with the demands of permissive gatekeepers. In this sense, comments on the sociology of theorising by Cox (1992/1996: 178–9), distinguishing between the consecrated discourse of 'groupies' – succumbing to a self-referential 'school' overlooking contributions from outside 'the group' – and 'loners' situated outside intellectual camps, has relevance here. The group pressure exerted by a 'school' may be conservative, revolving around implicit and yet subconscious judgements that may inhibit critical engagement with alternative perspectives. What can evolve from the designation and labelling of a 'school' is, therefore, a series of meritocracies, professional tags, and membership in discourses and practices that remove the intellectual from the *cantus firmus* of everyday politics.

This stress is conveyed in the critique developed by Gramsci of cultural, artistic and intellectual manifestations that he termed 'neology'. Following Gramsci, neology refers to the manifestation of cliques, schools or clubs revolving around individual expressions of language and jargon separate from 'national-popular' sentiments (Gramsci, 1985: 111–12, 122–3). The term was also a generic counterpart to the expressions 'Brescianism' and 'Lorianism' used by Gramsci throughout the *Prison Notebooks*. Briefly, Brescianism takes its name from the Jesuit Father Antonio Bresciani (1798–1862), a nineteenth-century historical novelist, who indulged in a wordy and reactionary style in a novel published in 1848, *L'Ebreo di Verona* (*The Jew of Verona*). Similarly, Lorianism takes its name from Achille Loria (1857–1943), an Italian economist. These terms, along with neology, are crucial to understanding Gramsci's critique of Italian intellectual groups. They represent a rejection of reactionary and wordy posturing (Brescianism), a distancing from cliques (neology), as well as a rejection of positivism in the social sciences commonly involving the further clustering of intellectuals (Lorianism). Whilst referring to historically specific forms of cultural criticism, such terms have importance and relevance beyond their indisputable specificity (Buttigieg, 1982: 22). They raise awareness about the general activity of different social types of intellectual and in particular the problems associated with a detached, convoluted or wordy style, on the one hand, and a crude positivism, on the other. It is this approach, or ethos, to considering the social function of intellectual activity that can be developed by focusing on the sociology of theorising and the general problem of school formation. By capturing such an ethos or attitude it becomes possible to highlight how 'neologisms', in this case related to the labelling of a 'school', can potentially lead to the crystallisation of a particular interpretive community, meaning a constituency with a specialised language whose concerns become increasingly parochial. There may be less of an inclination to appeal to wider debates and issues beyond neatly delimited and limiting horizons. The work of Edward Said can instructively illuminate some of these issues in more detail.

Whilst engaged with specific factors, issues and events, the intellectual and practical engagement of Said has consciously aimed to elaborate general themes and principles in an attempt to highlight the interaction between a transitory universality and the local, or subjective, here and now (see *inter alia* Said, 1978/1995, 1985, 1993, 1994, 1997). As a result of this awareness, attention has been drawn to the very dangers of interpretive communities or the problems inherent in the consolidation of a 'school' abstracted from a steady connection with human society. Therefore the concerns of an interpretive community, or 'school', can become restrictively tight and more self-enclosed – involving a self-confirming authority – whilst achieving the status of a stable constituency or even acquiring the power and status of an orthodoxy. Subsequently, everything that cannot be absorbed by such a community or 'school' can be screened out through the repetitive production of the same sort of analysis (Said, 1983a: 15).

In combination, one may take these remarks about the problem of neology and interpretive communities and relate them to the politics of labels, the act of labelling, or the dilemmas associated with the 'schooling' of intellectual and political practices. They may, therefore, not only have a bearing upon the specific construction and production of intellectual enquiry but also generally relate to those analyses that have broadly shared neo-Gramscian commitments. It is thus imperative that the radical intent of neo-Gramscian analyses continues to engage with and contest orthodox analysis within IPE whilst maintaining a certain 'worldliness', remaining situated in relation to society to give form and materiality to actual situations (Said, 1983b). This task is especially important since James Mittelman's recent comment that neo-Gramscian analysis is beginning to occupy a place in the global 'scientific' community (1998: 89). The price of such status and acceptance could lead to an increase in forms of conventionality. In short there is a danger that a particular 'schooling' of intellectual interests might itself lead to forms of 'common sense' orthodoxy.[2] Instead, then, by maintaining a certain 'worldliness' and by rejecting the conventionality and closure of a single school, the chapters that follow attempt to engage with strategic sites of political struggle and possible forms of resistance in a focus on the restructuring of European social relations within the context of the global political economy.

Besides the politics of labelling, however, there is also a problem of self-recognition and self-identification across neo-Gramscian analyses. This is expressed by the diversity of labels used to describe common commitments within such analysis by the alleged adherents: for instance, a cursory examination of the literature reveals the designation of terms such as 'Gramscian Historical Materialism', 'Transnational Historical Materialism', 'Coxian Historicism', 'Gramscians', 'new Gramscians', 'new materialism', 'Open Marxism' or 'neo-Gramscianism'. Yet such labels tend to generate more confusion than clarity: for example, it might seem contradictory to assert a recent notion of historical materialism as transnational when the focus of historical materialism has always been pitched at a level of social relations aimed at understanding, transforming and transcending the historically specific form of the state. In this sense it might be worth reiterating a statement from *The Communist Manifesto* (Marx and Engels, 1998: 39–40):

The need of a constantly expanding market for its products chases the bourgeoisie over the whole surface of the globe. It must nestle everywhere, settle everywhere, establish connections everywhere... It compels all nations, on pain of extinction, to adopt the bourgeois mode of production; it compels them to introduce what it calls civilisation into their midst, i.e., to become bourgeois themselves. In one word, it creates a world after its own image.

Indeed, in terms of the politics of transformation that preoccupied Gramsci, in both theory and practice, international trends were the context whilst national developments were taken as the point of departure (Showstack Sassoon, 1990: 24). This means that Gramsci took a national point of departure whilst acknowledging the mediation of global and regional social power relations (see also Chapter 1 for this emphasis). As Gramsci states (1971: 350) in an oft-cited passage, 'Every relationship of "hegemony" is necessarily an educative relationship and occurs not only within a nation, between the various forces of which the nation is composed, but in the international and world-wide field, between complexes of national and continental civilisations.' Indeed, there was a constant and dialectical juxtaposition between the national and international realms in Gramsci's treatment of hegemony. This involved focusing on *'relations within society'*, involving the development of the productive forces, the level of coercion, or relations between political parties that constitute *'hegemonic systems within the state'*. Yet it also involved focusing on *'relations between international forces'*, involving the requisites of great powers, sovereignty or independence that constitute *'the combinations of states in hegemonic systems'* (Gramsci, 1971: 176). Hence:

> the internal relations of any nation are the result of a combination which is 'original' and (in a certain sense) unique: these relations must be understood and conceived in their originality and uniqueness if one wishes to dominate them and direct them. To be sure, the line of development is towards internationalism, but the point of departure is 'national' – and it is from this point of departure that one must begin. Yet the perspective is international and cannot be otherwise. (ibid.: 240)

Moreover, Gramsci himself discussed numerous features of 'Anglo-Saxon world hegemony' (Gramsci, 1977: 81) and referred to cultural movements linked to 'American global hegemony' (Gramsci, 1996: 275), such as the Rotary Club, that had an international character but would become rooted in different forms of state. The concentration on aspects of 'Americanism and Fordism', the expansion of Fordist assembly plant production beyond the USA, also bears out a preoccupation with the way world hegemony and a particular mode of production may consolidate itself locally within different national settings. Manifestations of 'Americanism', at the time, were therefore questioned in relation to:

> whether America, with the implacable preponderance of its economic production, will force or is already forcing Europe to undergo an upheaval of its socioeconomic alignment, which would have developed anyway, but at a slow pace – whereas now it looms as a repercussion of American 'overbearingness'. In other words, whether a transformation of the material bases of civilisation is taking place that in the long run (and not very long, because in our time everything is quicker than in past epochs) will bring about the overthrow of existing civilisation and the birth of a new one. (ibid.: 17)

In Gramsci's approach, then, the way in which the tension between national and international realms came together and the manner in which an international class would succeed in establishing social cohesion within specific configurations of national state–civil society relations, was through the concept of hegemony. To cite Gramsci once again:

> It is in the concept of hegemony that those exigencies which are national in character are knotted together; ... *A class that is international in character has* – in as much as it guides social strata which are narrowly national (intellectuals), and indeed frequently even less than national: particularistic and municipalistic (the peasants) – *to 'nationalise' itself in a certain sense.* (ibid.: 241; emphasis added)

Hence Gramsci's re-working of historical materialism was not limited to state-based conceptions of politics but was constantly aware of the dialectic between global and local relations (Rupert, 1995: 36, 1998: 431–2) or the internal and international organisational relations of the state (Gramsci, 1971: 243). It therefore seems contradictory to label or recognise a 'new' approach as *uniquely* capturing transnational dimensions of analysis. The task that still remains, though, is to decipher those changes taking place in the global political economy that indicate quantitative and qualitative shifts in the transformation of production processes; how identifiable social forces might be formulating increasingly transnational policies of consensus formation; and the manner in which the state, as an ensemble of social relations, plays a role in this process. It is to these questions that neo-Gramscian perspectives with a focus on instances of transnational phenomena turn their attention towards (see especially Chapters 3, 4 and 5 below).

In terms of further problems associated with labelling there is also confusion over the appropriation of the label 'Open Marxism'. This label has been coined to refer to the work of Robert Cox because the approach develops many of the insights of Marxist theory whilst displaying an openness to new questions and directions (Drainville, 1994: 126, n.2). Confusingly the same term, 'Open Marxism', has also been used to designate an approach that is critical of neo-Gramscian perspectives (Burnham, 1994).[3] Moreover, the appellation 'Gramscian' to a contemporary approach is equally problematic because it mistakenly conveys a parallel or co-existence, without any significant change, of the historical moment that Gramsci occupied. That is why, in the next section, the accent is placed on *neo*-Gramscian perspectives, with the implication of innovation, rather than falsely implying that we can occupy Gramsci's historical moment.[4] The aim is to try to appreciate the relevance of Gramsci in and beyond his historical context in order to think contemporary problems through in a Gramscian way rather than simplistically believing that Gramsci has the answers or holds the key to our present problems (see Hall, 1988a: 161, 1997: 24–41; Morton, 1999).

Furthermore there are important reasons for rejecting the collective convenience of referring to neo-Gramscian analyses as an '-ism'. There is a diversity of approaches which claim a common Gramscian lineage, or derive some licence from Gramsci, within IPE whilst also placing varying emphasis on a vocabulary of Gramscian concepts. As a result it is difficult to support the notion of a neo-Gramscian*ism* that not only implies a uniform and settled consensus but also has a certain totalising connotation. As such, the notion of a neo-Gramscian*ism* may convey a further form of closure as well as a degree of continuity with '-isms' of the past.[5] There is also the liability of an incipient slide from historical materialism within the notion of an '-ism' only loosely affiliated to Gramsci, usually relying on an interpretation by proxy of Gramsci's intellectual and strategic problematic. It has been argued that this tendency is represented in a 'hyphenated Marxism' (post-, ex-, or anti-) that partakes in revisionist 'cut-and-paste quotation wringing' (Petras, 1991: 58–9). Elsewhere this tendency has been referred to as a 'designer Gramscianism' that develops aspects of Gramsci's work, often abstracted and ceaselessly distilled, so that Gramsci exists simply as a source for handy and stylish quotes, phrases or metaphors (Harris, 1992: 190–1).

Overall, then, due to the politics behind labelling, awareness has to be generated about the consequences of establishing a neatly demarcated 'school' or '-ism'. Such labels are often uncritically essentialist categories that can hide historical change and the interests of those deemed to constitute such categories whilst nuances and subtleties are denied (e.g. German and Kenny, 1998). Also, rather than analysing concrete social relations between people, the above labels tend to reify and obscure social relations. This means that the diversity of social relations becomes translated into a single category, preventing any serious discussion of assumptions, contradictions and differences which are thereby covered up. There is therefore the liability that the consolidation of a 'school' or '-ism' could disable and disempower what was empowering and interesting about the original insights in the first place. More importantly the question remains how a 'school' can encompass other perspectives with sympathetic overlaps, emphases and purposes.[6] Hence there is a need to appreciate a variety of different perspectives that can co-exist in a spirit of diversification and renewal whilst at the same time avoiding imperial pretension and closure. Alongside this prerogative, to adequately conceive a space where contending perspectives may co-exist, there also needs to be critical engagement with political practice to connect with everyday lived experience in the move towards engendering progressive transformation. Hence the twin issues of adequately reflecting upon the way IPE is conceived *and* practised within a more appropriate label to appreciate the contributions neo-Gramscian analyses can make to the questioning of social and power relations in world order.

An alternative: neo-Gramscian *perspectives*

Rather than a *de rigueur* critique of those works commonly recognised as neo-Gramscian within IPE, this argument, concentrating on the political nature of labels and the awareness drawn to the implications of 'schooling' thinking and practice in a certain way, proposes something different. Instead of a rejection of those works recognised as neo-Gramscian, my contention is that it would be more prudent to discern how different themes arise in different authors whilst also acknowledging overlapping alignments. Therefore, just as one should accept the diversity of the critiques that are made *against* those works recognised as neo-Gramscian – with some overlapping similarities – the same should be appreciated of neo-Gramscian works *themselves*. In short, a focus on the very diversity and heterogeneity of commitments in the works recognised as neo-Gramscian can be maintained by advancing the notion of neo-Gramscian *perspectives* and thus rejecting the label of a neo-Gramscian 'school' or '-ism'. This acknowledges the demands of those scholars, such as Robert Cox, who resist being assimilated into a 'school' whilst nevertheless drawing attention to the strong lineage of adopted and adapted Gramscian concepts.[7]

The emphasis on the plural form of neo-Gramscian *perspectives* is especially pertinent. It immediately accepts the diversity of contributions *within* the perspectives whilst also permitting the flexibility to realise commonalities and overlaps. It also offers the opportunity to appreciate intersections with forms of thought and action *beyond* the perspectives by maintaining the potential for intellectual engagement and openness across interdisciplinary sites, hence facilitating the convenience of naming one's position whilst signalling the intention to transcend disciplinary boundaries. By appreciating the diversity of neo-Gramscian perspectives it also becomes very difficult to substantiate critical generalisations about such perspectives. Similarly, by highlighting the specific efforts of social analysts to engage with concrete social forces within such perspectives, an alternative is also offered to the reification of a 'school'.

A recognition of the diversity of neo-Gramscian perspectives can also provide some basis for addressing criticisms made against those alleged adherents of the perspectives. It is not my specific intention here to deal with the diversity of such critiques but my argument does have relevance to how some of these critiques have been fashioned and it does reject some of the common assumptions on which such critiques are based. In contrast, though, it also has to be noted that, with few exceptions, there has been a staggering overall silence on behalf of the adherents of neo-Gramscian perspectives in dealing with such criticisms. This has resulted in a somewhat collective politics of forgetting when it comes to developing responses to criticisms.[8]

Those works that constitute what are referred to here as neo-Gramscian perspectives are quite often criticised as too unfashionably *marxisant* or, alternatively, too lacking in Marxist rigour. They are seen as unfashionable because many retain an essentially historical materialist position as central to analysis – focusing on the 'decisive nucleus of economic activity' (Gramsci, 1971: 161) – but without succumbing to expressions of economism. Hence the accusation that such analysis remains caught within modernist assumptions that take as foundational the structures of historical processes that determine the realms of the possible (Ashley, 1989: 275). Whilst this issue cannot be resolved within the current argument, the question remains open as to what degree there are modernist foundations underpinning any emancipatory commitment to historical materialism. However, it is worth noting that the fallibility of all knowledge claims is stressed across neo-Gramscian perspectives, which leads to a degree of diffidence about the foundations for knowledge. A minimal foundationalism is therefore implied based on a cautious, contingent universalism that combines dialogue between universal values and historically specific circumstances (see Cox, 1995; for a similar stress see Booth, 1995; or Rengger and Hoffman, 1996).

Alternatively, a degree of polemical sectarianism has arisen from certain quarters that decries the lack of historical materialist rigour within neo-Gramscian perspectives. According to Peter Burnham (1991), the work of Cox and others amounts to a 'pluralist empiricism' that fails to recognise the central importance of the capital relation and is therefore preoccupied with the articulation of ideology. By granting equal weight to ideas and material capabilities, it is argued that the contradictions of the capital relation are blurred which results in 'a slide towards an idealist account of the determination of economic policy' (ibid.: 81). Hence there is an inability to grapple with the dynamics of globalisation because the categories of state and market are regarded as opposed forms of social organisation that operate separately in external relationship to one another. This leads to a supposed reification of the state as a 'thing' in itself standing outside the relationship between capital and labour (Burnham, 1999). Instead, it is recommended that a 'totalising' theory, rooted in central organising principles, is developed that is attentive to the relations between labour, capital and the state.

In specific response to these criticisms, the social relations of production and the way these engender configurations of social forces are taken by neo-Gramscian perspectives as the starting point for thinking about world order (see Chapter 1). By thus asking what modes of social relations of production within capitalism have been prevalent in particular historical circumstances, the state is not treated as an unquestioned category. Indeed, rather closer to Burnham's own position than he might admit, the state is treated as an aspect of the social relations of production so that questions about the *apparent* separation of politics and economics or states and markets within capitalism are promoted (Burnham, 1994). Although a fully developed theory of the state is not evident, there clearly exists a set of at least implicit assumptions about the state as a form of social relations through which capitalism and hegemony are expressed. Therefore, akin to arguments elsewhere (Holloway and Picciotto, 1977), it is possible from within a neo-Gramscian perspective to raise questions about how different forms of state are established and how – through the contradictions of capital – the functions of the state are revised and supplemented.

Additionally, Burnham also states (1991: 76) that the account of hegemony developed across neo-Gramscian perspectives 'is barely distinguishable from a sophisticated neo-realist account'. Yet this undervalues a critical theory approach to considering hegemony and the insistence on an ethical dimension to analysis so that 'questions of justice, legitimacy and moral credibility are integrated sociologically into the whole and into many of its key concepts' (Gill, 1993: 24). Ideas are accepted as part of the global political economy itself, which facilitates recognition of the ideology and latent normative element underpinning a perspective. As a result it can be argued that Burnham tends to undervalue the production of intersubjective meanings within this theory of hegemony. Whilst Burnham's critique does rightly point to the danger of overstating the role of ideas within neo-Gramscian perspectives (Bieler, 1996), the function of intellectual activity across state–civil society relations and the role of consent as a necessary form of hegemony should not be overlooked. The point is therefore not to take the position of 'Theological Marxists', who focus on the 'law of value' and the 'law of motion of capital' as absolute knowledge rather than as hypotheses (Cox, 1992/1996: 176). Rather than upholding a fixed notion of historical materialism, following the spirit of Raymond Williams (1977: 3–4), the point is to remain open to a body of thinking that is active, developing and unfinished. Therefore, whilst neo-Gramscian perspectives cannot be separated from historical materialism, they may be distinguished within it.[9] This latter assertion is based on the assumption that neo-Gramscian perspectives implicitly accept, incorporate and advance upon the argument that Gramsci enables us to read Marx in the conditions of modern capitalism so that:

> In Gramsci, as he reworks the significance of Marx's Preface to 'A Contribution to a Critique of Political Economy', we find an historical materialism which sets out an agenda for research and for politics. We encounter a Gramscian materialism which escapes any simple causal explanation, which provides the basis for an analysis which is capable of comprehending a dynamic, contradictory, multi-faceted reality, in which material conditions indicate what is possible (Showstack Sassoon, 1987: xvii).

It is through neo-Gramscian perspectives that such a historical materialist research agenda for analysing contemporary society is being realised by asking questions about social, political and economic developments – in short, by illuminating the nature of capitalism in the present juncture – whilst remaining engaged with daily life. The point, therefore, is that by introducing the diversity of neo-Gramscian perspectives within a broadly historical materialist framework, all-encompassing statements and criticisms about such perspectives can rarely be sustained with confidence or conviction. It might be one thing to question the attachment to historical materialism across such perspectives, or assert the necessity of maintaining an active engagement with Gramsci (Germain and Kenny, 1998), but it is quite another to sustain a critique of *all* neo-Gramscian perspectives on such a basis. The difficulty is related to the diversity of appropriations and sequestrations that claim a Gramscian imprimatur within IPE. Thus, by drawing attention to and highlighting diversity alongside forwarding the alternative of neo-Gramscian perspectives, the argument is that criticisms need to be specific, in relation to the issues under discussion and with reference to specific adherents within the perspectives. This is part of the utility that is afforded by the alternative of recognising diverse neo-Gramscian perspectives. It now remains to sum up the discussion and give an account of how the notion of perspectives can assist efforts to transcend disciplinary boundaries in an endeavour to maintain openness and engage with forms of thought and action beyond self-enclosed analytical positions.

Conclusion: knowing something about something[10]

This argument has contested some of the taken-for-granted or 'common sense' assumptions associated with the proliferation of labels related to an alternative theoretical approach developed within IPE that advances upon (and therefore goes beyond) the general conceptual framework of Antonio Gramsci. At grave risk of confusion and oversimplification, it should be difficult to presume a single current of thought defined and labelled as a neo-Gramscian 'school'. There is no neo-Gramscian 'school' in IPE. The convenience of catchy labels can mask issues and generate theoretical and practical confusion rather than yield greater clarity. Moreover as we carry certain labels around in our thinking and express them through our everyday actions, the sedimentation of inappropriate labels can develop so that they become unconsciously accepted and even regarded beyond question. As a result labels are political, and that is why they matter.

Rather than affirming the virtues of a 'school', or particular interpretive community, and the guild consensus that this can engender revolving around the canonisation of certain notions, texts and authorities, an alternative emphasis was placed on the suitability of highlighting neo-Gramscian *perspectives* in IPE. The very plurality of the term compromises any status as a discrete 'school' indifferent to issues and debates beyond self-defined boundaries, and yet it also affords the opportunity to recognise a variety of opinions that have become a collective social element with innovative commonalities and overlaps. Whilst we need to be sceptical about all categorical designations, including those developed in this chapter, it is felt that a general recognition of broad and diverse neo-Gramscian perspectives furthers the effort to maintain openness to issues defined intellectually and practically rather than following certain rituals and preconceptions. There is a necessity to appeal to a plurality of audiences by offering common ground for analysis rather than locating oneself within a single group: hence the possible suitability of the alternative label of neo-Gramscian perspectives. Despite some of the advantages that this alternative provides, however, the important issue is to be able to move beyond the realm of ideas. A determining sphere of action certainly involves ideas but these have to be understood in connection with material power relations (cf. Hall, 1988b). As Edward Said has noted (1993: 407), 'Labels... are no more than starting-points, which if followed into actual experience for only a moment are quickly left behind.' This means that at the intertwined levels of ideas and material reality there is still much more work to be done.

This demands developing an analysis of a concrete conjuncture. The following chapters undertake such a task by deriving from specific social relations an appreciation of historical movement and political change as part of theoretical reflection. Through the realisation of knowledge in practice, conceptually informed historical research can thus promote particular ideas that both constitute and explain social reality. In lieu of discussing these issues within the present argument, the crux is that it is possible to raise and develop the above points, as well as similar questions to those posed by Gramsci, within a series of neo-Gramscian perspectives. This also includes moving towards suggesting agents and sites for change through a discussion of strategies of resistance (Bieler and Morton, 2001). Analysis, notes Drainville (1994: 125), 'must give way to more active sorties against transnational neo-liberalism, and the analysis of concepts of control must beget original concepts of resistance' (see also Chapters 3 and 10 below). Analysis of *specific* instances of the discipline of capital and resistance to capitalist social relations within the *general* local, national, and regional impact of neo-liberalism might also provide a necessary corrective to those searching for a single, unifying, grand historical political cause around which to rally (M. Cox, 1998). By developing an explicitly theorised account of concrete historical activity, the following empirical chapters therefore analyse social forces that have been involved in the making of the 'New Europe' and the restructuring of European social relations within the global political economy.

Notes

1. Many thanks to Andreas Bieler, Pinar Bilgin, Robert Cox, Randall Germain and Stephen Hobden for their comments on drafts of this chapter. Similar thanks are due to the participants of a research colloquium organised by Don MacIver and Brian White at Staffordshire University, as well as those present at a panel during the 23rd Annual Conference of the British International Studies Association, University of Sussex (14–16 December 1998), during which previous versions of the chapter were presented.
2. Also see the curmudgeonly disagreeableness directed by Andre Gunder Frank (1997) towards a collection of essays in Gill and Mittelman (1997) that brims with invective against some forms of conventionality. For responses see Mittelman (1997) and Gill (1997).

3. For a development of this alternative see Bonefeld, Gunn and Psychopedis (1992a, 1992b) and Bonefeld *et al.* (1995).

4. It has been queried what the 'neo' adds or subtracts within the overall scheme of neo-Gramscian perspectives (Robert Cox, personal correspondence, 28 December 1998). As argued, it helps to avoid committing the error of literally applying Gramsci whilst placing importance on developing constantly renewable ideas in relation to present political conditions.

5. Elsewhere, with very different issues at stake, see the battle over vocabulary and the need to abandon the use of particular '-isms' discussed in Said (1990). The crucial point here is that certain labels lose force, or are inappropriate, and hence the necessity of providing alternatives to prevailing notions in the attempt to question what passes as the accepted taken-for-granted or 'common sense' view.

6. For example, in addition to those works mentioned in Chapter 1, a glaring issue that needs to be raised is how the following Gramscian-inflected works can be situated within an easily demarcated 'school': see, *inter alia*, Agnew and Corbridge (1995); Birchfield (1999); Cafruny (1990); Gale (1998); Lee (1995); Murphy and Tooze (1991); or Sklair (1997).

7. Robert Cox conveyed to me his unrest at being assimilated within a 'neo-Gramscian school', declaring that the notion was someone else's and not his. The interpretive framework of ideas that Cox draws upon owes as much to thinkers such as Giambattista Vico, Ibn Khaldun, Karl Marx, Georges Sorel, Karl Polanyi, E. H. Carr, R. G. Collingwood, Fernand Braudel or Max Weber as to Antonio Gramsci and yet, as he argues, no one associates him with a 'school' deriving from any of these other thinkers (personal correspondence, 28 July 1997).

8. In addition to those critiques already referenced, it is important to mention the recent insights of Germain and Kenny (1998). Responses to criticisms, albeit very recent and related to a specific debate, include those of Murphy (1998), Rupert (1998) or Morton (1999). An intervention dealing with wider issues has been made by Bieler (1996). Despite these contributions, though, there does seem to be a more general tendency, in relation to criticisms, to resort to what can be called a politics of forgetting.

9. This seems to be the position of Hazel Smith (see H. Smith, 1996).

10. This phrase was asserted by Susan Strange as an essential part of broadening one's outlook in the endeavour to look closely at specific issues or episodes as a point of reference on larger issues (see Strange, 1984: 196).

Part II

Transnational Capital and the Neo-Liberal Restructuring of European Social Relations of Production

3
Constitutionalising Capital: EMU and Disciplinary Neo-Liberalism[1]

Stephen Gill

This chapter seeks (i) to conceptualise aspects of the emerging relationships between public and private patterns of authority or neo-liberal governance in the European Union (EU) and the global political economy, and (ii) to trace associated power structures and relations in terms of their coercive and consensual (material and normative) dimensions. In addition, some policy alternatives to neo-liberalism will be sketched.

New constitutionalism is an international governance framework. It seeks to separate economic policies from broad political accountability in order to make governments more responsive to the discipline of market forces, and correspondingly less responsive to popular-democratic forces and processes. New constitutionalism is the politico-legal dimension of the wider discourse of disciplinary neo-liberalism. Central objectives in this discourse are security of property rights and investor freedoms, and market discipline on the state and on labour, to secure 'credibility' in the eyes of private investors (e.g., those in both the global currency and capital markets).

The Maastricht Agreements and Economic and Monetary Union (EMU) are interpreted here as commensurate with this neo-liberal discourse. To explain the principles, practices and consequences, and more broadly the social power of this discourse, is complex. In Europe it partly involves analysis of fiscal crisis, the globalisation of and competition for financial sources for funding deficits, and instabilities associated with the European currency regime. Maastricht and EMU seek to minimise the threat of currency turbulence by moving to a single currency and by 'locking in' political commitments to orthodox market-monetarist fiscal and monetary policies that are perceived to increase government credibility in the eyes of financial market players.[2] Nevertheless, the social forces in support of EMU are not confined to *haute finance*. They are broad-based, and cut across social classes (some involving a *rentier* perspective and interest). These interests help form what, in neo-Gramscian terms, would be called a transnational historical bloc (see Chapter 1), that operates within and across nations and regions and seeks to politically embed neo-liberal hegemony. Therefore, what is significant about the present restructuring and globalisation of capital is that it involves redefinition of principles of political action and accountability, or patterns of power and authority, within and across state and civil society. In this way, EMU can be understood as part of a wider system of multi-level governance in the emerging world order.

At the same time, the Achilles heel of the European political economy, and one of the principal costs of the neo-liberal, market-monetarist austerity policies is persistent mass unemployment. Concentrated heavily among younger and less skilled workers, it partly explains tough immigration and asylum policies and, at least for the movement of (most) people, a 'fortress Europe'. It contributes to a potent admixture of social and economic dislocation, physical risks, racism and xenophobia. Indeed, corporate and state 'downsizing' now threatens the more protected workers, reflected in growing protests across Europe (e.g., in France in December 1995). Indeed, the vast majority of leading economists claim that EMU, like the orthodox policies of the 1930s, will drive up unemployment and intensify social polarisation with unpredictable political effects.[3] Hence, resistance is taking place. However, there is a lack of clearly articulated left-wing alternatives to the orthodoxy which can command credibility with voters. More than simple resistance is needed. So, in the next several years, EMU will pose acute questions of governance, political identity and social solidarity, probably under conditions of austerity and political alienation. What, then, are political alternatives to EMU from a European left that has recently taken heart from electoral victories in Italy, Britain and France?

Aspects of globalisation, regionalisation and EMU

EMU is a much less politically flexible or pragmatic approach to regionalisation than that which is found in North America or East Asia. However, it can be analysed in a similar way, by using an approach that views regionalisation as a part of a set of social forces and transnational class formations that are politically contested, contradictory and in movement. Thus it is important to place EMU (and other liberalisation measures in the EU) in the context of global patterns of power and production, as aspects of the political economy of globalisation. The emerging accumulation patterns are linked to the rising power of internationally mobile capital. They confirm some of Marx's predictions, particularly the tendency towards centralisation and concentration of capital. Of particular note in this regard is the acceleration in foreign direct investment and the deepened integration of capital markets over the past 20 years, especially since the late 1980s.

One of the key aims of the Marshall Plan and the NATO arrangements was to ensure political conditions for the expansion of American capital into Europe, and it would appear that this aim still holds with the expansion of NATO as new markets are created in the former Eastern bloc. The reach of transnational capital has now become global, as the former Soviet Union collapsed and the statist patterns of development in Latin America, parts of East Asia, India and China have shifted to create so-called emerging markets. A key difference from the early post-war years is that today the national identities of post-war state capitalism (e.g., the idea of 'national champions' within the context of protectionist and nationalist developmental policy) have changed and become more transnational. This is due to cross-investments, strategic alliances, and transnational political and social networks, especially at the level of the globalising elites of corporate capital and the state (Gill, 1994: 169–99).

The Maastricht Agreements form a political response to some of these developments. They seek to institutionalise a new currency and mandate strict fiscal discipline as part of the new practices of economic governance that will give credibility to governments and confidence to investors. It is part of an expansion of state activity to provide greater legal and other protections for business, and to try to stabilise the investment climate in Europe. European governments have sought to expand the scope of free enterprise as the primary motor of accumulation, and to de-socialise risk provision. In this way they are changing the institutional balance between state and civil society (e.g., through privatisation in pensions, health, education). Restructuring of state–civil society activity is also linked to international governance practices beyond the EU. Key agencies here are the Group of Seven, or G-7 (particularly at the level of central banks and finance ministries forums) as well as in the Organisation for Economic Co-operation and Development (OECD). Others are the international financial institutions such as the International Monetary Fund (IMF) and World Bank, as well as the regional development banks, although their impact is most profound in the transformation of the former Eastern bloc and the Third World (see, e.g., World Bank, 1997).

With regard to the role of the discourse of disciplinary neo-liberalism in the policy frameworks of globalisation, the following passage from the recent IMF publication, *World Economic Outlook 1997*, illustrates in part what I have in mind: a world in which the actions of governments, as well as firms and workers, are internally and externally disciplined by market forces, or, to put it differently, by the power of capital. The *World Economic Outlook* deals at length with the issues of globalisation and its implications for policy, and it concludes that economic globalisation limits the scope for countries to pursue:

> policies that are incompatible with medium-term financial stability. The discipline of global product and financial markets applies not only to policy-makers, via financial market pressures, but also to the private sector, making it more difficult to sustain unwarranted wage increases and markups. If markets adopt too sanguine a view of a country's economic policies and prospects, however, this could relax policy disciplines for a time and result in a high adjustment cost when market perceptions change... [and then] markets will eventually exert their own discipline, in such a way that the time period for adjustment may be brutally shortened (International Monetary Fund, 1997: 70–1).

The examples given by the IMF include those of the Exchange Rate Mechanism crises of 1992 and 1993, as well as the experiences of EU countries such as Sweden and Italy (1993–95). As the *World Economic Outlook* notes, 'these experiences show [how] international financial markets can serve to "discipline" governments (either by raising default premiums or by forcing adjustments in exchange rates), encouraging the adoption of appropriate policies' (International Monetary Fund, 1997: 66). I suggest, therefore, that EMU needs to be interpreted within this general framework, where 'appropriate policy' is understood in terms of disciplinary neo-liberal discourse. As such, it can be comprehended as part of a set of policies that have shifted the EU towards a neo-liberal and financial, as opposed to a social market or social democratic model of capitalism. This viewpoint favours tight monetary and financial discipline in a rules-based economic constitution as a means to deliver low inflation and to protect savings.[4]

This constitutional framework involves the separation of the economic and political in ways that lessen the possibility for democratic accountability in economic and social policy-making: a key example of this concerns the making and implementation of macroeconomic policy. A significant trend in economic governance is the way that monetary policy world-wide is increasingly placed in the hands of (more) independent central banks, or other mechanisms such as currency boards that are designed to prevent inflationary monetary policy. In EMU monetary policy is conducted by an independent central banking system. Moreover, EMU mandates strict control over fiscal policy (the USA's equivalent of this in fiscal terms is the attempt to pass a balanced budget amendment to the Constitution). Thus EMU would constrain EU governments from using fiscal policy for counter-cyclical reasons to offset recession.

Such changes involve political agency and active government in a process that is intended to more deeply institutionalise the power of capital within state–civil society formations in the context of economic globalisation, liberalisation and the restructuring of the state. Put differently, economic liberalisation is not necessarily the same as 'rolling back' the frontiers of a particular state, or indeed its 'retreat'. It involves actively remaking state apparatuses and governmental practices *and* the institutions of civil society. The central goal of neo-liberal reforms is to make state and civil society become more permeated with market practices, values, discipline, transparency and accountability (the creation of the European Single Market was intended to foster this). In Europe, then, some of the sources for such changes have been fiscal crisis, currency instability and economic stagnation, as well as fears of a loss of the EU's competitive edge relative to East Asia and North America. For example, because of fiscal crisis, many EU states raised interest rates to defend their currencies, and sought to reduce government expenditures, notably for social and welfare programmes, in large part to satisfy traders in the currency and bond markets.

In sum, what is at issue is a set of governance initiatives and political processes which reformulate and redefine the public sphere and rules for economic policy. Here it is important to stress that these initiatives and the policy discourses they entail involve both macroeconomics (e.g., the main focus of EMU) as well microeconomics and structural policies (e.g., trade, labour market and industrial policy; Gill, 1992).

As such, international agreements on trade and investment can be understood as reinforcing national and regional policies to restructure the state and thus to politically lock-in neo-liberal reforms; in short, as part of an attempt to secure the rights of investors and property holders. Some of these multilateral reforms, stemming from the Uruguay Round, are being institutionalised through the new World Trade Organisation (WTO). Moreover, measures such as the OECD's intended Multilateral Agreement on Investment attempted to go well beyond the Uruguay Round measures on Trade-Related Investment Measures (TRIMS), Trade-Related Intellectual Property Measures (TRIPS) and the General Agreement on Trade-in-Services (GATS) by reinforcing legal and other sanctions in support of a deepening of economic liberalisation. Other counter-party arrangements involve the adoption of standards and product rules that condition the terrain of competition in a global economic system that is dominated by giant knowledge-intensive corporations (with huge numbers of suppliers and retail outlets dependent upon them) and financial services firms.[5]

What is important here, on an ideological level, is not only the IMF's *World Economic Outlook 1997*, which is subtitled 'Globalisation: Challenges and Opportunities', with its discourse of disciplinary neo-liberalism, referred to above, but also the World Bank's 1997 *World Development Report: The State in a Changing World*. The Bank stresses the need for a strong state with an efficient public administration to institutionalise market forces, support economic liberalisation, and promote public–private partnerships not only in service provision, but also in the enforcement of contracts and the prevention of corruption. The World Bank sees the context for such changes as a world-wide market revolution that creates new obligations for the state.

What are the social forces in support of EMU?

The first point to note when considering which social forces support EMU is that European integration is not simply an economic project. It is much more fundamentally a strategic project, but not simply in the sense of a unified Europe as a means for Germany and its key allies to forge geopolitical strategy. Of course, European integration is connected to this broader goal, at least for many advocates of the federal view of Europe, such as Jacques Delors. They tend to represent EMU as an attempt to produce an economic union that might lead to political union, so as to generate more political cohesion and European competitiveness relative to North America and East Asia. But the key issue is the form and substance of regionalism and its link to the global political economy. Thus if we place EMU in the context of the gradual shift towards economic liberalisation, we can argue that it reflects more a strategy for reconciling regional integration with globalising forces. Indeed, the global aspect is illustrated by the fact that much of what is normally referred to as 'European' capital involves American, Japanese and other transnational firms. In short, as outlined in the introduction to this volume, the revival of European integration in general, and EMU in particular, is part and parcel of the global restructuring processes.

In this context, what social and political forces operate in support of EMU within its state and civil society, and why? France and other European nations moved gradually towards a 'German model' of economic policy during the 1980s and especially during the 1990s. This is because of the predominance and centrality of Germany, specifically due to its added political and economic weight and size following unification. Indeed, despite the reluctance of the Bundesbank and the majority of the German electorate to give up the D-mark, and their doubts about the wisdom of a single currency, the German government pushed towards the introduction of EMU. Chancellor Helmut Kohl in particular has pressed for European integration, provided that other nations were willing to accept EMU on largely German macroeconomic criteria and institutional principles. Yet, while it is the case that Germany has set the convergence and institutional conditions for entry to the inner core of the EMU project, there is confusion about the weight and scope of the social forces that support a tough anti-inflationary stance. Many have pointed out the dangers of an inflexible approach to fiscal and monetary policy when mass unemployment scars the European social landscape. In fact, there are powerful social forces operating in Europe that stand in support of the German perspective.

One way to explore this question is to start with Bastiaan van Apeldoorn's research on the European Roundtable of Industrialists (ERT). This work shows that neo-liberalism was in large part a strategic project of globally-oriented finance and industrial capital, rather than of European companies primarily producing for the European market. Van Apeldoorn shows how the ERT shifted from a perspective that sought to encourage the development of European champions (an inward-looking and defensive Euro-mercantilist strategy), to a more neo-liberal and global orientation during the 1990s. During the early 1980s, most firms that were the national and European 'champions' generally tended to perceive globalisation as a threat rather than as an opportunity and pressed for a relaunch of the European project on very different terms to neo-liberals. Van Apeldoorn calls this a defensive strategy of 'protective regionalism'. This strategy failed to win support in part because of the perceived success of the Single Market Initiative after 1986. Its final defeat within European ruling-class circles came with the conclusion of the General Agreement on Tariffs and Trade (GATT) Uruguay Round in December 1993, the international counterpart to the Single Market Initiative (van Apeldoorn, 1997a and Chapter 4 below). EMU was part of the European unification project under Delors, who sought ways to overcome and incorporate Bundesbank opposition to the potential loss of its cherished D-mark.

In neo-Gramscian terms what is occurring is the political and legal reconstitution of capital through the agency of a neo-liberal transnational historical bloc and a process of elite international policy-formation, with high-profile fora such as the G-7 and international financial institutions at the apex of an on-going and differentiated policy process. This transnational historical bloc is a political synthesis of interests and identities drawn from across social classes and nations that mediates and seeks to co-ordinate national, regional and global dimensions of accumulation and legitimation. It thus generates the ideas, institutions and material capabilities that are associated with the global shift towards more neo-liberal forms of state. The broad political aim is to restructure and consolidate state forms so that they become internally and externally more hospitable to the dominant forces in modern capitalism (notably large transnational corporations, financial services firms and institutional investors).

Thus the international policy-making apparatus operates in concert with private agents: for example, International Relations Councils such as the Trilateral Commission (which has a large EU membership, with elite political and economic interests represented), the World Economic Forum, the Group of Thirty (particularly important in money and finance), and think tanks such as the UK's Institute of Economic Affairs and the Adam Smith Institute, the American Brookings Institute and the American Enterprise Institute, as well as the fora for leaders of large corporations. It involves European fora associated with corporate influence on the making of public policy, such as the ERT which involves among its membership 20 of the top 100 firms in the world, according to the United Nations Conference on Trade and Development's *World Investment Report* of 1995 (see van Apeldoorn, 1997a).

This neo-liberal transnational historical bloc thus has a significant basis within the EU. It includes state interests associated with the German-dominated unification project, large-scale finance and productive capital of global reach, as well as European companies, and associated privileged workers and smaller firms.[6] The European Commission's (EC) 1995 *Green Paper*, moreover, illustrates that backing for EMU is strongly linked to the interests of large financial houses and firms, government bureaucracies and EU organisations, with the governments of Germany and France pressing strongly for its realisation. Thus the concept of historical bloc enables us to understand how the present political formations, based on the dominance of transnational capital, are also constituted by and incorporate a wider range of interests and identities, including many privileged workers, members of the professions and small business people. That is to say, the bloc comprises interests of both capital and labour, and elements of the state apparatus, although it is dominated by the largest and most internationally-mobile transnational firms and their political and economic networks. The bloc also includes small investors, many of whom have come to adopt aspects of a *rentier* mentality in the context of the world-wide stock market boom that has characterised the 1990s. As a result, the interests and perspectives of many blue- and white-collar workers correspond to the *rentier* perspective noted above. And, indeed, until recently, these workers have been less concerned with the plight of the unskilled and unemployed than they have been with maintaining their own living standards (see European Commission, 1995b). This bloc forms the primary political formation that promotes neo-liberal restructuring in Europe and supports EMU.

Not surprisingly, the EU's implementation strategy for EMU is partly based on mobilising this set of forces: it stresses the need to involve the most powerful economic agents first, and to draw in local/national interests associated with the EMU project to deepen its social basis. This entails working through the banking and financial sector, public administrations, enterprises and consumers (savers) to widen public support. The strategy assumes an economic order dominated by knowledge-intensive, internationally mobile capital (institutional investors, banks and transnational corporations, especially those that have large financial services arms). It also links to the growing salience of the discourse of the information society, and the practical interests of software and computing firms, since the change to a single currency will involve huge outlays in computer programming and software design.

Of course, some *rentier* interests will be damaged by EMU: for example, commercial banks, notably in the City of London, make large profits from intra-European currency transactions, particularly in the retail markets. The City is engaged in the lion's share of European foreign exchange transactions and thus some of its business will disappear with a European single currency. However, other interests contribute to a continued influence of a *rentier* perspective on policy. Many workers from the wealthier micro-regions are employed in successful firms that are at the vanguard of new patterns of innovation and accumulation. Such workers are often impatient with the redistributive welfare policies of their national governments, and of the EU itself (see *New York Review of Books*, 13 June 1996). This helps to explain why the Maastricht provisions have so far involved little by way of the creation of employment opportunities despite chronic mass unemployment across Europe. Here it is also noteworthy that redistributive funds are not being spent as members of the EU strive to reduce budget deficits to meet the Maastricht convergence criteria (i.e., budget deficits must be less than 3 per cent of GDP) and are, therefore, unwilling to provide the required sums to match EU funds in order to assist their depressed regions (see the *Financial Times*, 29 July 1996).

Thus, although Alan Milward perhaps overestimates support for Maastricht's fiscal rectitude and for the single currency when he claims 'the interest in stability of savings is high everywhere', his basic point still stands: in an economically polarised continent, many of the more powerful social forces are in favour of strong anti-inflation policies, almost regardless of the scale of unemployment (Milward, 1996: 62). This is particularly the case in Germany, where the broad-based fear of inflation harks back to the hyper-inflation of the Weimar Republic. The German fear of inflation meshes well with the interests of bond-holders and has forced other countries to accept the very tough convergence criteria for EMU. The dominance of the German position was indicated at the Amsterdam summit in June 1997. Here the newly-elected French Socialist government could not force a renegotiation of institutional and economic arrangements put in place at Maastricht, despite its electoral promises to deal with the problem of mass unemployment at the European level. In fact, other EU members pressed the French Socialists to deliver the opposite of what it has promised its electorate: more budget cuts and more austerity (see the *Financial Times*, 18 June 1997).

In sum, it needs to be re-emphasised that the neo-liberal perspective which dominates European public policy is not simply 'economic': it is deeply political and it involves new forms of governance. It is stressed that the state itself must be redesigned so that it operates in a more marketised way. State agencies are made to compete with the private sector in, for example, service provision, and behave as if they were market-place animals. The change in patterns of incentives and of governance is also reflected in the proliferation of quasi-governmental organisations or quangos. Quangos are charged with the administration and financial control over large areas of state activity, (e.g., in health and education), such that collective provision is subject to quasi-privatised forms of governance and accountability. In many cases, these quangos have come to be dominated by corporate interests, with Britain as the exemplar in the age of Thatcherism/Majorism. Such restructuring of the form of state has repercussions for the notion of the public sphere and the substantive nature of democracy, which thus undergoes a change in a neo-liberal framework. Certain interests are empowered by some of the neo-liberal innovations that separate the 'political' and the 'economic'.

What are the key principles, practices and consequences of EMU?

The rationale for EMU is based upon orthodox market-monetarist assumptions concerning the conduct of economic policy. It mandates state policies geared to maintaining business confidence through delivery of a consistent and credible climate for investment and the accumulation of capital (see, e.g., European Commission, 1995b: 34). Indeed, this discourse contains a normative commitment to a particular form of market civilisation dominated by investors and disciplined by market forces. In what follows I outline five components of this stance: sound policy; debt sustainability; surveillance and normalisation; the attenuation of democracy; and the prioritisation of market efficiency over equity and social solidarity. I will then explore challenges to this set of governance principles and practices, and consider the prospects for alternatives.

Sound policy and independent central banks

Bond traders and institutional investors and public agencies such as the IMF, World Bank, the Bank for International Settlements and the EU tend to press for 'sound policy' by governments. Whilst the market agents are on the whole agnostic about the processes for the delivery of such soundness, there has been support in the investor communities for the separation of monetary policy (and to a degree, fiscal policy) from the pressures of domestic politics and accountability. Investors seek low inflation and preservation of the value of currencies in which bonds are denominated (hence 'sound money'). According to neo-classical economists, high inflation has a negative impact on growth rates (although there is some debate as to whether this is the case at lower rates of inflation). To achieve lower inflation, the most favoured means is one that insulates (or, even better, removes) monetary policy entirely from the political process. The main mechanism for this involves central bank independence with the requirement of pursuing a low or zero inflation target and rules that prohibit the monetisation of government deficits (i.e., printing money and applying an inflation tax to reduce the real value of state debts).

According to Stanley Fischer, First Deputy Managing Director of the IMF, the question of prioritising the war on inflation (a priority that gradually emerged at the top of the G-7 agenda from the mid-1970s on) is ultimately a *political* one. It is 'a political judgement, supported by political and economic theory and evidence, that control over inflation should…be made the central goal of monetary policy' (Fischer, 1996: 35; emphasis added). Whilst the theoretical and empirical claims in this statement are open to contestation, it also means that a 'political judgement' to emphasise growth and to make the new European Central Bank structures more representative of wider social and political interests could be made, too. This is the position staked out by the government in France under Prime Minister Lionel Jospin, and it was also linked to Oskar Lafontaine in Germany (see below). This position seems certain to attain wider resonance if economic stagnation continues in the EU.

Debt sustainability

The next element in this broad policy stance associated with EMU is fiscal: the requirement that budget deficits must be 'sustainable'. It means that they must be seen by market operators and bond-holders in particular as consistent with low and stable ratios of debt to GDP. This would minimise the risks of default, as occurred in the 1930s. Again this goal is spelled out in the Maastricht convergence criteria on overall government debt levels and permissible fiscal deficits. The big market operators (institutional investors, hedge funds) are sceptical about the will or ability of governments to raise taxes (in an era of actual or potential tax revolts). They look for the willingness of governments to privatise assets and to cut public services by as much as is necessary. A subsidiary argument put forward by the supporters of EMU is related to debt-management and funding. It is said that a combination of policies that moves fiscal deficits closer to the Maastricht convergence criteria, allied to a Bundesbank-style tight money policy, is likely to induce the private bond-rating agencies to reward a number of governments with an improved credit-rating. This would lower the cost of funding new government debt. But again, we do not have a crystal ball. An improved credit-rating is unlikely if European growth is low and depresses tax receipts, especially in a world of capital mobility.

Surveillance and normalisation

Government policies, especially those which might influence the rates of return on capital (e.g., the rate of inflation, risk of government default) are placed under consistent and virtually instantaneous scrutiny (surveillance) by market operators. They are also monitored by public international financial institutions such as the secretive Bank for International Settlements, the IMF and the OECD. In this sense, market transparency only applies to some types of public financial operations but, when it does, it is meant to produce something akin to a Foucauldian condition of surveillance. Normalisation of this framework of surveillance reinforces statutory and other institutional provisions of new constitutionalism. The aim is to harmonise state policies by policing deviance from orthodox neo-liberalism, and, *en passant*, to move towards the further depoliticisation of questions of money and finance. Discursively this is also achieved partly through the insistence that low inflation plus flexible markets provides greater economic prosperity for all, and in more negative terms, by claiming that there is no credible alternative to EMU.

Attenuation of democracy

Put differently, 'new constitutionalist' initiatives are designed to lessen short-run political pressures on the formulation of economic policy, by re-defining the boundaries of the 'economic' and the 'political'. Such boundaries police the limits of the possible in the making of economic policy. Legal or administrative enforcement is required, since the power of normalising discourse or ideology is not enough to ensure compliance with the orthodoxy. The initiatives thus presuppose a system of unequal representation in the institutions of the economy and in politics. Unequal representation gives more political weight to 'technocratic' cadres, such as neo-classical economists, financial administrators and central bankers, who are hardly representative of broader societal interests. The least democratic levels of governance in the emerging multi-level system tend to be in local government (where participation at the local level often tends to be quite low) and more acutely at the level of regional and global governance in, for example, the EC and the international financial institutions, where there are significant 'democratic deficits'.

Due to the pressures of Maastricht, some national governments in the EU, which are more accountable to electorates than is the European Commission, may be tempted to resort to government by decree if normal measures to gain support for their policies fail. An extreme example of this logic (i.e., of subordinating democracy to the dictates of a neo-liberal restructuring of state finances) was seen in Belgium in 1996. Here we witnessed a peculiar combination of austerity and absolutism in order to meet EMU convergence criteria (*The Guardian Weekly*, 11 August 1996). The future may be worse. As the prominent American economist, Richard Cooper, has put it (1994: 70):

> Maastricht...creates a body of Platonic monetary guardians, accountable to no one, to frame and execute one of the most important aspects of policy in modern economies, affecting hundreds of millions of people. This was done in the name of insulating monetary policy – and its primary objective of price stability – from political pressure, and of endowing the new European central bank with political independence.

In this context, EMU has come to have a peculiar political logic, which to be charitable could be described as Homeric: in order to return safely home whilst on his epic journey Odysseus insisted on being bound to the mast (of fiscal and monetary rectitude) so he would not be lured by the song of the Sirens (and debauch the currency). In political terms the effect of such measures, when implemented, would be to prohibit a wide range of policies to defend national or local interests. Indeed many redistributive policies that a more ecologically and socially-oriented policy perspective might seek to promote would be made more difficult, or even illegal. These measures could be opposed as being in restraint of trade or freedom of investment/repatriation of profits and so on.

Prioritisation of market efficiency over equity and social solidarity

One consequence of the implementation of these principles is that a more narrowly defined efficiency goal is prioritised over equity in the making of public policy. At the same time, it tends to erode old forms of social solidarity and generates, for the majority of the population, increased personal insecurity and uncertainty as social inequality increases. This has meant, amongst other things, that European social institutions are redefined more comprehensively by possessive individualism, the protection of private property rights and the ideology of market society.

Some alternative policy perspectives

None of what I have written above is intended to suggest that processes of disciplinary neo-liberal restructuring are uncontested or complete. In order to conceptualise alternatives to EMU we have to look beyond the issues of macroeconomic policy. We need to restate the debate in terms of the way that the restructuring of policy impacts on the everyday lives of people in fundamental ways. Moreover, policies associated with a new political economy need to be cast in terms of a time-horizon that is linked to the creation of an alternative form of state for Europe in the new century. In my view this form of state needs to be a more democratic, 'green' and social one. This is opposed to the arid financial vision of Europe associated with EMU. Proposals need to be justified in terms of creative economic and political (democratic) potentials. Credibility, however, needs to be redefined as not only financial but also social. Moreover, proposals from the left must overcome the argument that since governments are in fiscal crisis or virtually bankrupt, we have to adjust our expectations downwards. The general point to be emphasised here is that, in conditions of unprecedented affluence, new policies are affordable and can be financed. Nevertheless they need to be thought through carefully in terms of appropriate timeframes for political action.

The immediate frame includes influence over the electoral process. Nevertheless, given the dominance of prevailing orthodoxy within the political cadres, even when the socialist and social democratic left has been successful in recent elections (e.g., in Britain and France in 1997), their governments did not deviate far from neo-liberal austerity (Italy under its present left-wing coalition government illustrates this trend). The continued commitment to Maastricht was reflected in the Amsterdam summit of June 1997. Very little, if anything had apparently changed since then in the plans for EMU and in the current logic of austerity policies which force the most significant adjustments on the most vulnerable in society.

Thus, over the next few years, social and political tensions are likely to increase. On the one hand, this timeframe allows for the development of more institutionalised left alternatives and initiatives that might feed into government policies. On the other hand, this development would pose great dangers to the left. This is because, first, the left could be associated with the continuation of austerity. The left might thus be discredited further after it has been weakened on a world scale by the combination of the collapse of Communist rule and the growth in the power and mobility of capital. Moreover, powerful alternatives to a neo-liberal order in the EU may, of course, not necessarily be progressive ones, and they might further weaken the left. This is especially the case given the resurgence of the reactionary right in the last 20 years, and the vein of xenophobia and racism that exists across the political spectrum in several European countries, such as France and most recently in Austria, where the Neo-Nazi Austrian Freedom Party (FPÖ) joined the right-wing governing coalition, causing consternation and confusion in other European Union capitals.

With regard to the remobilisation of economic activity to deal with unemployment, Alain Lipietz, in the context of a wider eco-socialist strategy for European renewal, offers a pragmatic alternative to Maastricht. Lipietz's proposals (1996: 377–8) are based upon a strengthening of European social policy and a neo-Keynesian programme of European-wide co-ordinated expansion. His proposals were partly reflected in the stance of French Prime Minister Jospin at Amsterdam, and in a somewhat different manner by Oskar Lafontaine, the former Finance Minister of the Social Democrat government in Germany, who abruptly resigned after strident opposition from German business neo-liberal forces elsewhere in the European Union under mysterious circumstances in early 1999, thus signalling a defeat for pragmatic Keynesianism in German policy circles.

However, clearly, other solutions to mass unemployment are necessary, based on a renewal of civic responsibility and the formation of counter-hegemonic forces that gain a stronger foothold in states and civil societies, thus promoting a more socialist-ecological format of European and global politics. This requires a combination of parliamentary pressure and the weight of social movements to make it happen and to widen the EU agenda. In some senses this is already happening: for example, Lipietz's other proposals to impose uniform taxation of capital at source throughout the Union have been taken up initially by Lafontaine and now by European Union member states. They are, of course, opposed by the UK because of the importance of low taxes for the financial interests of the City of London, which means for investors world-wide, since the City is dominated by American and Japanese, as well as continental European banks and financial firms. This is because key elements of the tax base have become more internationally mobile, and less taxable as a result.

The problem needs considerable international co-operation, in order to reverse the trends towards 'tax competition' which brings about a downward harmonisation of taxes on mobile economic agents and, as such, the British veto becomes crucial to European Union reforms in this area (International Monetary Fund, 1997: 70). So we return to a more general question: can hyper-mobile capital be controlled? If so, how? To answer this question requires study of how the dominant agents in transnational capital generate self-regulation as well as formal institutions, and how these relate to the international governance of capital mobility. Under different political conditions EMU might allow the possibility of a more democratic form of surveillance and potential political control and channelling of global movements of capital. There are two arguments to be made here, one that appears technical and one that seems political. In reality, the two are interconnected.

One argument which sustains the present situation is that the speed and ingenuity of financial innovation will always outstrip the ability of governments to react. It is said that new information technology allows for international transfers of funds beyond nation-states in the span of a nanosecond. Thus governments must subordinate policy to this techno-logical imperative. In response, the left needs to emphasise that technol-ogy is always implemented in a social and political context and can therefore be used for a variety of social purposes, including the re-regulation of capital. Indeed, paradoxically, with regard to capital mobility, much of the complex theoretical and practical work in under-standing these questions has actually been done by private interests and high-level research fora such as the Group of 30 and, as such, can be used by the left. The 30 largest banks have begun to create their own global payments-matching and -monitoring system and have expressed concern that EMU may actually increase the systemic threat of a breakdown in financial payments systems (e.g., in the repurchase markets for bonds and other securities). Such a breakdown would have potentially far-reaching, perhaps even catastrophic, consequences for the European and perhaps the global political economy. Much of the work done, and sys-tems actually implemented, has therefore been carried out in response to banks' and institutional investors' expansion of cross-border invest-ments. Major figures in the financial world, such as George Soros (who profits from currency speculation), have expressed worries about contain-ment of financial crises when reserves of central banks may be inade-quate, and when their mutual responsibilities in a crisis are unclear.

In other words, finance and money are much too important to be left to the central bankers. Here it may be significant that the largest global capital and money flows, especially currency payments, are routed through a relatively small number of mainframe computers in the USA and the EU. Under different political conditions their software systems might be reconfigured to allow not only for monitoring of capital and money flows, but also for taxation. Given that one of the hidden costs of the implementation of a single currency is very large outlays on new software, this software could be written to allow for this type of surveillance, and subsequently more democratic control. More specifically, though, political criticism of the costs of free capital mobility and globalisation is rising, as even the IMF has noted.[7] Indeed, if there was to be a significant breakdown in the financial system, as almost happened following the collapse of the Long-Term Capital Management hedge fund in August 1998 following a Russian bond default, pressure for re-regulation might well become politically unstoppable. This needs to be set alongside disquiet in some political circles that surrounds the perceived loss of government autonomy *vis-à-vis* the global capital markets (an autonomy that, in my view, could be regained at the European level through political co-operation). Many government leaders and bureaucrats have concerns about the sustainability of the tax base under conditions of capital mobility. Even the G-7 leaders discussed the possibility of a Tobin Tax on cross-border financial transactions as a way of throwing 'sand in the wheels' of hyper-mobile capital movements at the Halifax Summit in 1995 (the IMF's *World Economic Outlook 1997* flatly rejects such a tax as impractical). More generally, the massive increase in economic and social polarisation associated with globalisation is giving way to widespread political and social unrest, and not just among unskilled workers. All of the above may result in more politically powerful demands for more state action to control market forces. This might even lead to international discussion of what has seemed to be a taboo in the 1980s: the reimposition of progressive income taxes and attempts to ensure that transnational corporations could not engage in regulatory and tax arbitrage and use devices such as transfer pricing as a means of tax avoidance. This might, in fact, complement some of the European-wide measures suggested by Lipietz.

Strategic alternatives: from resistance to counter-hegemony

In other words, there seems to be growing support for heterodox policy initiatives. As many commentators have pointed out, the deflationary bias of Maastricht is also being challenged politically from below in the shape of mass politics. A key reason for this is that expenditure cuts mandated by the need to hit the convergence criteria have begun to undermine powerful interests among privileged workers. These include public servants in France and Germany and many members of the powerful German unions. Of course, some of these workers have, until recently, been to some extent incorporated into the transnational historical bloc of neo-liberal forces sketched earlier. A key question is whether they will continue to support the neo-liberal project in the coming years. However, neo-liberal retrenchment of social provision in much of Europe is less than many have claimed, and levels of popular support for social security and decommodification are very high in the EU. Thus further austerity poses significant legitimacy problems for European integration as it is currently constituted. It also provides a terrain where potential political allies, some within the ranks of capital, might be found for a reconstituted red-green political counter-offensive against neo-liberalism.

In short, the potential for counter-hegemonic forces *may* be strengthening. Generally, by contrast, the mainstream political parties of the left do not propose measures fundamentally different from the original EMU model, except that they re-prioritise employment and growth. The dominance of neo-liberalism is such that all the left-wing governing parties in the EU (with the possible exception of the French, and briefly Germany, when Lafontaine was in office) seem to operate within new constitutionalist assumptions. However, it seems that the next few years will prove to be crucial for the future direction of Europe, east and west, particularly since the Amsterdam Summit was partly concerned with the enlargement of the EU.

Here we might make an analogy with the 1920s, when in the aftermath of the First World War and the Russian Revolution there was an attempt, led by the USA and the UK, to restore aspects of nineteenth-century international economic governance, most notably the international gold standard and free trade: antecedents of the new constitutionalism of globalising neo-liberalism. However, the political and economic contradictions and conflicts of the period meant that this attempt was unsuccessful, especially following the Wall Street crash of 1929. There was a political revolt by productivist and planning-orientated social forces against the re-introduction of *laissez-faire*. The various state forms thereby produced included, in the context of the convulsions of the 1930s, the Nazism of Hitler and the fascism of Mussolini. Imperial spheres-of-influence consolidated into 'imperial-regionalisms', which clashed and helped to produce the political conditions that led to the Second World War. Of course, there are many differences between the 1930s and today, one of the key elements of which is the very existence of the EU itself. The Union institutionalises inter-state conflict (notably Franco–German rivalry) with European security, primarily defined within the framework of the North Atlantic Treaty Organisation (NATO). This makes European inter-state war seem a remote possibility, but does not necessarily mean that the political situation is cast in stone.

From the viewpoint of a broad European left, however, part of what is needed is to theorise not only resistance but also the conditions for a wider coalition of counter-hegemonic forces. This would connect polit-ically with the goal of constructing credible political, economic, social and ecological alternatives. Some of Lipietz's work on macroeconomics and the work place is an example of the type of re-thinking that needs to be done. However, the scope of what is required is much wider than this. It is partly indicated in an argument made by Kees van der Pijl (1998). He suggests that, as the discipline of capital is imposed more strongly on labour and on social institutions, it encounters resistance within three processes of class struggle. The first concerns what Marx called 'original accumulation', where the commodity form incorpo-rates previously non-commodified goods and services into the reaches of capital (e.g., through privatisation and commercialisation of public services or the 'commons'). The second relates to production relations. Much recent evidence shows that in the brave new world of high tech-nology and knowledge-based capital, instead of a leisure society being created, the pattern of labour for core workers is one of intensification, often involving longer hours and a rising rate of exploitation. There is a growing section of precarious workers, often working part-time or under temporary contracts, and under more extreme forms of exploita-tion. Beyond these, there are (often unprotected) immigrant workers in the secondary or informal labour markets. For the rest – and it seems that in the EU their numbers have grown rapidly in the past 10 years – there is the prospect or the reality of mass unemployment and margin-alisation. The third set of forces of resistance is more diffuse and relates to social reproduction. For example, microeconomic rationality and the influence of neo-liberal restructuring is spreading into the home, the schools and the institutions of civil society more generally. This raises the issue of a crisis of social reproduction. Part of the reasoning here is the pressure on the home linked to the growing feminisation of the European labour force in recent decades. Political disquiet is felt at the level of everyday life as public provisions intended to support the processes of social reproduction are reduced. These trends also raise a series of ethical questions concerning the responsibility of the state, and indeed the very nature of European society.

Conclusion

What the left and other progressive forces need to do, beyond resistance, is to reconsider their criteria of action and of political agency and to consider how to synthesise and channel the potentials for resistance into a creative political project that has a new form of the 'modern prince' as its mobilising myth, understood in the sense of Sorel and Gramsci (see Augelli and Murphy, 1997). We need to ask, in other words, what will be the new principle(s) of social justice that could be used as the criterion (or criteria) for judging the adequacy of policy that can challenge the counter-myths of progress and endless accumulation and consumption associated with neo-liberalism? What forms of potential political community and identification can be envisaged that can mobilise and consolidate support for such initiatives? As Gramsci put it (1971: 129), 'the modern prince, the myth-prince, cannot be a real person, a concrete individual. It can only be an organism, a complex element of society in which a collective will, which has already been recognised and has to some extent asserted itself in action, begins to take concrete form.'

Whilst this chapter has emphasised the power and reach of a transnational historical bloc, the sustainability of its political power should not be overestimated. As we have noted, there are at least three dimensions along which we can conceptualise resistance to disciplinary neo-liberalism. Another dimension is ethical and concerns questions of social justice linked to the growing public outcry at the truly staggering concentration of wealth and income that reflects the growing power of capital in its struggle with labour on a world scale, and its reflection in the politics of disciplinary neo-liberalism. A recent United Nations Development Programme Report, the *Human Development Report 1996*, noted for example that 358 billionaires had combined assets that exceeded the total annual income of 45 per cent of the world's population (i.e., of 3.2 billion people). Indeed, in one day in mid-July 1997, the personal wealth of Bill Gates, now the richest man on earth, rose by well over one billion US dollars (to about US$37 billion) simply because of appreciation in the stock market value of Microsoft. This took place in a nation where the real wages of the majority of Americans have stagnated or fallen over the past 10 years. Similar, though less extreme, examples can be found in the European context.

In this context, the left needs to call for a politics based on greater equity, social justice, responsibility and democracy, as well as a more ecologically sustainable form of development. This strategic perspective needs to be linked to concrete policy initiatives that deal with immediate and medium-term issues. For example, one issue that involves both questions of finance and social reproduction concerns the trend towards an ageing population. This trend will go much further in the first three decades of this century, according to virtually all demographic predictions. So far the fiscal crisis has been primarily related to the mobility of capital and skills, but there is every reason to expect that the question of the age structure of the population will become a much more dominant element of fiscal crisis over the next 30 years.

Stepping back from particular issues we need to know how far and under what conditions a truly European policy could emerge. Which social forces might support it? How would these relate to the problem of capital mobility and the sustainability of the tax base? Related to this is the need to break down the false dichotomies concerning work and retirement, productive and unproductive members of society, and the young and the old. Further, proposals should take account of distributional effects of changes in the pattern of taxation. This more selective approach would be preferable to the more blanket use of indirect taxes in Lipietz's proposals since, on the whole, indirect taxes are regressive and tend to hit the poor the hardest. So there needs to be much re-thinking of the nature of social reproduction and its interface with traditional questions of political economy, that is, a discourse that goes well beyond the economism of 'financial Europe' with the EMU as its totem.

Changing this situation requires more than mere resistance. Real change presupposes an intensification of political pressure and new forms of political organisation from below to alter the structures of unequal representation that have emerged in the era of disciplinary neo-liberalism. It also implies a radical shift in the thinking among left political parties, a shift that needs to go beyond a negative response to create a counter-hegemonic potential with real and practical policy alternatives. Such alternatives should seek to link short-term measures to remobilise the EU political economy with longer-term policies (e.g., to deal with structural unemployment and ageing populations). Finally, the strategy needs to address the logic of our present lifestyles and associated patterns of consumption. We need to adopt a new and longer-term perspective on our civilisation which is not that of the emu or, more to the point, that of the ostrich with our heads in the sand. Otherwise, we are likely to meet the fate of the dodo (like the emu and the ostrich, another large, clumsy flightless bird that was rendered extinct in the seventeenth century).

Notes

1. My thanks are due to Heikki Patomäki, Petri Minkinnen, Magnus Ryner, Jacqueline True, Adam Harmes and Kees van der Pijl for comments on earlier versions of this chapter. Permission is gratefully acknowledged to edit and reprint, in substantially revised form, a previous version of this chapter, originally published as Stephen Gill, 'European Governance and New Constitutionalism: Economic and Monetary Union and Alternatives to Disciplinary Neoliberalism in Europe', *New Political Economy*, 3:1 (1998), 5–26.
2. The phrase 'locking in' is taken from World Bank (1997), 51.
3. 'Open letter from 331 European economists to the heads of government of the 15 member states of the European Union', published 12 June 1997 in several European papers. Source: iire@ANTENNA.NL. I am grateful to Scott Redding for this reference.
4. *Rentier* interests dovetail with capital engaged in foreign direct investment. Both seek stable longer-term conditions for private investment with demands for legal frameworks to constrain governments to fully guarantee rights and freedoms to holders of private property irrespective of national needs or circumstances (see OECD, 1996a, 1996b).
5. This process is partly arbitrated by non-state actors such as institutional investors and private credit-rating agencies such as Moody's that provide assessments for the fund managers and speculators in the capital and exchange markets.
6. E.g., small and middle-sized businesses who often work as contractors or suppliers to large corporations, import–export businesses, service companies in advertising, public relations, computing, stock broking, accountancy, consultancy and, increasingly, educational entrepreneurs, architects, urban planners and designers, and many top sports stars who help market corporate images and identities.
7. 'Globalisation has been viewed with concern in many advanced economies, with the belief common that it harms the interests of workers, especially unskilled workers, either directly through immigration or indirectly through trade or capital outflows' (International Monetary Fund, 1997: 59).

4
The Struggle over European Order: Transnational Class Agency in the Making of 'Embedded Neo-Liberalism'[1]

Bastiaan van Apeldoorn

Introduction

This chapter presents an analysis of *transnational* social forces in the making of what is interpreted as a new European socio-economic order emerging out of the relaunching of the European integration process of the 1980s and 1990s. This transnational struggle over European order is seen as taking place within the context of a changing global political economy in which the social relations of capitalist production are increasingly constituted beyond the nation-state. As the editors stress in their introduction, it is only by putting the process of European integration within a global context that one can fully capture present dynamics and see how that process has been bound up with a *transnational* restructuring of European state–society relations. This has, in turn, involved a transformation of the historical bloc underpinning the European project. In this perspective, European change is seen as linked to global change through the mediating agency of transnational social forces, understood as collective actors whose identities, interests and strategies take shape within a changing global structural context, and who struggle over the direction and content of the European integration process.

In this chapter, I thus conceive of the European integration process as a struggle between transnational social forces. This struggle may express itself ideologically, or on what Gramsci called the 'universal plane' of hegemony (Gramsci, 1971: 182), in the form of rival 'projects' contending for the construction of European order. On the one hand, these projects serve as rallying points around which disparate actors may coalesce into broad transnational coalitions. On the other hand, they are also consciously articulated and propagated by certain elite groups at the apex of (fractions of) transnational social forces. I argue that in this respect a particularly critical role is played by the agency of an emergent transnational capitalist class.

The chapter is structured as follows. The first section briefly elaborates the theoretical framework that informs my analysis, thus defining my position within the broad array of neo-Gramscian perspectives that have inspired this volume. The second section then identifies three contending projects – identified as neo-liberalism, neo-mercantilism and 'supranational social democracy' – in the struggle over European integration as that process was relaunched in the mid-1980s. These are then linked to different transnational social forces, and especially to rival 'fractions' of an emergent European transnational capitalist class. The third section analyses the struggle between these rival projects up to the Treaty of Maastricht, emphasising in particular the struggle within Europe's transnational capitalist elite. In the final section I argue that, as the ideological orientation of this class (fraction) has, into the 1990s, definitively shifted away from its earlier neo-mercantilist tendencies and towards neo-liberalism, one witnesses the rise of a new comprehensive concept for European socio-economic governance. This is denoted as 'embedded neo-liberalism', which is neo-liberal at its core and reflects the outlook of the most globalised sections of European capital, while at the same time seeking to accommodate the orientations of other social forces.

'Gramscian transnationalism' as an approach to European integration

European order has both a particular institutional *form*, and a particular socio-economic *content*.[2] Established approaches to European integration, particularly those bound up with the still dominant perspectives of intergovernmentalism (Moravcsik, 1991, 1998) and supranationalism/ neo-functionalism (Haas, 1958; Sandholtz and Zysman, 1989; Sandholtz and Stone Sweet, 1998), have always focused rather exclusively on the institutional form of the integration process. In contrast, the primary concern here is with the socio-economic content of, or the social purpose underpinning, the European project. Understanding the social purpose underlying the emergent European order requires, I argue, an analysis of its social underpinnings, which remain hidden from established perspectives inasmuch as these narrowly define power in terms of political authority of either states or supranational/international public bodies (cf. Ruggie, 1982). In order to overcome this narrow focus, one should add a concept of *social* power, in both its material *and* ideological dimensions, derived not from political authorities, or from the state in a narrow sense, but from the social forces that underpin state power. As a result, any analysis of the *problématique* surrounding the social purpose of European integration necessarily demands an alternative approach to the study of European order. A neo-Gramscian perspective within the field of International Political Economy (IPE) can, in my view, provide fertile ground for such an alternative. This approach to European integration, which one might refer to as 'Gramscian transnationalism', integrates the following three elements: a focus on social forces; an emphasis on the role of ideas; and, finally, a radical abandonment of state-centrism in favour of a transnationalist view of (global) politics.[3] Let me briefly discuss each of them.

The first element, then, calls for a focus on social forces within the process of European integration and views these as engendered by the capitalist production process. I thus proceed from a historical materialist understanding of 'the social' in which the social relations of production are seen as critical for an understanding of social power in capitalist societies.[4] Such a perspective also ought to consciously reclaim the centrality of the concept of class in the study of political economy. The point of departure of any class analysis should, however, be that the class domination by which capitalist societies are characterised cannot be understood from a structuralist perspective. Instead, the reproduction of the structural power of capital – and of the capitalist class – has to be explained in terms of collective human agency within concrete social power struggles.

Although it is the relation between capital and labour that engenders the basic class division in capitalist society, the class approach adopted here does not take classes as unified social actors. In particular, following the pioneering work of Kees van der Pijl and others (van der Pijl, 1984, 1998; Overbeek, 1993), I conceptualise the process of *capitalist* class formation as one in which the different concrete groups within the capitalist class crystallise into rival class *fractions*. The elites of such fractions might aspire to represent the capitalist class as a whole, articulating a 'general capitalist interest' from their own fractional perspective. Two primary structural axes along which class fractions are concretely formed may be identified: first, that of industrial (productive) versus financial (money) capital, and, second, that of domestic (or national) versus transnational capital, which becomes particularly relevant for analysing divisions *within* industrial capital (see also Chapter 1 on this point). Within the latter, one can further differentiate with respect to the degree of globalisation: that is, whether the transnational activities of an enterprise take place on a truly global scale or are rather more confined to a particular macro-region (e.g., Western Europe).

A neo-Gramscian perspective also emphasises the ideological dimension of the struggles between social (class) forces (and indeed of the process of class formation). Entering what Gramsci called 'the most purely political phase' (Gramsci, 1971: 181), the struggle between social forces becomes a struggle between competing ideologies aspiring to hegemony. The second element of our approach is the critical role accorded to the power of ideas and ideological practices in the construction of European order and in defining its social purpose. This approach thus transcends the narrow rationalism of established approaches to European integration. The link between ideas and particular social forces is critical, however, inasmuch as ideas are produced by human agency in the context of social power relations, and are as such bound up with the strategic action of social actors.

The third element is the transnational dimension. Whereas intergovernmentalist accounts of European integration ignore the transnational level altogether, supranationalist (neo-functionalist) approaches do explicitly acknowledge the role of transnational actors. However, they tend to see that role as subservient to the alleged functional logic of the integration process and/or to the supranational leadership of the European Commission, thus denying the autonomy of these actors. The point of departure for the present analysis is that the social forces underpinning European order are not necessarily internal to the European Union (EU), or to its member states, but are rather located within a global political economy in which capitalist production and finance are undergoing a sustained transnationalisation and globalisation. This is reflected *inter alia* in the increasing dominance of transnational corporations (TNCs) as actors in the world economy (see, e.g., United Nations Conference on Trade and Development, or UNCTAD, 1997), and in the concomitant growing structural power of transnational capital (Gill and Law, 1993). These structural transformations thus engender *transnational* social forces, and indeed a process of *transnational class formation* (van der Pijl, 1998). It is from this perspective that in the sections below I will examine what can be seen as the transnational dynamics of European integration in the 1980s and 1990s.

Transnational struggle over European order: contending projects and rival class fractions

In Western Europe, throughout the 1970s and early 1980s, there was a period of 'Euro-pessimism' as both the integration process and the post-war Fordist growth engine came to a rather sudden grinding halt. In what soon came to be the conventional view, the world economic crisis was regarded to have affected Europe in ways that traditional (Keynesian) policies could not answer as well as revealing structural weaknesses within the European economy which made it lag behind the competing blocs of Japan and the USA. It was within this context that the European integration process was relaunched as social and political forces – in particular sections of European big business – organised themselves at a European level, re-activating the political process. Here, different visions, different projects, came to compete with one another, each of which must be seen as linked to specific transnational social and political forces, and as constituting contending responses on the part of these forces to the crisis of European capitalism within the context of global capitalist restructuring.

The neo-liberal project

In the context of European integration, the rising power of neo-liberal ideology became first of all manifest in the 'Euro-sclerosis' discourse according to which the stagflation of the European economy was the result of 'institutional rigidities'. These, it was claimed, were engendered by 'excessive' government intervention, 'too powerful' trade unions and an 'overburdened' welfare state, among other things, that all hindered the efficient allocation of resources through the market mechanism, thus impeding necessary adjustments to the changing global environment.

In the neo-liberal conception of European integration, then, the process should be restricted to negative integration, resulting in more market and less state at all levels of governance. The benefits of the Internal Market project were thus seen as principally deriving from the freer market it would create, emphasising its deregulatory effects and expected efficiency gains. In the neo-liberal view, European integration should subordinate Europe's socio-economic and industrial space to what are seen as the beneficial forces of globalisation: Europe as an advanced free trade zone within a free trading world.

It was, however, only at the end of the 1980s and the beginning of the 1990s that neo-liberal adjustment really started to become a reality in continental Europe, moving beyond right-wing rhetoric. Indeed, as this analysis intends to show, neo-liberalism was not the only ideological force playing a role in Europe's relaunch.

The neo-mercantilist project

The world economic crisis also gave rise to a different discourse on Europe's alleged decline and how to reverse it. Whereas the neo-liberal ideology was primarily propagated by social forces bound up with global financial capital and industrial TNCs with a truly global reach, most of continental Europe was still dominated by firms that, although maybe no longer domestic, had yet to develop into 'global players'. The crisis of international Fordism, in the context of a deepening transnationalisation of production, provoked a global restructuring race – with the rise of Japan further intensifying global competition – that had profound impacts upon European industry (Van Tulder and Junne, 1988). These former national champions and 'would-be European champions' therefore perceived the forces of globalisation more as a threat to their market shares and competitive position than as an opportunity to force a structural transformation of Europe's 'sclerotic' socio-economic system. Within this perspective, the loss of international competitiveness was blamed less on labour market rigidity, trade union power or the welfare state, and more on the fragmentation of the European market, the (resulting) insufficient economies of scale and the perceived technology gap *vis-à-vis* the USA and Japan.

It was thus these forces that came to promote the creation of a European home market as the centre-piece of their strategy for a relaunching of Europe. As Grahl and Teague note, in the neo-mercantilist interpretation of the Internal Market project, 'national rivalries and the fragmentation of Community market, have … deprived European companies of a key element in competitive success, which the 1992 programme will correct' (Grahl and Teague, 1990: 172). A strong European home market was expected to serve as both a stepping-stone to conquer the world market as well as a protective shield against outside competition. The neo-mercantilist project thus constituted a defensive regionalisation strategy oriented towards the creation of a strong regional economy, not only through the completion of the Internal Market, but also through an industrial policy aimed at the promotion of 'European champions', if necessary protected by European tariff walls (Pearce and Sutton, 1986).

The social democratic project

The social democratic project for Europe's socio-economic order developed within the context of the initial success of the Internal Market programme as pro-European social democrats came to see European federalism as the answer to the dilemmas of the European left in the era of globalisation. As a concrete political strategy, this project was first and foremost formulated and pursued by Jacques Delors and his entourage during Delors's presidency of the European Commission (for a detailed account of the 'Delorist' strategy see Ross, 1995). For Delors, as for other social democrats, a united Europe offered an opportunity to protect the 'European model of society', and its traditions of the mixed economy and high levels of social protection, against the potentially destructive forces of globalisation and neo-liberalism (on this see, e.g., Delors, 1992; Grant, 1994: 86–7; Ross, 1995: 15, and *passim*). Delors had accepted the creation of a competitive home market (and the market liberalisation that went with it) as both an economic and political *sine qua non* for a successful relaunching of the European integration process but, at the same time, he warned the neo-liberals that 'the Community is not and will not be, a free trade zone. It is up to us to make a *European organised space*' (Delors in Krause, 1991). As George Ross notes, it was 'for this reason [that] the backbone of Delors's strategy was to promote state-building programs on the back of market-building successes' (Ross, 1995: 109).

Transnational class formation within the European arena

As indicated, all three projects – including the social-democratic one – developed within a transnational setting. It is particularly the process of transnational class formation, as engendered by the transnationalisation of global capitalism, that is the key to understanding such a setting. Processes of class formation must always be located within concrete historical and institutional contexts. One can argue that the EU provides one such context: a political arena in which an emergent transnational capitalist class – consisting of the top managers and owners of Europe's largest TNCs – takes the European region as its primary frame of reference and organises itself to influence the (socio-economic) governance of that region. The organised power of this transnational capitalist class within the European arena contrasts starkly with that of European labour, which remains fragmented and weak (see, e.g., Streeck and Schmitter, 1991), and certainly does not constitute a transnational class as such.

A basic divide that has structured this European process of transnational class formation as it evolved in the 1980s has been the division within European capital between that part already integrated into global production networks, operating on the world market and having a concomitant 'globalist' outlook, and that part which was still much more exclusively oriented towards, and dependent upon, the European 'home market', thus adopting a more European 'regionalist' perspective. This has engendered the tendential formation of two rival fractions within Europe's emerging transnational capitalist elite. These are here denoted, first, as a 'globalist' fraction, deriving from the most mobile and most globalised parts of transnational capital, i.e., global financial institutions and other (industrial) 'global players'; and second, as a 'Europeanist' fraction consisting of those who control large industrial enterprises which, although operating on a transnational scale, nevertheless primarily serve the European market, competing against the often cheaper imports from outside Europe (in particular East Asia).[5] As demonstrated below, the perspective of the former fraction has tended towards neo-liberalism, whereas the latter came to promote the neo-mercantilist project. It is maintained here that in the 1980s the opposition between neo-liberalism and neo-mercantilism was the central axis around which the ideological struggles within the emerging transnational European capitalist class revolved. The outcome of this struggle, in interaction with the so-called social democratic project, has been critical in shaping the emergent European socio-economic order.

This struggle will be analysed by examining the case of the European Round Table of Industrialists (ERT), one of the leading bodies within the organisational network of the European capitalist class, and at the same time a prime organisation through which that transnational capitalist class has formed. Founded in 1983 by a group of 17 major European industrialists, the ERT today consists of around 45 chief executive officers (CEOs) and chairmen leading Europe's biggest and most transnational industrial corporations. The membership of the ERT is personal (rather than corporate) but the fact that its members together control a large part of European transnational capital – a majority of the members' companies are Fortune 500 firms[6] and about half are amongst the 100 biggest TNCs in the world (UNCTAD, 1997) – of course contributes to explaining the large political influence that this group of people can command.[7] Generally recognised as 'the single most powerful business group in Europe' (Gardner, 1991: 47–8), the ERT is in particular credited with bringing the completion of the

Internal Market back on to the European agenda. It thus represents one of the driving forces behind Europe's relaunching (see especially van Apeldoorn, 2000; Cowles, 1994, 1995; Holman, 1992).

The ERT can be viewed as an elite organisation of Europe's emergent transnational capitalist class in which – transcending the more conventional forms of corporate lobbying in the EU – the interests of that class (fraction) are organised, shaped and synthesised into a comprehensive strategy. Yet, while effectively representing the perceived material interests of European big business, the ERT ideologically transcends those interests as well by appealing to a wider set of interests and identities (for a more elaborate account, see van Apeldoorn, 2000). In contradistinction to the Union of Industrial and Employers' Confederations of Europe (UNICE, the EU's official employers' organisation which represents a more 'corporatist' class interest, defending the vested interests of the European employers' class), the ERT, as a private club of transnational capitalists, seeks to elevate its class strategy towards a higher, more universal level: that is, to the 'universal plane' of hegemony. The role of the ERT must thus be seen as operating primarily at the level of ideas and ideology formation. It is at this level that the ERT has been an important actor in the struggle over the socio-economic content of the relaunched European integration process.

Transnational struggle over European order: from Europe 1992 to Maastricht

The rivalry between the neo-liberal and the neo-mercantilist concepts of a relaunching of European integration was also manifest within the ranks of the ERT, in turn reflecting what constituted the central axis of intra-capitalist struggle in the Europe of the 1980s. After an early walk-out of three 'globalist' members (the British CEOs of Unilever, Shell, and ICI), the ERT became dominated by representatives of the Europeanist fraction. Thus its strategic orientation in the 1980s tended towards what one could call a protective regionalism, at the heart of which was the promotion of a big European home market, in which Europe's regional TNCs could grow to resist and challenge the rising global competition. Premised, albeit ambivalently, on a neo-mercantilist project for European order, this strategy included the advocacy of a European industrial policy – centred around European technology programmes and infrastructure projects – focused on the nurturing of European champions as well as a limited form of protectionism at the European level. The Internal Market was thus seen by a majority of the early ERT members in neo-mercantilist terms as the creation of a big home market that would enable European industry to reach 'the scale necessary to resist pressure from non-European competitors' (ERT, 1983).

The ERT's campaign for a European home market has indeed significantly contributed to, and was probably critical for, the successful relaunching of the integration process through Europe 1992. Yet the Internal Market that was created on the basis of the Commission's White Paper did not turn out to be the kind of home market that many of the early ERT members (of the Europeanist fraction) had envisaged in several respects: namely, a relatively protected home market in which Euro-champions could prosper in order to confront global competition. The latter turned out to be an illusion as most initiatives for a European industrial policy failed, in the end, to take off. The more straightforwardly protectionist measures met resistance from (neo-)liberal governments (e.g., Germany, the UK, and the Netherlands) which reflected in part the dominance of the globalist fraction of European capital in those countries. Although sectors of European industry – cars and electronics – lobbied hard for protectionist measures and had their demands partially met, these limited protectionist policies (such as anti-dumping duties and import quotas) were gradually ended and external trade liberalisation in the EU has progressed steadily ever since (Hanson, 1998). Therefore, as the internal barriers came down, no external barriers were erected and the Internal Market provided as much opportunity for US and Japanese as for European firms (Wyatt-Walter, 1998). Hence, the regionalisation of the European economy, in the sense of the further integration of its national economic systems, went hand in hand with a further globalisation of the European region.

In the transnational struggle over Europe's relaunching, neo-liberal social forces, strengthened by the on-going and deepening globalisation process, were gaining the upper hand over those that had favoured a neo-mercantilist interpretation of the Internal Market programme. This struggle had also been fought out within the ranks of Europe's transnational capitalist class in which the Europeanist fraction was slowly losing its dominant position and, moreover, gradually abandoning its own earlier neo-mercantilist perspective. This neo-liberal shift on the part of Europe's capitalist elite was also reflected in the changing strategic orientation of the ERT at the end of the 1980s and into the 1990s, when its membership witnessed a significant change in the balance of power between the globalist and Europeanist 'fractions'.

From 1988 onwards, one can witness a change in the composition of ERT's membership that made the globalists the dominant group within the ERT. Not only did many globalist companies, such as Shell, Unilever, ICI, BP, La Roche, BT and Bayer, (re-)join the ERT, but older ERT companies, formerly producing primarily for the European market and competing against non-European imports, became more global themselves (see van Apeldoorn, 1999: ch. 6). This globalisation of European industry took place within the context of intensifying global competition, as well as the political failure of the neo-mercantilist project, in the light of which neo-liberalism gained appeal as an alternative strategy.

These structural changes enabled (but did not determine) a transcendence of the earlier opposition between Europeanists and globalists. The shift in the ideological and strategic orientation of the ERT – and of Europe's transnational bourgeoisie more widely – did not, however, come about without internal struggles. Indeed, in the final analysis it was through these struggles that this shift was achieved. The expansion of membership that had swelled the ranks of the neo-liberal globalists initially brought about a renewed opposition between the two camps, in which conflicts about trade policy occupied once more a central place. According to one representative of ERT's globalist fraction at that time, the (then) chairman of Unilever, Floris Maljers, the 'struggle between liberals and protectionists' became a constant feature of the internal policy debates at the end of the 1980s and beginning of the 1990s.[8] Rather than leading to a break-up of the ERT, this internal strife was in fact a (probably necessary) phase that preceded the emergence of a new consensus. In 1991 – when the ERT in the context of the Maastricht negotiations published its report, *Reshaping Europe* (ERT, 1991) – this new consensus still had the form of a rather unstable compromise between the two competing perspectives of protective regionalism and neo-liberal globalism; yet this compromise was later to develop into a new synthesis reflecting the dominance of the neo-liberal perspective (see below).

With regard to the Maastricht Treaty, which set the EU on course for Economic and Monetary Union (EMU), the ERT did not play the same initiating role as it did with regard to the Internal Market programme. When one analyses the (socio-economic) *content* of Maastricht, however, one encounters several of the ideas that the ERT, or at least part of the ERT membership, had been pushing for years, in particular ideas related to monetary union as a necessary complement to the Internal Market,[9] as well as an enhanced European role in infrastructure and research and technology (for further details, see van Apeldoorn, 2000).

The socio-economic content of Maastricht can in fact be interpreted as reflecting the transnational configuration of social and political forces within the European political economy at the beginning of the 1990s. The ERT here represented important sections of the ruling elite within that configuration and as such was one important forum from which that elite could shape the debates that at the ideological level conditioned the political bargaining process. However, transnational social-democratic forces, which under the leadership of Delors temporarily gained momentum around the end of the 1980s, also played a significant role in this respect. Next to the social chapter, EMU in fact became an equally important centre-piece of the social democratic project. It was seen as serving the double function of regaining some democratic control over the global financial markets (Holland, 1995: 12), as well as paving the way to a (federal) political union that could then further advance the cause of 'organising European space'. The social democratic interpretation of Maastricht has, however, largely failed to materialise. The social chapter has not gone much beyond mere symbolic politics (even if such symbols do matter), thanks in large part to the lobbying efforts of big business (Rhodes, 1992; Streeck 1995a). Political union has for all intents and purposes been indefinitely postponed, and the Treaty of Amsterdam of 1997 notably failed to deliver on this score. Also, the hope that EMU might restore democratic control over policy making continues to be contradicted by the reality of a monetarist consensus among the European elite. This is expressed, in addition to the stability pact, by the ability of monetarist elites to rebut the challenge posed by a powerful figure such as the former German finance minister, Oskar Lafontaine (on EMU, see Chapter 3 below; on the challenge by Lafontaine, see Chapter 9 below).

Maastricht was not a triumph for Thatcherite neo-liberalism, or for the social-democratic vision, or even, for that matter, for the neo-mercantilist strategy. In fact, it contained elements of all three rival projects, even though it was biased in favour of the neo-liberal project due to the neo-liberal orthodoxy underpinning EMU. At the same time, however, chapters on 'Trans-European [infrastructure] Networks' and 'Research and Technological Development' did provide a basis for some form of European industrial policy or *Ordnungspolitik*, clearly more in tune with the German model of Rhineland capitalism (Albert, 1993) rather than the (UK) neo-liberal model. These policies did not amount to a neo-mercantilist strategy, but they did speak to the interests of that part of European industry that – in its dependence on a strong European home base – had propagated a more mercantilist conception of the European project in the past. Finally, the albeit rather weak 'social chapter' nevertheless succeeded in incorporating European social democracy and the trade unions into the 'New Europe' (for the reasons behind, in particular, export-oriented unions' support of the Internal Market and EMU, see Chapters 5 and 6 below).

The emergent new European order: 'embedded neo-liberalism'

The Maastricht compromise reflects the gradual rise of what can be termed an 'embedded neo-liberal' synthesis that also points to the social purpose underpinning the emergent European order. Embedded neo-liberalism is neo-liberal inasmuch as it emphasises the primacy of global market forces and the freedom of transnational capital. Yet, as a result of such processes, markets become increasingly *disconnected* from their post-war national social institutions. Embedded neo-liberalism is thus 'embedded' to the extent that it recognises the limits to *laissez-faire*, and thus to the disembedding process, and accepts that certain compromises need to be made; hence at least a limited form of 'embeddedness' is preserved.[10] This means that within most European countries the dismantling of the welfare state has so far been limited, and that established corporatist institutions have not been abolished but rather – as in the case of the celebrated Dutch model – maintained and strengthened to implement neo-liberal labour market reform while maintaining social consensus (cf. Rhodes, 1997, see also Chapter 5 below). Such a reformulation of the original neo-liberal project, which had been developed in the Anglo-Saxon heartland, was necessary within the (continental) European context for a number of reasons. For instance, the neo-liberal offensive had to overcome the resistance of the institutionalised traditions of corporatist class relations, the social and industrial protection offered by an often interventionist state, and other elements of 'embeddedness' in a context within which rival social democratic and neo-mercantilist projects had developed.

On the one hand, then, one may interpret embedded neo-liberalism as the outcome of the transnational struggle between the three contending projects of neo-liberalism, neo-mercantilism and supranational social democracy. This was a struggle in which the neo-liberal project became dominant but still had to accommodate the concerns of both the former neo-mercantilists and of the social democrats that promoted a social dimension to the new European market. The neo-liberal project incorporated these rival concerns in such a way that they were ultimately subordinated to the interests of globalising capital (on the neglect of social democratic concerns in this compromise, see also Chapter 5 below). On the other hand, though, embedded neo-liberalism can also be interpreted as the emerging hegemonic project of Europe's transnational capitalist class. It is this class that has become dominated by the leadership of a globalist fraction both in terms of financial firms and global industrial TNCs.

It is in particular within global *industrial* capital that one can observe the dialectical conflict – captured so brilliantly in Polanyi's classic analysis (Polanyi, 1957) – between, on the one hand, the drive of capital for market liberalisation and, on the other hand, a recognition of the need for social protection. Pure *laissez-faire* policies would only harm the interests of this capital fraction as it still needs the state to educate the workforce, to provide infrastructure, to pursue macroeconomic policies that favour growth and investment, or to maintain social and political stability; in short, to sustain both economic and political hegemony.[11] At the same time that globalising capital seeks to detach itself from the constraints imposed by (national) institutions, it is also 'aware' that it cannot in fact become fully 'footloose' in this sense, and continues to need supporting institutions itself.

In sum, embedded neo-liberalism is here interpreted as a potentially hegemonic project unifying Europe's transnational capitalist class and expressing its collective interests, while at the same time appealing to a wider set of interests and identities. As such it is also reflected in the discourse and strategy of the ERT as it continued to play an important role in the evolving regime of European socio-economic governance into the 1990s.

Transnational class strategy and European governance in the 1990s

The post-Maastricht period witnessed the further consolidation of ERT's neo-liberal shift, reflecting a general re-orientation of the European transnational bourgeoisie, of which now both the (former) globalist and Europeanist fractions were united within the ERT's ranks. Whereas, in the early 1980s, the response to the world economic crisis (and the concomitant global restructuring race) was still defensive, and indeed protectionist, the deep recession of the early 1990s (which also saw the temporary return of 'Euro-pessimism') met with a rather unambiguous call for further neo-liberal restructuring. This means deregulation, labour market flexibility, 'downsizing' the public sector and an unequivocal commitment to global free trade (see ERT, 1993a, 1993b, 1994).

With regard to ERT's strengthened free trade orientation, the crucial battle was probably that over the conclusion of the Uruguay Round of the General Agreement on Tariffs and Trade (GATT) talks (in December 1993). This was because free traders within the ERT established a position of leadership and persuaded the French members to take a stance against the wavering position of their own government.[12] In retrospect, the Uruguay Round and the subsequent founding of the World Trade Organisation (WTO) signalled the 'final' defeat of the Euro-protectionists, both within the ERT and the European corporate elite more widely.[13] The post-Maastricht period also witnessed a strengthening of the consensus in favour of monetary union. This was not only because the crises of the European Monetary System (EMS) of 1992 and 1993 showed that only a single currency could provide European business with sufficient stability, but also because the convergence criteria were increasingly showing their 'salutary' disciplinary effects.[14]

Yet, just as ERT's original 'Europeanist' orientation was never unequivocally neo-mercantilist (although some members came close to this ideal type), the ideological outlook of ERT capitalists in the 1990s is not one of orthodox neo-liberalism either. Indeed, it rather reflects the potentially hegemonic synthesis of embedded neo-liberalism. Within ERT's own discourse, the limits of its neo-liberalism become most apparent with regard to the field of industrial policy broadly conceived. Within a pure neo-liberal model, the only legitimate industrial policy is the policing of the free market by competition policy. Whereas such a perspective may suit the interests of transnational financial capital, industrial capital, even its most transnationally mobile fraction, needs the state to go beyond this passive role, in an attempt to actively seek and secure the 'conditions for competitiveness' (ERT, 1993a). Hence, rather than the British neo-liberal model, it was the liberal German alternative of an active *Ordnungspolitik* that became the preferred concept around which all fractions could rally.[15]

The embeddedness of ERT's neo-liberalism also transpires from its attitude towards European social policies, and in particular from those that came out of the so-called social chapter of Maastricht. Although the ERT at the time waged war on the social chapter, it was also recognised by (at least part of) the ERT that, given the balance of social and political forces at that time, its inclusion (albeit as an 'appendix') was inevitable. Hence acceptance of the social chapter was possible given the extent to which it had been watered down. Most ERT members remain keenly aware of the need for social consensus by rejecting the neo-liberal (confrontational) mode of labour relations (characteristic of, say, British industrial relations), and emphasising that some degree of basic social harmony is indispensable for European industry to prosper (see ERT, 1993b: 9). Although transnational capital will of course remain categorically opposed to any form of European collective bargaining, it has not refused to participate in the 'neo-voluntarist' (Streeck, 1995b) European Social Dialogue. This was another initiative that was started under Delors and represented a form of 'social partnership' that fits well within the embedded neo-liberal model.

Still, the 'embeddedness' of ERT's neo-liberalism remains thin in this respect and seems to be primarily geared towards the creation of the 'conditions for competitiveness', and thus to serve the interests of transnational and globalising capital, rather than to protect subordinate social groups and classes. Indeed, the ERT bluntly states that the burden of 'adjustment' will have to be carried by labour. In the ERT's own words, 'a very large amount of the effort to adjust European labour markets will rely on labour' (ERT, 1993b: 16). The ERT is well aware that this 'adjustment' – which is offered as the only way to restore growth and employment – implies a fundamental restructuring of state–society relations and that this in turn calls for the construction of a new hegemonic project capable of producing consent across social classes (and class fractions):

Enabling Europe to return to high employment growth requires more than replacing policy instruments, it calls for a change of our economic and social structures. But governments are only able to change structures when there is a *new social consensus*, i.e. the convergence on principles and, ultimately, agreement on the goals for that change among the social partners, governments, the opinion leaders and ultimately, the population ... We need a consensus on the European level that *only a healthy, efficient and competitive private sector is able to provide sufficient jobs, and that markets should be left to allocate labour efficiently.* (ERT, 1993b: 9; original emphasis)

In creating this new consensus, a key role is played by the concept of *competitiveness*. Appealing equally to neo-liberals, neo-mercantilists and social-democrats, this concept enables the articulation of a predominantly neo-liberal ideology with elements of the alternative ideological discourses of the social democratic and neo-mercantilist projects in such a way that their opposition is neutralised. Hence the construction of hegemony.

Competitiveness, like globalisation, has become a key word in European socio-economic discourse. From the Delors White Paper on 'Growth, Competitiveness and Employment' (European Commission, 1994) onwards, it has become the unofficial key policy objective of the EU. In 1995 – following an initiative by the ERT – a Competitiveness Advisory Group (CAG) was set up by the Commission, which since then has been 'keeping competitiveness in the forefront of the policy debates' (ERT, 1993a: 27). Crucially, as transpires from both ERT and Commission publications, the meaning of the concept of competitiveness has now, first of all, come to be bound up with the (albeit embedded) neo-liberal project. This constitutes a break with the past in which the concept had tended to be defined more in neo-mercantilist terms, as in the case of the ERT, or in more social-democratic terms (i.e., mixed with Keynesian and other 'progressive' elements), as in the case of the (Delors) Commission.

As an operationalisation of this new competitiveness ideology, the ERT has, in tandem with the CAG, started to promote the concept of 'benchmarking' *vis-à-vis* the Commission and the member states. Bench-marking means not only 'measuring the performance' of individual firms, or sectors, but also that of nations against the other 'best competitors' in the world (ERT, 1994: 4). In its report, *Benchmarking for Policy-Makers*, the ERT is very explicit about how policy-makers should 'measure' competitiveness. The country or (macro-)region that is most competitive is the country that is most successful in attracting mobile capital: 'Governments must recognise today that every economic and social system in the world is competing with all the others to attract the footloose businesses' (ERT, 1996: 15).

Competitiveness and benchmarking have also become the key concepts within the public (socio-economic) policy discourse of the EU. Analysing the policy documents of the Commission one can also see how these concepts are mobilised to promote a programme of neo-liberal restructuring, aimed at removing, in the words of the Director-General for Industry, the still remaining 'rigidities and distortions... that prevent Europe from fully exploiting its potential' (European Commission, 1997c: 5). Invoking the inevitability of globalisation, and 'hence' the need for adaptation, the Commission defines benchmarking as a tool for improving competitiveness and 'for promoting the convergence towards best practice' (European Commission, 1996: 16). This involves the global 'comparison of societal behaviour commercial practice, market structure and public institutions' (European Commission, 1997a: 3). The 'High Level Group on Benchmarking' – chaired by a board member of Investor, the investment company controlling the global Wallenberg empire – reinforces this stance. As it makes clear in its first report, the object of all these 'comparisons' is to promote rapid 'structural reforms' that will allow Europe to adapt to the exigencies of globalisation: 'this involves further liberalisation, privatisation, ... more flexible labour laws, lower government subsidies, etc.' (High Level Group on Benchmarking, 1999: 13). Inasmuch as this neo-liberal restructuring programme will be successfully implemented, the contradictions of embedded neo-liberalism will of course become more acute.

Conclusion

This chapter has analysed transnational social forces in the making of what has been interpreted as an 'embedded neo-liberal' European order. Embedded neo-liberalism was interpreted as the outcome of the transnational struggle between the three rival projects of neo-liberalism, neo-mercantilism and social democracy. The 'embedded' component of embedded neo-liberalism addresses the concerns of both the former neo-mercantilists as well as those of the European labour movement and social-democratic political forces. But this incorporation is done in such a way that these concerns are, in the end, subordinated to the overriding objective of neo-liberal competitiveness. As Gramsci has put it (1971: 182), 'the development and expansion of the particular group are conceived of, and presented, as being the motor force of a universal expansion, of a development of all the "national" energies'. Indeed, the 'universal expansion' of neo-liberal competitiveness increasingly seems to be formulated as the primary goal of European socio-economic governance whilst intertwined with the development of '"national" energies'. This is apparent, first of all, in the competitiveness discourse that is now underpinning the Commission's strategy with regard to industrial policy and macroeconomic management. Second, it transpires from the relative failure of the social dimension. Third, it follows from the way the EU has fully committed itself to global free trade. Finally, it is apparent from the neo-liberal character of the EMU, at the heart of the current integration project.

The European socio-economic order that is being constructed thus subordinates the European region to the exigencies of the global economy and global competition, and hence to the interests of global transnational capital. Under the banner of 'competitiveness', the EU pursues the, by now, familiar neo-liberal policies of budget austerity, deregulation ('freeing' the market), and 'flexibilisation' of the labour market. These are pursued even whilst also seeking to preserve the social consensus model that is still prevalent in most European countries. The limited elements of 'embeddedness' that one may discern in, for instance, the discourse of the ERT, as well as within that of the Commission and within similar elite discourses (such as that of the 'Third Way'), thus seem to be primarily oriented towards the interests of globalising transnational capital. The question remains, then, to what extent the social purpose of the emergent European order may yet be constructed on a different normative basis from that contained in the idea that the ultimate 'benchmark' for the 'performance' of a society is its ability to accumulate wealth in private hands.

Notes

1. This chapter draws in part on an earlier and longer version, see van Apeldoorn (1998b).
2. Here I borrow the words of John Ruggie (1982) in his critique of the international regimes literature. Form and content are of course interrelated, but in this chapter I will focus on the latter.
3. For a much more extensive development of this approach, see van Apeldoorn (1999: ch. 1). Also see Chapter 1 above for a more elaborate discussion of the limitations of conventional integration theories and how a neo-Gramscian perspective might provide an alternative. The neo-Gramscian perspectives developed, for example, by Overbeek (1993) or van der Pijl (1998) most closely inspire my own approach to European integration.
4. A historical materialist perspective on global politics is defined by Robert Cox as 'examin[ing] the connections between power in production, power in the state, and power in international relations' (Cox, 1981: 135). To be sure, it is not suggested here that 'the social' is exhausted by 'social relations of production'. However, in my view, the latter are primary in the production and distribution of wealth and thus central to both the constitution of forms of social power and the question of socio-economic content that concerns me in this chapter.
5. This division of European capital has been partly inspired by a similar one developed by Holman (1992).
6. *Fortune's* 1998 Global 500; see http://cgi.pathfinder.com/fortune/global500. For a list of current ERT members (as well as other up-to-date information on the ERT), see the ERT website: http://www.ert.be.
7. Commenting upon this, former EU Commissioner (for competition), Peter Sutherland, stated that because membership 'is at head of company level, and only the biggest companies in each country of the European Union are members of it...by definition each member of the ERT has access at the highest level to government' (telephone interview, 27 January 1998).

8. Interview with Floris Maljers, by Otto Holman and author, Rotterdam, 3 September 1993.
9. Although the ERT in its 1991 report did call for a single currency and a 'clear and unambiguous timetable to achieve this goal' (ERT, 1991: 46), it largely left the lobbying for monetary union to a big business forum especially set up for that purpose (in 1987), the Association for Monetary Union in Europe (AMUE).
10. 'Embeddedness', then, does not denote a re-embedding in the sense of Polanyi's (1957) 'double movement' (in which 'society and politics' re-assert their control over the market). It must rather be seen as anticipating and preventing (we speak mainly about effects here, and only in a very limited sense about intentions) such a societal backlash.
11. Of course, this applies to capital in general as well, but, ideally speaking, productive capital is closer to the moment of the accumulation process with which these functional needs are bound up with than financial capital. Abstractly, productive capital is more concerned with the principle of social protection than financial capital, and national capital is more so than transnationally-mobile 'global' capital (cf. van der Pijl 1984, 1998).
12. Interview (by Otto Holman and author) with former ERT Vice-Chairman Floris Maljers, Rotterdam, 3 September 1993.
13. At least this was the perception of former ERT Vice-Chairman, David Simon (interview, London, 12 September 1996).
14. Interview with former ERT Vice Chairman, André Leysen, Antwerp, 21 May 1996.
15. Interviews.

Part III

European Trade Unions and the Problems of Neo-Liberal Integration

5
European Constitutionalism and Industrial Relations

Hans-Jürgen Bieling

European industrial relations in the age of competitive restructuring

European industrial relations have undergone fundamental changes from the early 1980s onwards. This is mainly due to a range of structural shifts in the mode of economic, social and political reproduction. Most important among them are the following: the reorganisation of work and production (involving new technologies, rationalisation and labour shedding, flexible working conditions, changes in the production chain, or new logistic concepts); sluggish economic growth, high rates of unemployment and a highly fragmented workforce; an expanding service sector; and an accelerated transnationalisation of trade, production and finance. Two other significant factors are the increasing influence of banks, investment funds and insurance companies, and a transformation of the 'Keynesian welfare state' into a 'Schumpeterian workfare regime', which implies restricted opportunities for social and economic intervention. Most scholars agree that the re-launching of European integration since the mid-1980s should be seen as an integral part of all these tendencies of socio-economic restructuring (Ferner and Hyman, 1998; Martin and Ross, 1999). Without doubt, its core economic projects – the European Monetary System (EMS), the Internal Market, and Economic and Monetary Union (EMU) – have had a serious impact on the transformation of industrial relations. This applies to the accompanying constitutional reforms: that is, the Single European Act (SEA) and the Treaty of European Union (TEU), as well as concrete legislation – rules, directives and recommendations – and juridical decisions.

However, in view of a whole mosaic of different tendencies, the European mode of regulative transformation and governance seems to be far from unambiguous. On the one hand, it is characterised by a structural asymmetry between strong initiatives for 'negative integration', such as intensified market-competition, and only tenuous attempts to embed these competitive pressures in a socially oriented institutional framework of 'positive integration' (Scharpf, 1999: 47–80). This does not mean that European integration is only a market-making and market-deepening process, but that polity-creating measures are primarily aimed at securing a highly integrated market economy. Hence, a deregulatory and monetarist bias as well as a macroeconomic co-ordination deficit seem to be engraved in the European economic constitution. Even after a stepwise extension of social regulations and agreements on modest European re-distribution – European funds for regional development and cohesion – we can witness a 'persistent gap between the reality of economic and social Europe' (Cressey *et al.*, 1998: 60). Consequently, industrial relations systems have to adapt to intensified competitive pressures. Against the background of expanded cross-border activities of mobile industrial and financial capital, it is no exaggeration to argue that the logic of 'regime-competition' (i.e., the competition between the different national systems of industrial relations regulation) has become a main feature and a driving force of current industrial adjustments within the European Union (EU) (Streeck, 1998).

On the other hand, however, the European mode of governance is not only an engine to reinforce competition. The efforts to strengthen the social dimension within the EU cannot be reduced to a matter of simple lip service. Of course, the content of European social policy is highly symbolic. In the course of the past fifteen years, however, supranational social regulation, particularly in the area of industrial relations, has made some progress. Although the different national regimes still represent the most important level of regulation, the European level is becoming increasingly relevant. In the meantime it is not completely wrong to speak of an emerging supranational regime of industrial relations regulation, characterised by common principles, norms and regulations, co-ordinating the mode of interaction between capital and labour. In principle, the European regime consists of two complementary pillars: *regulatory legislation*, involving the Commission, Parliament and the Council, and the *social dialogue* between the so-called social partners (Rhodes, 1995). Regardless of all social improvements, however, both pillars are still much too weak to hinder the competition between existing regimes of industrial relations. Within the given framework there is virtually no possibility for trade unions, employers and governments to elude the more or less evident downward pressure on wages, employment contracts, working conditions or social security regulations. Despite the extension of majority voting and the involvement of the social partners in the process of decision making, the preliminary results are meagre: some new social minimum standards and low quality framework agreements will probably serve at best to avert the worst forms of 'social dumping'.

These contradictory tendencies – intensified regime-competition and modest social regulations – already indicate that the socio-economic dynamic of European integration cannot be grasped by applying dichotomous categories. The mode of European governance includes market-deepening and polity-creation, deregulation and re-regulation, decentralisation and centralisation, economic competition and political co-operation. The composition and interaction of these different but complementary dimensions constitute the emerging European socio-economic order. To understand its content and mode of reproduction as well as its impact on industrial relations systems, it makes sense to analyse the success or failure of competing political ideas and strategies. This chapter deals first with the political process by which 'regime competition' as a core feature of European integration was established, intensified and socially embedded. Then, in a second step, it tries to outline the emergence of rather weak forms of corporatist interest mediation at the national and European level. Both tendencies refer to the incorporation of trade unions into a transnational historical bloc (see Chapter 1) involving the hegemony of neo-liberal forces. The effect of this incorporation is twofold: it simultaneously helps to consolidate the current neo-liberal configuration and it hinders a more rapid disembedding of social relations. Whether trade unions can thereby realise their aims, however, is uncertain or even doubtful. Therefore, the chapter asks why trade unions still support the chosen path of integration, despite all the evident disadvantages. The argument will conclude with some reflections on the prospects for a rearrangement of the 'European bargain'.

Capital and labour in the process of European constitutionalism

The transformation of industrial relations systems is inextricably linked to governance mechanisms engraved in the European multi-level system. Some of the significant basic features of the socio-economic order are, above all, the dynamics of 'regime competition'. Their market-driven acceleration can be traced back to the completion of the Internal Market programme and the realisation of EMU, two pivotal milestones in the 'making of the new Europe'. In highlighting the underlying ideas, intentions, forces and strategies, the main focus of this chapter is thus the strategic dimension of hegemony involving the construction of concrete hegemonic projects. In this argument, hegemony relates to specific class configurations united behind 'comprehensive concepts of control' – or hegemonic projects – that lend cohesion and cogency to the rule of particular classes and fractions of classes by becoming an expression of the general interest (van der Pijl, 1984). Such hegemonic projects combine ideational and material aspects of social reorganisation in a complementary way. In this sense, hegemonic projects have a situational focus within class fractions, meaning groups unified around a common economic and social function in the process of capital accumulation, that aspire to represent the general interest through ideological action (see Chapter 1). In referring to the very fundamental causes, dynamics and effects of concrete political initiatives, they not only take into account the socio-economic and organisational context, but also the relation of forces, the public climate and the dominant discourses. The analytical focus on hegemonic projects is promoted by the fluidity of processes in the configuration of European social relations. Since the early 1980s strong social and political forces have pressed vigorously for the emergence of an economically based transnational power structure. Some of its basic features are already evident. To provide a deeper understanding of them, it is instructive to analyse the dynamics – the challenges, problems, ideas, interests and strategies – of the current hegemonic project of economic integration.

The Internal Market programme and the Single European Act

After the failure of the 'Werner plan', a first attempt to establish a single European currency in the early 1970s, Western Europe entered a decade of stagnation. Later this period was called the age of 'Europessimism'. It was characterised by a 're-nationalisation' of politics fostered by economic recessions, slow recovery, rising unemployment and growing problems of social regulation. Despite an increasing awareness of losing ground in the triad competition, governments and politicians in the EU remained locked into a politics of muddling through. This climate of European standstill began to change, however, after the German and French governments agreed to establish the EMS. The EMS was primarily created as a mechanism to control the fluctuation of currency rates, externally spurred by high volatility of the US dollar

(McNamara, 1998). Its asymmetrical mode of operation, however, engendered an important side effect. Due to the dominant role of the German Bundesbank – the D-mark was the anchor currency – the EMS enforced the generalisation of monetarist objectives (i.e., compliance with the imperatives of transnational financial markets and the priority of anti-inflation policies) (Gill, 1992: 169). In the early 1980s, after the failure of national roads to economic recovery became evident, the EU experienced, step-by-step, a change of political priorities and increasing consent to policies of deregulation, privatisation and flexibilisation. One result was not only the success of right-wing parties, but also, as happened in France, a political turnaround of parties on the left. These developments indicated that against the background of fundamental socio-economic changes, persistent problems of European competitiveness and growing pressures for institutional adjustment, European economic and political elites became more receptive to neo-liberal ideas (Sandholtz and Zysman, 1989). In a way, the Internal Market can be interpreted as the result of 'policy learning' (Wallace and Young, 1997): that is, as a complex interaction of pressing socio-economic problems, a redefinition of interests and emerging new ideas, eventually leading to concrete political initiatives.

Depending on the model of explanation, the change of economic and political strategies is generally ascribed to 'epistemic communities' (P. M. Haas, 1992) and 'advocacy coalitions' (Sabatier, 1998). Both are part of a broader structure of 'policy networks', in which the ideas of intellectuals are backed by politicians and private interest groups. In contrast to idealist tendencies inherent in some policy analyses, a neo-Gramscian perspective regards 'policy networks' primarily as channels of communicative and political interaction, ensuring the hegemony of ideologically more cohesive political leadership. This leadership role is thereby always related to the structural dimension of social development. In the crisis-prone atmosphere of the early 1980s, this process of hegemonic construction was unambiguously captured by transnational European corporations and their representative organisations, above all by the European Round Table of Industrialists (ERT) (van Apeldoorn, 1999 and Chapter 4 this volume; Cowles, 1995). They provided the European public and political decision-makers with a simple but obviously convincing interpretation concerning the causes of socio-economic difficulties. Accordingly, the EU was 'too bureaucratic and too expensive' (Dekker, 1989: 28), and suffered from home markets which were too narrow, and a lack of internal competition which hindered technological progress and economic growth. This means in turn that Europe, in order to facilitate new economies of scale, required a unified European market without non-tariff trade barriers. It was generally acknowledged that a competitive Europe must be based on a closely integrated economy and a business-friendly socio-political framework, to enable European-based transnational capital to exploit hitherto unrealised eco-nomies of scale and scope in order to keep pace with global competitors (Jacquemin and Wright, 1994).

At first, the concrete content of the Internal Market programme was not clearly defined. As Rhodes and van Apeldoorn (1997) point out, it was initially subjected to competing neo-liberal, neo-mercantilist and social democratic ideas (see also van Apeldoorn, Chapter 4 this volume). Although its final shape therefore represented a compromise, the design of the SEA, above all its core project of the Internal Market, already reflected the implicit primacy of neo-liberal elements. Irrespective of some political flanking through regional and social policy compensation, European big business, the European Commission and national governments have been almost exclusively concerned with the issue of market integration by pulling down physical, technical and fiscal trade barriers. Lord Cockfield (1990: 8), the Commissioner responsible at the time, stressed very bluntly the supremacy of intensified market competition:

> one thing I would not accept, and I was supported by the Commission as a whole, was that progress on the Internal Market should be linked to progress on other policies, particularly regional and social policy. Linkage would simply be a recipe for delay and manoeuvre. If the Internal Market programme were allowed to go ahead unfettered it would in fact provide both the catalyst and the stimulus for progress elsewhere.

Eventually, however, the assumption of political 'spill-over' turned out to be wrong as far as more substantial social regulation was concerned. The SEA was still in line with the old European treaty, which provided limited social regulation with respect to agricultural politics, labour market mobility and equal opportunities for men and women. Thus it contained only a few new articles enabling directives in the area of health and safety regulation at the work place. Irrespective of all public declarations, the scope for European social regulation remained very restricted. Up to the present, its content is still defined on a fairly narrow basis (Majone, 1998; Pierson, 1998). While market-breaking measures are almost excluded, most social regulations are directed towards a smooth functioning of the Internal Market. Of course, wretched supranational social regulation and intensified market competition does not necessarily mean that the European agenda is neo-liberal. This is rather the result of a more fundamental transformation of global capitalism and the accordingly altered operation of (financial) markets and political regulations. The weak forms of social regulation are only a constitutive element, insofar as they fail to soften the competitive pressures to deregulate national regimes of industrial relations regulation. In this context, deregulation is not always an advantageous strategy, not even from a short-term point of view. In general, however, it tends to become more likely, because of increased market integration, high capital mobility and a generalised application of the principle of 'mutual recognition'. This principle, without any supranational framework of substantial social regulation, encourages deregulatory pressures on national forms of 'product regulation' as well as on the regulation of production and social affairs (Sun and Pelkmans, 1995).

The political discussion revealed that the intentions and anticipated effects linked to the project of the Internal Market has been highly controversial. It is no surprise that it was strongly supported by neo-liberal politicians, employer organisations and big business. In addition to the stimulus for increased productivity, they approved or even deliberately welcomed the side effects of social dumping and 'regime competition' (Grahl and Teague, 1989: 48). In contrast to this stance, many employees, trade unions and Social Democratic (as well as Green and Communist) parties have all been more sceptical. In the mid-1980s there was a common awareness that liberalised capital and financial markets and the generalised principle of 'mutual recognition' have necessarily profound and – from a trade union point of view – adverse repercussions on labour markets and industrial relations. Nevertheless, and this seems at first glance surprising, most of the left-wing parties and trade unions by and large accepted the SEA. Although the vision of '1992' – above all the foreseeable effects of deregulation, cross-border capital mergers, and accelerated rationalisation – represented a threat to trade unions, they partly even solicited for its completion.

This indicates that many employees and trade unions – primarily those of export-oriented industrial sectors – have already been drawn into a transnational historical bloc of hegemonic social and political forces. Until now this bloc has been strongly influenced by neo-liberal ideas, but it was still open to combine them pragmatically with social and ecological issues. In order to understand this process of incorporation, it is necessary to take into account some further developments.

Some factors have been particularly relevant for the strategic orientation of trade unions: first, in addition to some serious socio-economic difficulties, there was the changed political climate of the early 1980s (P. A. Hall, 1987). Against this background many trade unions and their rank and file had already accepted the basic neo-liberal arguments when the Internal Market was discussed in public. The situation was characterised by a tacit agreement that intensified market competition, deregulation, and even measures of privatisation, were economically beneficial or at least unavoidable. Most trade unions have only been interested in how to link extended and intensified market competition to social concerns. Second, the mood of 'Euro-phoria' favoured all those within the trade unions, who argued from a sometimes rather naive 'Euro-optimistic' standpoint. Accordingly, the Internal Market was considered as a first step towards an age of new social progress, since it encouraged monetary integration, which would in turn lead to a common European economic policy, a political union, and finally also to a social union. Third, and probably the most immediate reason for trade union support, the Internal Market was not simply the product of neo-liberal hard core politicians. Even if it was stimulated and attentively monitored by transnational big business, it was finally institutionalised and shaped by the Commission, the Court of Justice and national governments. On the basis of some far-reaching suggestions for an extensive social regulation (Venturini, 1989), it was first of all Jacques Delors who, by leadership and political charm, involved the trade unions in supranational European affairs, however belatedly and even then only as junior partners.

Delors was not only famous for his bargaining skills (i.e., his talent to tie up so-called 'packages' and to take care of weaker interests by providing 'side-payments') but also for his strategic capability to provide the European constitution with a social dimension. According to George Ross (1995), the Delors Commission pursued a kind of 'Russian doll strategy': that is, it pressed steadily for more social regulation on the European level subsequent to closer economic integration. The SEA itself can be seen as the first 'Russian doll'. While social policy concerns have not been mentioned at all in the Internal Market White Paper, the then new Article 118a of the SEA subjected the harmonisation of safety and health regulations to qualified majority voting. The second 'Russian doll' was then constituted by the 'Paquet Delors' (i.e., the reform of agricultural and structural policies in combination with a new budgetary programme of financial redistribution). It complemented the Internal Market by enhancing – at least partially – economic and social conversion. A few years later, in 1992, a second 'Paquet Delors' followed, which added a new fund for cohesion and doubled again the financial volume available for regional policy. And finally, the initiatives for extended social regulation – the 'Community Charter of Basic Social Rights for Workers', a Community Social Action Programme, and the Social Protocol of the Maastricht Treaty – represented a third 'Russian doll', strongly linked to the project of EMU.

EMU and the treaty revisions of the 1990s

The EMU project itself was launched in the late 1980s. In June 1988 at its meeting in Hanover, the European Council assigned an expert group chaired by Jacques Delors to prepare a plan for realising economic and monetary union. The results, a three-stage process towards monetary convergence, were presented in April 1989 as the so-called 'Delors Report' and were confirmed at the Maastricht European Council in December 1991. As the course of events made clear, it was first not so much a political project of transnational big business – even if groups such as the Association for Monetary Union in Europe (AMUE) lobbied for it – but an alliance of national governments, central bankers and European technocrats concerned with the prospective development of the integration process (Sandholtz, 1993). Despite the fact that the EMS had been generally successful in stabilising currency exchange rates, the expectation was that it would become overburdened. Within the general trend to deregulate financial markets in the course of the 1980s (Helleiner, 1994: 146–68), the Internal Market was among the initiatives that almost immediately arranged complete liberalisation of capital movements. The stimulus for new waves of financial flows implied not only the risk of powerful speculative attacks on national currencies, but also serious difficulties in pursuing monetary policy for the benefit of domestic objectives. The Commission, most central bankers and national governments regarded the incompatibility of fixed exchange rates and free capital movements as a serious problem. In order to overcome it, they pushed for EMU as a necessary completion of the 1992 programme (Cameron, 1998: 196–7). The threat of losing control of financial affairs was perceived above all by the weak currency countries. Since they suffered from an asymmetric distribution of adjustment burdens within the EMS, they were strongly in favour of a common European currency. For them it represented a chance to break the diktat of the German Bundesbank.

Of course, there have been further aspects which led social and political actors to support EMU: for example, an improved European home base in the global currency competition *vis-à-vis* the US dollar and the Japanese yen, or stronger European control of a unified Germany. According to Tsoukalis (1997: 295), it was a culmination of various motives which finally led to a Community compromise:

> The French secured a clear commitment enshrined in the treaty, as well as a specific date. The Germans made sure that the date would be distant, with little happening in between, and that the new European model would be as close as possible to their own. The British secured an 'opt out' for themselves, followed later by the Danes, while the poor countries obtained a more or less explicit link with redistribution.

This clearly shows that nationally defined interests cannot be neglected in the process of decision making. Nevertheless, it would be wrong to reduce EMU to an exclusively inter-state bargain mediated by suggestions on the part of the Commission. At least with respect to the broadening of public support after the difficulties of the Maastricht referenda in Denmark and France, the Commission started to involve explicitly more economic experts, opinion leaders and the business community in campaigning for the common currency.

At first glance, large corporations and banks have been in favour of EMU, since they 'believed that removing the uncertainties of currency fluctuations would help them realise the full promise of a single European market, and give them a larger effective home base from which to confront outside competitors' (Frieden, 1998: 26). Yet lower transaction costs, more market transparency and better management calculation were only the immediate effects influencing transnational corporations (TNCs) to support EMU. For most of them it was more important that the project of the single currency had a monetarist content and confirmed the on-going socio-economic transformation along the lines of a 'competitive shareholder society'. At least with the benefit of hindsight, such a tendency comes more and more to the fore. First, TNCs, banks, insurance companies and institutional investors pressed for the deregulation of European capital markets. As a consequence, this encouraged the spread of *rentier* interests and the discourse of neo-liberal adjustment within state and civil society. Then, step-by-step, the new *rentier* mentality broadened the social and popular basis for monetarist principles. This in turn provided an additional incentive for governmental agencies to subject themselves to the discipline and surveillance of financial markets (see Chapter 3 this volume).

It is often emphasised that governmental interests, inter-state power relations, and anticipated tensions within the EMS have been very important for launching EMU. However, this is only half the story as, eventually, the movement towards EMU by and large turned out to be also an attempt to accommodate fiscal and monetary politics to the imperatives of global financial markets and the interests of European *rentiers* (i.e., above all, that of TNCs, large banks and insurance companies). Moreover, the agreed schedule for monetary integration represents a transnational initiative to strengthen the European policy agenda of regulatory competition and austerity. It is a truism that the extension of competition as a side effect of EMU has been welcomed by the European business community and neo-liberal politicians. In particular, two consequences are regarded as very promising: first, it establishes a direct link to further deregulation of industrial relations systems, since the new common currency intensifies the pressure on trade unions in terms of collective bargaining (Altvater and Mahnkopf, 1993; Busch, 1994). Due to more visible and therefore comparable wage cost differentials, national and regional bargaining regimes are subjected more explicitly to the dynamics of regime competition. Besides, the general downward pressure on working and income conditions is exacerbated by the fact that EMU forecloses the opportunity of currency depreciation. Thus, in a short-term perspective, economic and political actors have only a few adjustment mechanisms at their disposal to compensate for poor economic performance and competitive disadvantages. The choices are wage reduction, longer working hours or an intensification of work. Second, EMU affects industrial relations regimes more indirectly by compelling governments to pursue more or less rigorous politics of austerity. This fosters not only the dismantling of the welfare state, reduced social provisions and services, a poor public sector, or insufficient infrastructure, but also an economically depressive situation characterised by poor business performance, high unemployment and weak trade unions.

In short, the envisioned consequences of EMU in its planned and realised shape have been generally detrimental to employees and trade unions. Hence, it was no surprise that, against the background of persistent mass unemployment, the Maastricht Treaty became a symbol of the crisis of European legitimacy. The fragile approval of the population in referenda and opinion polls was only one indicator, followed later by a series of protests, demonstrations and strikes against the social consequences of tough fiscal discipline. In almost every member state the number of people engaged in anti-Maastricht campaigns increased (Obradovic, 1996). This was of course a sign of growing distrust as regards the further course of European integration as well as towards neo-liberal adjustment strategies of national governments. Since governments refused to give up the primacy of monetarist objectives, they suffered electoral defeat. Hence, in the mid-1990s, in a range of member states – above all in France, Great Britain and Germany – parties exhibiting a more social rhetoric have been more successful.

The changing public climate is perhaps one reason for extending the engagement of the EU in social affairs. The Maastricht Treaty contained the 'social protocol', which augmented EU competencies, subjected more issues to qualified majority voting and strengthened the role of the 'social partners' (Falkner, 1998: 78–155). As this turned out to be insufficient to secure public consent, the Commission pressed strongly for using the new legislative opportunities to pass directives on European Works Councils, parental leave and part-time employment. Moreover, and perhaps more important, it took the initiative to tackle the unemployment problem. In publishing the White Paper on *Growth, Competitiveness, Employment* (Commission of the European Communities, 1993) it started a relatively intense European discussion on the political management of economic modernisation and employment creation. Afterwards, with the support of the Commission and some Social Democratic governments, the employment issue was placed again and again on the European agenda, albeit redefined more and more in neo-liberal terms. Finally, it became firmly established as a permanent theme in the revised TEU of Amsterdam, in which the 'social protocol' was also incorporated.

From the angle of national and European elites these very modest modifications of the socio-economic constitution of the EU serve mainly two purposes. In general, they operate as 'flanking policies' to facilitate a smooth process of market integration. In this context, one central aim is the avoidance of serious social distortions and political upheavals. Besides, the measures of social regulation have a strong symbolic impact, since they are aimed at strengthening the approval of the EU. Above all, the Commission is engaged in an EU that pretends to be more than an agency for neo-liberal deregulation; yet so far, most corrections have been marginal and hardly improve the overall appearance. Despite some disputes on the institutionalisation of a European economic government as suggested by the French, the basic traits of the neo-liberal configuration remain untouched. As we have seen, one of the main purposes of an accelerated European integration was to establish and to widen, not to close, the gap of macroeconomic co-ordination (Teague, 1999: 165–88). For such a far-reaching goal, the measures taken until now have been too timid and mistaken. They are almost exclusively concerned with a regulative framing of a primarily market-determined adjustment of welfare regulations, wage costs and working conditions.

All in all, despite initiatives to strengthen the 'social dimension', most employees and trade unions have been fully aware that EMU has a detrimental impact on social and working conditions. In all member states the convergence criteria and the 'stability pact' reinforced both public expenditure cutbacks and a deregulation of labour markets and collective bargaining systems; hence it was not surprising that the campaign was accompanied by much public criticism and political protest. The conundrum was, rather, why the trade unions nevertheless buttressed monetary integration. Against the background of political weakness, their attitude towards EMU was based on similar considerations as that towards the Internal Market. Without any powerful European voice they have been reliant on co-operation with stronger organisations in the political arena, first of all with Social Democratic parties and the European Commission. In principle, both showed an interest in co-operating with trade unions as well. Eventually, however, they were only willing to do so if the unions accepted the given socio-economic conditions, i.e., the primacy of monetary stability and an intensified market competition. In view of public discussions, Social Democratic parties have already accepted these objectives in the course of the 1980s and 1990s (Dyson, 1999; Sassoon, 1996: 730–54). The Commission as a whole was even a major initiator of the creation of the new European economy. To be sure, the motives of both organisations are not thoroughly identical. In general, however, most Social Democrats as well as the Commission seem to be convinced that European integration can only progress smoothly if some new flexible forms of national and European regulation accompany it. In this context, they regard the involvement of consensus-oriented trade unions as an advantage.

The neo-liberal configuration: industrial relations besieged by 'regime competition'

The preceding argument should not be misunderstood as suggesting that the political involvement of trade unions in the process of European integration was without any positive result in the form of social compensations. However, there is no reason to ignore the fact that European integration so far has been primarily a business driven project. In fact, the dominating economic initiatives have not simply been an expression of hard-line neo-liberalism (i.e., a radical deregulation of the existing social security mechanisms) but rather, in terms of economic policy, an unmistakably European supply-side agenda has been evident. In this context, two features of the new European mode of socio-economic governance operate as an implicit lever for neo-liberal adjustment strategies. Both are closely connected with the pivotal projects of economic integration already outlined above: first, the Internal Market project marked a qualitative shift in the mode of capitalist reproduction by accelerating the transition from simple trade liberalisation to the integration of capital-markets (Simmons, 1999). Now, cross-border capital mobility and the emergence of a European economy have a significant impact on the development of industrial relations and national bargaining structures. They stimulate a logic of 'competitive deregulation', which fosters a step by step deregulation of industrial relations and the retrenchment of welfare systems, even if they are further embedded in specific institutional settings, cultural traditions and power relations. Second, the project of EMU engraved monetarist targets (i.e., low inflation, fiscal discipline and an internationally strong currency) into the TEU. These objectives have been guaranteed first by the 'Maastricht' criteria of fiscal and monetary convergence. Since the start of stage three of EMU, the so-called 'stability pact' has taken care of the fulfilment of austerity measures. As far as intra-European currency management is concerned, this movement describes an at least partial transformation of the logic of 'competitive austerity' into one of 'decreed austerity'. Thus, in principle, the restrictions on governments to provide social security and tackle the unemployment problem by means of Keynesian state intervention remain unchanged.

As already indicated, the neo-liberal European configuration is detrimental to trade unions inasmuch as the twofold pressures of 'competitive deregulation' and 'competitive or decreed austerity' nurture 'social dumping' and 'regime competition'. Unions, therefore, have some reason to be rather critical of the EU. Actually, however, this applies only to a few of them, which are either rooted in a stronger socialist or Communist tradition (e.g., the Confederation Générale du Travail in France) and/or try to defend a comprehensive welfare state and an extensive public sector, as in some Nordic countries (Martin and Ross, 1999). Most unions, particularly if they are based in export-oriented sectors, hope to benefit from economic gains achieved in intensified competition. Besides this, they are mainly concerned with securing immediate political influence (i.e., being heard by governments, employers, and the business community). For both reasons they support the new European constitution, even if they are only accepted as junior partners without any influence in macroeconomic affairs. In other words, European trade unions have agreed to a new 'competitive bargain', which is strongly asymmetrical. They are principally willing to approve the basic neo-liberal goals – market deregulation and monetary stability – in exchange for involvement in negotiations about their concrete realisation and political framing. In this sense, trade unions are an active force in the current multi-level structure of 'co-operative deregulation'.

First, at the firm or regional level, employees become more and more involved in local productivity coalitions, whereas trade unions are regarded as an external source or irritation (Dörre, 1999: 312–15). As a consequence of such internal tensions within the working class, pressures to agree to lower payments and worse working conditions intensified. In view of imminent dismissals or threatening bankruptcy, there is widespread readiness to renounce existing social employment conditions. Thereby, the fear of losing jobs is not only a phenomenon found in crisis-prone branches and enterprises: it seems to be more and more common in high-tech TNCs as well, which may take advantage of playing off the employees of plants in different industrial relations regimes (Cressey *et al.*, 1998: 54–5). Although the directive on European Works Councils improves the opportunities of the employees to counteract the most extreme forms of such practices (Schulten, 1996), in the age of transnational capital mobility the chance to pursue 'regime-shopping' and shift production sites remains a permanent threat.

Second, in contrast to the firm level, where employees and unions can only react defensively, there seems to be a more proactive involvement at the national level of political decision making. From the late 1980s onwards, governments and the so-called social partners often became involved in new corporatist arrangements, which are aimed at improving the competitiveness of national institutions and regulations (Rhodes, 1998). In contrast to the corporatist arrangements of the 1970s, 'material rewards for workers and institutional influence for labour are...tied to the acceptance of a joint commitment with employers to success in competitive markets' (Streeck, 1998: 15). In a way, the new 'competitive corporatism' is based on a 'peace formula', which is substantially different from the old 'Fordist class compromise'. The old compromise of 'embedded liberalism' (Ruggie, 1982) was characterised by restraint of the labour movement with regard to socialist political issues (work place democracy, the extension of public control of the economy) in exchange for income growth and full employment. Nowadays, the new bargain – if there is one at all – is based on the renunciation of social security and specific forms of work place regulation in exchange for restricted employment guarantees for established workers. Sometimes such guarantees are connected with the promise of investment. In this sense, in most European countries trade unions agreed on a range of 'social pacts' (Hassel, 1998), which are primarily directed to three issues:

1. With respect to *collective bargaining*, the guiding principles are wage restraint and wage flexibility. First of all, this means that wage increases should remain clearly below productivity gains in order to improve competitiveness, investment and employment. Besides, agreements on wages and working conditions should become decentralised to a certain degree in order to react to the specific requirements of singular regions or firms.

2. With respect to *labour market policy*, the 'social pacts' try to improve the employability of the national workforce. For this reason, they provide stronger economic and administrative incentives to work by means of decreases in social expenditures, restricted entitlements and more flexible employment regulations. This last point can be realised through an extension of restricted or part-time employment or a flexible reduction of individual working hours. Moreover, additional programmes for training and education are directed to particular social problem groups (young people, long-term unemployed), who run the risk of becoming permanently excluded from the employment system.

3. With respect to the *reform of social welfare*, the social partners try to arrange the reduction of social contributions to lower labour costs and stimulate employment. One important side effect of this should be a relief of social insurance systems (pension funds) and public budgets later on.

Obviously, the new 'competitive corporatism' is a result of an emerging European 'best practice capitalism'. The dynamics of 'regime competition' and its corporatist management can be seen as two sides of the same coin. In this context, however, one should not ignore the fact that, because of intensified competitive pressures, the new forms of national corporatism remain rather weak and fragile (Crouch and Menon, 1997: 160–3).

Organisational weakness is even more typical for the third level of 'co-operative deregulation': that is, the new supranational forms of interest mediation. Even those who argue that recent treaty revisions show the initial stages of European tripartite bargaining (Dølvik, 1999; Falkner, 1998), are also cautious about deriving from this any substantial modification of the European socio-economic order. This is mainly due to the constricted scope for supranational negotiations. From the start, fundamental issues of financial and monetary politics have been excluded from tripartite meetings. Even after the EU summit in Cologne in 1999, which agreed on an 'employment pact' and a macroeconomic co-ordination approach, there was no real bargaining process. The only issues which are at stake are modest wage settlements and further adjustments of social regulations and security systems. Obviously, neither the European Central Bank nor national governments are willing to become involved in a new and powerful Euro-corporatism. As a result, the European Commission, as the only representative of an (at best) rudimentary supranational state, is not able to provide strong material incentives for either trade unions or employer organisations to make both willing to negotiate binding European arrangements. To be sure, the Commission has a strong interest in extending its own influence by attracting European peak organisations of capital and labour into relationships. Nevertheless, the 'type of exchange' may resemble corporatism in form, but the issues concerned rarely move beyond 'symbolic business' (Crouch and Menon, 1997: 167–8). In other words, at the European level the emerging 'corporatist policy networks' are strongly subjected to the neo-liberal and monetarist objectives of improved European competitiveness.

Impasses and pitfalls of trade union strategies

The various forms of 'productivity coalitions' and different types of corporatist interest mediation can be interpreted as the incorporation of trade unions and employees into an emerging transnational historical bloc dominated by the hegemony of neo-liberal ideas. Of course, such a view is strongly rejected by most Social Democrats and trade union leaders. They emphasise incessantly that the involvement of trade unions in the process of economic and social decision making, in principle, makes room for a new, more socially oriented path of economic restructuring. At root, however, this perspective seems to be based on rather vague hopes: first, it is quite unclear whether the new focus on employment policy and the reform of national welfare systems will not only generate an improved economic environment for companies, but also some 'social benefits' for employees and the unemployed; and, second, there is some reason to believe that the 'organisational benefits' derived from union involvement will prove as insubstantial in times of economic recession.

Hence, even if the new role of trade unions is an indication that neo-liberal hegemony is far from complete, it reveals at the same time that its prevailing strategies are sub-optimal. Of course, there is no easy and direct way to overcome the European framework of neo-liberal and monetarist imperatives. As the Lafontaine experience suggests, the path towards an alternative macroeconomic configuration is cumbersome and causes many troubles (see Chapter 9 this volume). The problem with most leaders of Social Democratic parties and trade unions is rather that they do not even seriously take such a possibility into account, when thinking and talking about a socially cohesive Europe. Eventually, this means that the dynamics of 'competitive deregulation' and 'competitive austerity' will unravel further by simultaneously giving precedence to microeconomic strategies to manage problems of competition. In this context, contrary to the first impression, the new type of national 'competitive corporatism' represents no disapproval, but rather a concrete, politically mediated form of microeconomic restructuring. Its main concern is to improve investment conditions by reforming labour markets and welfare systems. Thereby it encourages a productivist (neo-liberal) redefinition of progressive social issues. For trade unions, such a narrow perspective is not without difficulties. It contains at least two major pitfalls: first, it tends to undermine the already fragile ties of working-class solidarity, for, in principle, it accepts the deregulation of industrial relations and more social inequality; and, second, with respect to European integration, it seems to be risky, since it operates as a self-fulfilling prophecy (Bieling and Deppe, 1999), which from the start excludes and therefore blocks a more socially oriented, macro-economic strategy of growth and employment creation.

So far, there is no indication that the microeconomic (i.e., basically neo-liberal and nationalist) approach to improve competitiveness is balanced or even corrected by the emergence of 'Euro-corporatist' policy networks. Such a possibility is excluded as long as tripartite supranational bargaining is restricted to only a few, rather vague, agreements on the 'social flanking' of market integration. As outlined above, such a limitation is completely in accordance with business interests. The dominance of business interests can be explained partly through the economic, political and ideological power of globally oriented TNCs.

Moreover, it is also the result of an advantageous lobbying and bargaining position, which is reflected in a particular, very successful division of labour between main European business organisations: the 'big business troika' consisting of the ERT, the EU Committee, and the European Enterprise Group (EEG) that plays a very decisive role with respect to the launching of major strategic initiatives (Cowles, 1997; Greenwood, 1997: 101–32). It takes advantage of very good formal and informal ties to the European Commission and, thus, a privileged access to the European arena of political agenda-setting and decision making. On the other hand, for a long while the Union of Industrial and Employers' Confederation of Europe (UNICE) has been in an enviable position with respect to the prevention of more binding supranational regulations. In this context, unanimity voting in a range of areas was certainly beneficial. It was necessary only to convince one government – usually the British one – to oppose drafts on social regulation, and to refuse any negotiation of binding agreements with the European Trade Union Congress (ETUC). Of course, this changed after the electoral success of the British Labour Party and the Amsterdam Treaty (Dølvik, 1999). Nevertheless, UNICE still has the opportunity to organise the disapproval of social regulation by a qualified minority blockage in the regular legislation process or to pursue delaying tactics within the 'social dialogue'.

This clearly indicates that the trade unions are in a fairly difficult position at the European level. In lacking the power to push through any autonomously defined initiative, they become more and more involved in the prevailing strategy of 'co-operative déregulation'. Thereby the weak, often only symbolic, forms of an emerging 'Euro-corporatism' represent the outcome of interaction between a range of competing influences: the weak support of European trade unions on the part of national federations; detrimental lobbying and bargaining conditions; and some financial and organisational assistance on the part of the European Commission to build transnational union networks (Martin, 1996). This last influence might support the somewhat naive view that after the completion of the Internal Market and EMU the EU, above all the Commission, will concentrate its energies on the extension and improvement of the so-called 'social dimension'. In the meantime, however, such an expectation has proved to be misleading. It has become evident that the attention of European economic and political elites is directed above all towards eastward enlargement (see Chapter 8 this volume) and the consolidation of EMU. Hitherto it seems to be rather unlikely that the definition of these priorities will imply a more substantial Europeanisation of trade unions and social regulation. In other words, despite their participation in the EU, trade unions seem to be locked into an unfavourable position. The fundamental problem is that they have subjected themselves almost unconditionally to the prevailing functionalist (i.e., neo-liberal and technocratic) path of European integration. This might have made possible some social progress – regulations and directives – and some involvement of trade unions in the process of European decision making. Nevertheless, this strategic orientation also implies some often ignored, but remarkable, political costs. With respect to further political initiatives, it may turn out to be a huge burden as the recognition, legitimacy and influence of the ETUC becomes derived more from European institutions (such as the Commission) than from its own affiliations and their rank and file.

In lieu of a conclusion: prospects for a rearrangement of the European bargain

At first glance, there is no reason to believe that the conditions which are necessary to overcome the current neo-liberal configuration will improve. This might be surprising, since in the mid-1990s trade unions mobilised against austerity measures and social democracy had electoral success in most European countries. Yet despite this temporary political upswing, there was an apparent lack of more far-reaching demands for democratic control and social regulation of the new European economy. Instead, most trade union leaders and Social Democrats have been primarily engaged in curtailing their visions and accommodating them to the given neo-liberal European framework of economic and social regulation (Dyson, 1999). In this sense, monetarist imperatives have been either acknowledged or neglected in public discussions and electoral campaigns. At the same time, political initiatives of left-wing forces have been primarily reactive and defensive. They are neither linked to a new political vision nor to a new concept of European governance. Such a concept would require that alternative projects of democratic political control and solidaristic reorganisation exceed the narrow perspective on social regulation at the European level. At any rate, it is not sufficient to pursue a political strategy which aims at mitigating some of the most damaging consequences of intra-European 'regime competition', while simultaneously accepting the 'terms of the neo-liberal consensus' (Crouch, 1997).

A more vigorous left-wing strategy implies transforming the fundamental principles of the European socio-economic order. This requires, particularly for trade unions, shifting the focus from participation in different kinds of 'flanking' or so-called 'soft politics', which are at the heart of the European partnership approach, but often only of a symbolic nature, to more fundamental policy issues dealing with macroeconomic co-ordination within the European economy. Of course, there are many obstacles to more far-reaching Europeanised trade union strategies. Most important are the ideological differences within the union movement, the institutional diversity of national social standards and regulations, and specific socio-economic conditions on the national and regional level. Besides, it seems to be impossible to cause employers to consent to binding supranational agreements. Nevertheless, in principle, trade unions have good reasons to avoid a competitive deterioration of wages, working conditions and standards of living. Consequently, there is at least the option of much closer transnational co-ordination of trade union strategies with respect to wages, working conditions, and social regulation (Marginson and Sisson, 1998).

In such a process, the sectional European trade union committees have a decisive role to play. They have to expand their institutional structures in order to support a European system of comprehensive mutual information, so that the processes of collective bargaining would be effectively co-ordinated. The European Metalworkers' Federation (EMF) has emphasised such co-ordination since the 1970s, but only in the 1990s did the measures and agreements become more concrete: since 1996 national members have to justify themselves, if confronted with real losses of income in three consecutive years. Also, only in 1998 did all European unions of the metal sector commit themselves to a guideline for wage bargaining, which is determined by the compensation of the rate of inflation plus a balanced share of productivity increases (Schulten and Bispinck, 1999).

The co-ordination of collective bargaining might be an important initial stage, but obviously it is insufficient to resist the pressures of European regime competition. Hence, it must be complemented by a much closer co-ordination of national economic and social policies. This requires not only more binding agreements but also changes in political content (i.e., a macroeconomic approach of economic development transcending the 'neo-liberal configuration'). According to a Memorandum of European Economists (1997), this should be achieved by carrying out four sets of political objectives:

1. With respect to monetary policy, the European Central Bank and member states should agree on less tight criteria of monetary stability to stimulate economic growth and employment.

2. With respect to fiscal policy, the revenue base of the EU should be enhanced in order to invigorate investment, infrastructure and employment programmes. On the other hand, an initiative for tax harmonisation should encourage a moderation of tax competition among member states.
3. With respect to labour markets, a flexible approach to cuts in working time is suggested (see also Lipietz, 1996), since active labour market policies – education and training programmes – can only partly contribute to a reduction of unemployment.
4. With respect to welfare policy, the memorandum also demands more supranational regulation – i.e., minimum standards or social rights of participation – and a reversal of social redistribution that in past decades has been in favour of profits, interest and high income groups.

Whether such a perspective will be possible in the near future is, however, far from certain. The prospects are rather gloomy. Against the background of the existing legal requirements of the TEU and currency competition *vis-à-vis* the US dollar, it seems very unlikely that the neo-liberal and monetarist agenda will be changed. Nevertheless, there are also some grounds for optimism. First, the eleven economies that have participated in EMU from the beginning do not constitute an exclusive club of enthusiastic advocates in favour of austerity measures. Since there is still a lack of rules concerning the interaction of the European Central Bank (interest and exchange rates) and national governments (fiscal and economic policies), European bargaining on economic issues is still far from complete. Second, such tensions might become more evident in times of economic recession, when national governments are tempted to resort to divergent strategies of crisis management. Then the concrete content of these strategies will be determined more directly by national public controversies. While the political right will probably turn towards more nationalist solutions, trade unions and the left have at least a chance to bring more explicitly the issue of transnational macroeconomic co-operation on to the political agenda. And, in reopening the debate on a re-arrangement of the European socio-economic order, they might initiate the emergence of a transnational counter-hegemonic bloc of social and political forces.

6
Strength Through Unity? A Comparative Analysis of Splits in the Austrian, Norwegian and Swedish Labour Movements over EU Membership

Andreas Bieler and Stina Torjesen

Introduction: globalisation and the challenge of revived European integration

Austria, Norway and Sweden had always been sceptical about European integration. Instead of the European Union (EU), they joined the European Free Trade Area (EFTA) in 1960. In particular, Social Democratic parties in these countries argued that the EU was dominated by 'big capital' and Christian Democratic parties. Supranational integration led by these forces would imply the danger of undermining social democratic achievements of full employment, social equality and generous welfare provisions (Kurzer, 1993: 207; Jerneck, 1993: 26; Cappelen *et al.*, 1994: 58). In addition, Austria and Sweden also rejected EU membership, because it was considered incompatible with their neutral status (Huldt, 1994: 111; Neuhold, 1992: 89). Nevertheless, from 1989 onwards, all three countries applied for membership and Austria and Sweden actually acceded to the EU on 1 January 1995, while membership was rejected in a referendum in Norway in late 1994. This chapter analyses the role of the Austrian, Norwegian and Swedish labour movements in the struggle over membership and assesses whether differences between the three were crucial for the different outcomes in the referenda.

In all three countries, the social democratic achievements were based on the possibility of small states being able to counter negative effects of international competition at the national level. Katzenstein (1985) has shown how these three states retained an economic openness to the international market throughout the post-war era, while at the same time providing domestic compensation for the costs of constant adjustment to international competition via an active investment and employment policy, restraint on wage and price increases and the maintenance of a large public sector. Globalisation, characterised by the transnationalisation of production and finance (see Chapter 1), has undermined the policy autonomy of states in this respect. While the end of the state has clearly been announced too early (e.g., Strange, 1996), to argue that there has been no substantial change apart from an increase in cross-border flows (e.g., Hirst and Thompson, 1996) is equally one-sided. Rather, it is clear that globalisation has, at least partly, been brought about by state action and that, as a consequence, the role of the state has not necessarily diminished but changed (Panitch, 1994). Instead of providing protection against negative effects of international competition, the state has to ensure the smooth functioning of a country within the global political economy. This restructuring of the state goes hand in hand with a general change at the level of ideas from Keynesianism to neo-liberalism. Hence, as a result of globalisation, not only are states less able to fulfil a protective role, they are also less willing to do so. Overall, whatever the exact nature of globalisation and the new role of states, it is clear that the pressure on traditional compensatory measures has grown stronger.

The pressures of global restructuring have been intensified in the EU through the revival of European integration in the mid-1980s. As was argued in Chapter 1, the latter has been part and parcel of the former. The Internal Market programme fostered the transnationalisation of production in Europe and included provisions for the free movement of capital, thereby supporting the general tendency towards a global integrated financial market. The rationale of liberalisation and deregulation, further cemented by the Maastricht convergence criteria, clearly reflects the general shift towards neo-liberalism by forcing countries to adopt economic policies of this type.

The Internal Market presented Austria, Sweden and Norway with a dilemma. On the one hand, to stay outside implied a threat to the countries' general economic well-being. The Internal Market removed internal trade barriers between member states and implied higher barriers to countries from the outside. Hence, EU companies gained a competitive advantage *vis-à-vis* their Austrian, Norwegian and Swedish counterparts. On the other hand, it was argued that EU membership would lead to increased competition, while at the same time restricting national subsidies in support of disadvantaged and/or ailing industrial sectors. Furthermore, the neo-liberal EMU convergence criteria, with their emphasis on low inflation and price stability, would probably restrict high welfare spending. This would also limit national governments' ability to stimulate economic growth and higher levels of employment via budget deficit spending and other types of state intervention. EU membership, consequently, would both increase international competition and pose a threat to traditional compensation strategies.

To date, the role of trade unions has largely been neglected in the debate on globalisation. Nevertheless, as Coates makes clear, this is mainly the result of an undue focus on capital mobility as the core feature of globalisation. Capital is regarded in a fetishised form as a 'thing' instead of a 'social relationship', and thus it is overlooked that capital can only realise itself on a global scale to the extent that real production processes are created on this scale. 'The enhanced global mobility of capital in the last three decades has social rather than technical roots. Capital is more geographically mobile than it was in the past because it now has more proletariats on which to land' (Coates, 2000: 255). New strata of workers (e.g., women, rural workers and immigrants) have been employed in established capitalism, and by spreading production processes to developing countries new proletariats were additionally created, doubling the world proletariat to 3 billion people within a generation. Hence, 'capital...as it moves, does more than constrain the policy options of national governments: it actually alters the balance and character of social classes, and does so increasingly on a global scale' (ibid.: 256). In short, labour is part of global restructuring processes, and it is therefore necessary to analyse its position in the global economy, as well as the possibilities and opportunities it presents.

Katzenstein (1985) has stated that domestic compensation mechanisms are formulated and devised within corporatist systems, where trade unions (together with employers' associations) are co-opted into governmental policy making. Thus he includes labour in his analysis of small states in world markets. He does not, however, appreciate the possibility that there may be splits within the labour movement due to the location of various unions in different production sectors, differently affected by international competition. Gourevitch (1986) has pointed out that the international economy puts pressure on business, agriculture and labour within countries, which in turn lobby their governments in favour of policies intended to cope with these pressures.

In contrast to Katzenstein, Gourevitch acknowledges that these societal actors may be fragmented. Amongst other factors, he argues that both business and labour may be divided over the issue of international competitiveness. Business and labour at the cutting edge of international competition are likely to be in favour of free trade and intensified specialisation in international trade, while business and labour in less competitive areas may favour various forms of protectionism (ibid.: 55–60, 221–9).[1] Gourevitch, however, does not realise that the transnationalisation of production adds an additional dimension. Although he mentions the 'internationalisation' of production, he still only distinguishes between internationally-oriented capital and labour, based on domestic production but producing for export, and nationally-oriented capital and labour, also based on domestic production but supplying predominantly or exclusively the domestic market. A neo-Gramscian perspective, as outlined in Chapter 1, has an additional advantage because it takes into account transnational capital and labour, which stem from transnational production, producing for the global market.

In the next section, consequently, a brief overview of the three countries' production structure is offered to help identify the relevant social forces, meaning collective actors as engendered by the production process. For labour, trade unions are accepted as its organisational expression. They are not, however, treated as unitary actors, but as institutions, within which social forces struggle for predominance. Peak organisations are, therefore, divided according to unions representing particular industrial sectors (i.e., nationally-oriented, internationally-oriented and transnational unions). In the third section, then, the role in, and position on, the struggle over EU membership of the various social forces is analysed in detail. Finally, the conclusion briefly discusses trade unions' strategies and the chances of countering the negative effects of global structural change.

Globalisation and the production structure in Austria, Norway and Sweden

Globalisation is a general phenomenon. Its particular impact, however, differs from country to country, resulting in different configurations of social forces. In this section, the three countries' production structures are assessed in order to identify the different fractions of labour crucial in the struggle over EU membership.

Austria: a predominantly domestic production structure

Austria's post-Second World War production structure has been predominantly characterised by small-scale industry. In 1992, out of the 2.19 million working population, 55 per cent were employed in small-sized companies with fewer than 100 employees and 28 per cent in medium-sized companies with fewer than 1000 employees. This is a relatively high percentage in an international comparison. In general, these companies contribute only between one-third and two-thirds to the overall national employment (Breit and Rössl, 1992: 191). Importantly, about 50 per cent of Austrian domestic production was completely sheltered against international competition with regulated supplies and production quotas (Luif, 1994: 26). Siegel identified 21 Austrian transnational corporations (TNCs) in 1990, but only one of them, Austrian Industries – dissolved in 1993 – lived up to international standards. The 21 TNCs were mainly concentrated in Austria in their production structure, employing only 20 per cent of their workforce abroad (Siegel, 1992: 167). The low number of TNCs and their focus on Austria signals a low degree of transnationalisation of production.

This does not mean that Austria has been totally unaffected by globalisation. Although still modest in overall terms, both inward and outward foreign direct investment (FDI) rose during the second half of the 1980s. Outward FDI increased from US$66 million in 1985 to US$1601 million in 1990 and inward FDI from US$164 million to US$557 million during the same period (EFTA, 1991: 43–4). This tendency was underlined by the growth of the foreign private sector in Austria, where employment rose by 16 per cent between 1970 and 1985 (Pichl, 1989: 164). It indicates an increasing, albeit small overall, presence of foreign TNCs in Austria.

In general, however, Austria is linked to the global economy mainly via the traditional route of exports and imports in goods. As a consequence, the main line of division is likely to be between nationally-oriented capital and labour on the one hand, and internationally-oriented capital and labour on the other. While the former may reject EU membership since this implies the end of their protection against international competition, the latter probably support accession to the EU since this guarantees access to their primary export markets. The few transnational social forces can be expected to join forces with internationally-oriented capital and labour, as they too rely on international free trade and liberalisation.

Norway: the significance of the oil industry

Norway has an open economy with import and export ratios measured at 37 per cent of GDP (SSB, 1999b). Oil accounts for more than 30 per cent of total exports. Norway is the third largest oil exporter in the world with petroleum production providing more than 5 per cent of GDP and a substantial government income (Dølvik and Stokke, 1998: 120–1). In the 1970s and 1980s, in conjunction with European trends, recession hit parts of the mainland economy. The oil wealth, however, allowed a significant expansion of the public sector, thus easing the effects of negative economic trends (Organisation for Economic Co-operation and Development, or OECD, 1999: 51–3). Between 1970 and 1994 government expenditures, as a share of GDP, rose from 45 to 55 per cent (Freeman, 1997: 17). Oil revenues have also permitted continued high levels of regional subsidies and sectoral support to agriculture, fisheries and industrial sectors such as the food processing and energy intensive industries (OECD, 1999: 61–8).

Oil, together with fish, is the major export commodity. Employment in these sectors is, however, low and accounts for only 1 per cent each of total employment. The metal and mineral industry, chemical industry, paper industry and manufacturing industry produce the remaining goods entering international markets. Workers in industry make up 14 per cent of the workforce. Two-thirds of these are exposed to competition in domestic or foreign markets (SSB, 1998, 1999b). Employment in the government sector grew with increasing government expenditure. In 1998, 30 per cent of Norwegian workers were public employees, signalling a growth of 94 per cent since 1973 (SSB, 1999b; Freeman, 1997: 24).

The level of foreign direct investment in Norway has traditionally been low. In recent years, however, there has been a significant increase. In 1994, total FDI was US$12.5 billion, whereas the figure for 1998 is US$24.19 billion. The oil sector has received the largest bulk of investment. In 1998 it accounted for US$10.37 billion, or 42.9 per cent of total FDI (Hansen, 1999: 574). The flow of investments to industry has increased in the 1990s. In 1998 it amounted to approximately 20 per cent of total FDI (ibid.). Norway's outward FDI has also increased: in 1996 US$20 billion was invested abroad. Still, in relative terms, few workers are employed in foreign-owned companies or Norwegian TNCs. Hence, with the exception of the oil sector, few transnational social forces are identified. In the EU membership debate, Norway is expected to have powerful nationally-oriented labour forces opposing EU membership. They are centred around shielded home markets depending on protection policies and government subsidies. Public sector workers share the interests of nationally-oriented labour in their common reliance on continued high levels of public spending. These forces differ from internationally-oriented capital and labour situated in Norway's export sectors, which are heavily dependent upon unrestrained access to the European market.

Sweden: capital flight and increasing transnationalisation

Unlike Austria and Norway, Sweden's production structure has always been characterised by TNCs (Andersson, Fredriksson and Svensson, 1996: 27–47; Braunerhjelm *et al.*, 1996: 2). The degree of transnational-isation, however, increased dramatically in the second half of the 1980s, when there was a drastic upturn in outward FDI. While inward FDI had only risen from US$396 million in 1985 to US$2328 million in 1990, outward FDI increased from US$1783 million to US$14 136 mil-lion during the same period (Luif, 1996: 208). This is even more dra-matic if one takes into account that 'in 1989 for the first time ever, Sweden invested more abroad than at home' (Kurzer, 1993: 133).

The transnationalisation of Swedish production is also expressed in the change in the Swedish and foreign share of TNCs' employees and production. In 1965, TNCs employed 33.9 per cent of their employees abroad, where they achieved 25.9 per cent of their turnover. By 1990, the situation had drastically changed: 60.6 per cent of the workforce was employed in production abroad, accounting for 51.4 per cent of the turnover. This increased emphasis on production abroad was espe-cially apparent between 1986 and 1990. The percentage of employees abroad rose by 11.4 per cent (i.e., 42.7 per cent of the overall increase between 1965 and 1990), and the percentage of turnover abroad by 9.1 per cent (i.e., 35.7 per cent of the overall increase between 1965 and 1990) (Braunerhjelm *et al.*, 1996: 10; own calculations). Initially, foreign production by Swedish TNCs led to increased exports by these companies and, therefore, had no negative effect on the Swedish econ-omy (Swedenborg, 1979: 223). From the mid-1980s onwards, however, increased investment abroad was substituted for expansion at home and implied the transfer of production units (Andersson, Fredriksson and Svensson, 1996: 126). In some instances, this even included the transfer of headquarters. Asea Brown Boveri moved to Zurich/ Switzerland and Tetra Pak and IKEA to locations in the EU.

As a result, the main line of division in Sweden is likely to be between national capital and labour on the one hand, and transna-tional capital and labour on the other. Internationally-oriented social forces are less important and can be considered to be allies of transnational forces and their quest for EU membership and full participation in the Internal Market.

Trade unions in the struggle over membership

Austria: internationally-oriented labour wins the day

The Chamber of Labour (AK) and the Austrian Federation of Trade Unions (ÖGB) are the two peak organisations of Austrian labour. Both organisations are extremely concentrated and centralised. Though the ÖGB is divided into 14 individual trade unions according to different industrial sectors, they enjoy little independent power. Indeed it is the ÖGB which decides about personnel, finance and general union policies. By contrast, individual unions do not have an independent legal status on their own (Traxler, 1991: 339–41). Membership of the AK and financial contributions are obligatory for workers and the degree of unionisation is high in Austria, with more than 60 per cent of blue- and white-collar workers being ÖGB members (Tálos, 1996: 105).

The AK and ÖGB came out in favour of membership early on in the debate (AK, 1989; ÖGB, 1988). During high-ranking talks within the corporatist institutions, it had become clear that the trade unionists did not have an alternative plan that could counter the promised increase in general welfare resulting from EU membership put forward by the Chamber of Commerce, representing employers. Against the background of global restructuring and Austria's difficult economic situation, the opening of the sheltered sectors seemed to be the only way forward and EU membership was the best way of bringing this about. In other words, the trade union representatives agreed that membership was necessary for the revival of the Austrian economy (Interview 2; a list of interviews, giving more details, can be found at the end of the chapter). Globalisation and the limitations of state autonomy were accepted as economic facts, and national Keynesian solutions were ruled out as a possibility in this new international environment (Interview 1). Experts such as Heinz Zourek of the AK realised the problems for the sheltered Austrian sectors in case of accession, but pointed out that this would lead to lower prices for consumers and for inputs of the export-oriented industries, and thereby improve the overall economic situation (Zourek, 1989: 189). Once the Cold War had come to an end in 1989, the ÖGB leaders additionally had to take into account the prospect of new competitors in Eastern Europe. Therefore, these high-ranking officials accepted the bid for membership while focusing on a 'just' distribution of the expected welfare gains (Interview 2). Overall, it was argued that, due to economic imperatives, full participation in the Internal Market should be the aim. As membership seemed to be the EU's precondition for full participation, Austria's accession to the EU could not be excluded (ÖGB-Rednerdienst, 1988: 7).

Support for membership was, however, not unconditional. The ÖGB's Europa-Memorandum of December 1988 laid out the conditions. First, Austria's neutral status must be maintained (ÖGB, 1988: 2–3). Second, the economic benefits must be used to improve the income, employment and welfare of the general population with a commitment to full employment as the priority of economic and social policy. Additionally, decision making in social policy must remain at the national level (ibid.: 3), and the right for the ÖGB and AK to participate in all spheres of the decision-making process related to European integration and Austria's possible EU membership must be guaranteed (ibid.: 4). The ÖGB's position was echoed by the AK (1989).

Both the ÖGB and the AK strongly emphasised the importance of a European social dimension in addition to economic integration and demanded that the Austrian government worked towards this in case of membership (ÖGB, 1988: 2; AK, 1989: 5). The opinion of Jacques Delors, President of the European Commission, that a European social dimension was a necessary complementary part of the Internal Market, helped leading Austrian trade unionists in their support for membership (Interview 4). In view of the loss of national policy autonomy due to globalisation, exemplified by the failure of Keynesian policies in France between 1981 and 1983, it was pointed out that the EU, with its social dimension, offered some compensation at the European level and provided better possibilities for the control of TNCs (Vogler, 1991: 179).[2] In December 1991, Austrian trade unions were disappointed about the missing social dimension in the convergence criteria of EMU. Nevertheless, ÖGB President Verzetnitsch concluded that this made Austria's membership even more urgent, as one could only participate in the decision-making process as a member (ÖGB, 1991).

The AK's and ÖGB's pro-membership decision had been mainly taken by leading officials (Interview 1). At first, opposition arose across all industrial sectors against this position. Nevertheless, the trade unions linked to the export sectors soon offered their support, while the trade unions of the sheltered sectors remained opposed. The Union for Textile, Clothes and Leather was the driving force within the ÖGB. Globalisation, in the form of transferring production to developing countries resulting in increased international competition, had affected the sector since the early 1970s; hence, the access to a bigger 'home market' was deemed to be of vital importance. The union's president, Harald Ettl, became the head of the ÖGB Integration Committee set up in late 1987 (Interview 4). Industrial unions such as the Chemical and the Metal Workers' unions also supported participation in the Internal Market. On the other hand, the Rail, Postal and Public Workers' unions, and also the construction and wood workers, opposed such a move (Schaller, 1994: 94). The *Gewerkschaft der Privatangestellten* (White Collar Workers' Union, or GPA), which was the strongest individual union within the ÖGB – representing the white-collar workers in industry, crafts, money and credit, trade, social insurances, insurances, agriculture and forestry – was never positive about EU membership. Accession was opposed, especially in the sheltered and regulated areas of transport companies and the food processing industry because of the likely job losses. Information material in this sense was published by the GPA (Interview 5). The executive board of the Food Processing Union accepted that the maintenance of the sheltered position was unfair on the consumers, who had to pay for it via high prices. It was also realised that the General Agreement on Tariffs and Trade (GATT) Uruguay round would lead to further free trade, and therefore undermine the sheltered sectors anyway. Consequently, the union did not oppose membership but demanded financial restructuring help for the food processing industry before accession and the setting-up of so-called 'work-foundations' with the goal of retraining workers who had lost their jobs in the course of restructuring (Interview 3). Nevertheless, in a conference on the EU held by the extended executive board in March 1988, dissenting voices were raised. Representatives of the tinned food and the tobacco industries opposed membership, arguing that this would push Austrian products out of the market in their sectors and lead to job cuts (Food Processing Trade Union, 1988: 8). Representatives of the dairy and sugar industries rejected restructuring of their sectors via the closing down of production units.

Eventually, the pro-EU decision triumphed within the ÖGB, but a long campaign until 1992 was needed in order to convince members and work council officials at the company level (Interview 1). Objections and doubts were removed by the central organisation through the promise of financial restructuring help and retraining programmes (Interview 4). In the referendum campaign, the ÖGB and its affiliated unions operated as a united body in favour of membership.

Some GPA members, participating in joint information meetings held by capital and labour in companies, dared to outline their critical, hesitant position. This was controlled and criticised by ÖGB officials, who put the GPA functionaries under significant psychological pressure and accused them of left extremism. Considering the predominance of the ÖGB *vis-à-vis* its affiliated unions (see above), the GPA did not attempt to form alliances with other anti-EU actors and resist membership more openly (Interview 5). In the end, the yes-group won in the referendum on EU membership on 12 June 1994 with a clear majority of 66.6 per cent to 33.4 per cent.

Norway: the dominance of nationally-oriented labour

The Norwegian Confederation of Trade Unions (LO-N) is the dominant peak trade union. It covers 800000, or 54 per cent, of all unionised workers. The two other loose confederations, the Federation of Norwegian Professional Associations (AF) and the Confederation of Vocational Unions (YS), organise mainly public sector workers and cover approximately 15 per cent each of the unionised workforce. Union density is relatively low in Norway compared to Sweden and Austria, with a mere 56 per cent of the workforce unionised. LO-N organises a wide spectrum of the Norwegian workforce, including a substantial number in the public sector, but has a particularly firm foothold in core manufacturing industries. The affiliated unions in LO-N are organised according to the industrial principle (i.e., economic sectors) and operate under the guidance of a strong central authority vested in the LO-N leadership. LO-N, with its close links to the Labour Party and its organisational strength, sets the pattern for collective bargaining and political activity in the Norwegian labour movement (Dølvik, 1998: 9–12).

In the EU membership debate YS and AF chose not to give a recommendation. LO-N, on the other hand, had an active approach. It encouraged the Labour government's efforts to secure a European Economic Area (EEA) agreement in the EFTA–EC negotiations. The 1992 EEA agreement gave the EFTA countries access to the Internal Market but did not include them in the EU's political dimension (Gstöhl, 1996: 56–61). LO-N, taking into consideration Norway's open economy and the high export rate of 70 per cent of total Norwegian exports to the European market, deemed the EEA agreement and Internal Market access to be of vital importance (Interview 13). On the question of Norwegian EU membership, however, LO-N had a balanced view. The Maastricht Treaty's encouragement of non-interference by government in the economy was questioned, and the predominance of monetary targets over employment policies was feared (Interview 13). Still, arguments in favour were attributed more weight. Membership gave more influence over EU decisions and in turn justified the loss of sovereignty to a supranational body (LO-N, 1994: 33). LO-N further-more saw, in spite of worries over neo-liberal tendencies, a prospect of gaining more control over capital in the EU. Likewise LO-N argued that the social dimension and the possibility of strengthening trade union co-operation in Europe were features favourable to the labour movement (ibid.: 81). An additional factor was the decision of the EFTA partners – Sweden, Finland and Austria – to enter the EU. This weakened EFTA's institutional framework supporting the EEA agreement. In the end, LO-N favoured full participation in the EU, rather than co-operation built on a feeble EEA agreement (ibid.: 101).

The LO-N leadership encouraged debate and freedom of opinion within and amongst the 28 affiliated unions. Most of the exporting, private sector unions argued in favour of EU membership whereas the public sector unions, together with unions in less competitive or shielded private sectors, tended not to recommend EU membership. *Fellesforbundet* (FF) is the largest private sector union, with 160 000 members. It organises blue-collar workers in export industries such as the iron and metal industry, the shipbuilding industry, the paper industry and the building industry. FF argued that only full EU mem-bership would secure the interest of the export industries. These indus-tries depended not only upon access to the EU market, but also upon operating under the same conditions as their European competitors. Membership would provide an equal basis for competition. Moreover, it was seen as vital for Norway to participate in the future political processes setting the conditions for further developments in the Internal Market (FF, 1994). A common framework for production and trade was viewed positively and even judged particularly beneficial for a small and open economy such as Norway's (Interview 16). Before the national referendum, FF – together with eight other private sector LO-N affiliates – submitted an official declaration stating their arguments in favour of EU membership (Interview 12).

The union covering the oil industry, *Norsk Olje og Petrokjemisk Fagforbund* (NOPF), organising 18 000 workers, did not recommend EU membership. Above it was noted that the oil sector has a high degree of TNC penetration. At first sight one might expect to find trans-national labour forces endorsing EU membership with the aim of securing exports to this market as well as gaining better control over transnational capital. However, Norwegian oil is exported world-wide rather than primarily to EU countries. Similarly the transnational capital engaged in the Norwegian oil sector is primarily US-based TNCs (Hansen, 1999: 574). EU membership therefore would have little impact on the constellation of transnational forces in the oil industry. NOPF, although recognising the need to influence EU energy policy, still attributed greater importance to the danger of a possible lowering of work standards and increased competition for jobs in the off-shore industry within a deregulated European labour market (Interview 15).[3] Workers in Norway's second largest export sector, fisheries, were torn between securing market access and avoiding unfavourable changes in policy due to EU membership. Export considerations were, surprisingly, attributed less importance. *Norsk Nearings og Nytelsesmiddelarberiderforbund* (NNN) organised 36552 workers in a wide range of food processing sectors, including those attached to fisheries and agriculture. Initially, in 1987, NNN rejected both EEA co-operation as well as EU membership. The fishing industry feared that European fishermen would get access to national resources. This would put pressure on a fragile eco-system as well as pose a threat towards mainland processing units, should production be shifted to the continent (Interview 14). Moreover, fisheries are located in remote regions.

The industry, directly or indirectly, receives significant support from the government as part of the welfare state's strategy to maintain a decentralised population and production structure. These government transfers were perceived to be under threat with entry into the EU. First, EU competition regulations in the Internal Market might prohibit government subsidies and protection of domestic production. Second, the neo-liberal policies embedded in the Maastricht agreement were seen as a threat to the welfare state and its high levels of government support to the regions. Workers in the fisheries shared the above concerns with employees in dairy and meat production (LO-N, 1994: 126). The EFTA–EU negotiations for the EEA agreement had to a certain extent taken into account issues facing fisheries and agriculture, thus allowing for continued government support to these sectors (Gstöhl, 1996: 58). Hence, in 1993 NNN decided to approve of the EEA agreement but to oppose EU membership (NNN, 1993: 18–22). A number of other private sector unions engaged in domestic market activity, such as the transport workers' union (*Norsk Transportarbeiderforbund*, NTF) and the commercial sector union (*Handel og Kontor*, HK), opposed EU membership, but acknowledged the necessity of an EEA agreement (HK, 1994: 4; Interview 18).

The public sector union *Kommuneforbundet* (KF), Norway's largest sub-union with 240 000 members, took a similar position. It accepted the EEA agreement but remained sceptical about EU membership. KF saw the Maastricht Treaty as a straitjacket compelling states to implement distinctively neo-liberal policies (Interview 17). The consequences of EU economic policy would be a marked reduction in public sector income, rendering it impossible to finance the welfare state (LO-N, 1994: 60). It was particularly female public sector workers who opposed EU membership (Fagbladet, 1994). As in Sweden, the public sector expansion in the 1970s and 1980s saw an unprecedented number of women join the workforce (SSB, 1999a). EU labour market policies, however, seemed neither conducive to female participation in particular, nor full employment policies in general. Jan Davidsen, the KF leader, was one of the dominant figures within the labour movement arguing against membership. KF's 1994 national congress recommended the KF delegates to the LO-N congress to vote against a LO-N endorsement of EU membership.

The different segments of the Norwegian labour movement supported the two national political coalitions for and against EU membership. LO-N as a whole only gave an official recommendation at its national congress on 22 September 1994, less than two months before the national referendum. The congress voted against EU membership with the tiny majority of three votes. The vote in LO-N may have had a decisive influence on the final outcome in the national referendum (Dølvik, 1998: 135). The recommendation offered vital support to the national no-coalition, whilst at the same time leaving the LO-N leadership unable to campaign in favour of EU membership. The national referendum was held on 28 November 1994. It resulted in 52.2 per cent of votes against Norwegian EU membership and 47.8 per cent in favour.

Sweden: divisions between national and transnational labour

The degree of unionisation (at about 85 per cent of the total workforce) is very high. In contrast to Austria, however, there is no compulsory membership, more rank and file autonomy, and no individual peak trade union enjoys a representational monopoly. The Swedish Trade Union Confederation (LO-S) organises blue-collar workers and lower non-manuals and is, with over 2 million members, the main trade union. Nevertheless, the Swedish Confederation of Professional Employees (TCO), with over one million white-collar employee members, and also the Swedish Confederation of Professional Associations

(SACO), which mainly represents university-trained professionals with roughly 350 000 members, enjoy an independent voice (The Swedish Institute, 1994: 2). All three peak organisations consist of a whole range of affiliated unions, organised according to the industrial principle in the case of the LO-S and TCO, and the craft principle in the case of the SACO. The affiliated unions enjoy a considerable degree of autonomy *vis-à-vis* their peak organisation.

Both the LO-S and TCO assessed the question of membership against the background of the changes in the global economy. It was realised that 'capital and ownership have become almost completely mobile in international terms' (TCO, 1993: 4). Sweden's economy and welfare system depended on a few TNCs, and it would be impossible to remain outside the EU while the TNCs were part of the Internal Market through their investments (Interview 10); hence, a change in trade union strategy was required. 'Internationalisation in itself means that the Swedish trade unions must cooperate across national borders – primarily in Europe where we have the major part of our economic ties and commitments' (TCO, 1994: 5). Co-operation at the European level, it was argued, offered a way to regain some control over capital lost at the national level.

The acknowledgement of the pressures caused by the transnationalisation processes did not, however, imply that the LO-S and TCO accepted the neo-liberal logic. Competition was regarded as beneficial for economic growth and efficiency, but the importance of regulations at the EU level was stressed. Hence, great emphasis was put on the further development of the social dimension and the social chapter of the Maastricht Treaty was welcomed (Interview 8; TCO, 1993: 9). By the same token, the neo-liberal convergence criteria of EMU were criticised. The LO-S and TCO preferred a less austere monetary policy and wanted to include employment as a criterion for the convergence of European economies (LO-S, 1994: 6; TCO, 1993: 18). 'The clear political will must be expressed by the convergence criteria being made subordinate to clear employment goals' (TCO, 1994: 15).

Despite this criticism, the LO-S and TCO were satisfied with the negotiation results. Their individual concerns, such as the right to establish EU labour market directives via collective agreements and the maintenance of the higher Swedish health and safety regulations, had been met. Of course, the problem of the convergence criteria remained unresolved, and this was pointed out and criticised (TCO, 1994: 15). Eventually, however, it was accepted that the convergence criteria had not been up for negotiation. The focus should, therefore, be on future common initiatives for the creation of employment at the European level (Interview 6). In other words, while the peak trade union organisations were not entirely happy about neo-liberal policy co-ordination at the European level, considering the transnationalisation pressures, they did not see any viable alternative to membership. Nevertheless, many of their members and affiliated unions were opposed to membership. Since there is less centralisation and greater autonomy of affiliated unions in Sweden than in Austria, the LO-S and TCO could not recommend a 'yes' for the referendum. Instead, they decided to adopt a neutral position and to provide members with information to help them make up their minds.

Within the unions, there was a split between transnational sector, industrial unions in favour of membership and national sector unions opposing it. In particular the LO-S affiliates, the Paper Workers' Union and the Metal Workers' Union, supported EU membership. Both sectors were heavily export-dependent (the paper sector exports about 80 per cent of its products, and the engineering sector more than 50 per cent), and the engineering sector is also characterised by some of Sweden's most important TNCs such as Volvo, Ericsson and Electrolux. The Paper Workers' Union decided at its congress in autumn 1993 that it would recommend a 'yes' for the referendum on trade union grounds, but leave the final decision to its members on whether the consideration of other issues such as security policy still justified a 'yes'. This decision had encouraged the Metal Workers' Union. In early 1994, the union's committee decided that it would not give a recommendation, but it made clear that it was strongly in favour of membership. The argument was threefold. First, and most importantly, considering that the Swedish TNCs had already established themselves within the Internal Market and taking into account the export dependence of the two sectors, remaining outside the EU was economically impossible. Second, the EU regulations had to be accepted anyway due to the EEA. There was, consequently, no reason why the option of participating in the decision-making process via membership should not be taken. Finally, the EU was also regarded as a peace project, in which Sweden should take part. Eastern enlargement had already been on the agenda in 1993–4, and it was possible that the EU would bridge the divide between Western and Eastern Europe (Interview 11).

On the other hand, there were other LO-S affiliates, the Commercial Workers' Union and the Municipal Workers' Union, which came out heavily against membership, although they did not give a recommendation. The jobs, especially in the public sector, did not depend on exports or transnational production, and the increased structural power of capital consequently played a less significant role. Instead, it was feared that future decisions made in Brussels (e.g., with reference to the harmonisation of tax systems) could lead to rules which implied cut-backs in the public sector and which could thereby cause job losses. Moreover, both unions predominantly represented female blue-collar workers (up to 80 per cent in the case of the Municipal Workers' Union). The participation of women in the labour market of the EU members was, with the exception of Denmark, much lower, and these unions were afraid of experiencing a negative impact through member-ship. In short, the so-called Swedish Model, with its generous welfare system, full employment policy, large public sector and gender equality via high female participation in the work place, was considered to be endangered by the EU's neo-liberal economic policies (Interview 9).

A similar division along the production structure was apparent in the TCO. The Swedish Association of Supervisors (Ledarna), which repre-sented managers and supervisors working in production in both the private and the public sector, recommended a 'yes' on the ground of economic necessity. Moreover, the Swedish Union of Clerical and Technical Employees in Industry (SIF), and the Union of Financial Sector Employees, which organised white-collar workers in industry and finance respectively (i.e., transnational social forces), exhibited a strong yes-tendency without official recommendation. On the other hand, the Swedish Teachers' Union, which represented teachers throughout the entire education system from pre-school to university level (and thus public sector workers), had a tendency towards a 'no'. Its chairman even openly opposed membership. As in the case of the Municipal Workers' Union, EU membership was viewed as a threat to the Swedish welfare system and the equal treatment of women and men at the workplace (Interview 6).

The SACO considered the question of membership to be a matter of foreign policy and, therefore, to be beyond trade union concerns. There was no big internal discussion and no recommendation. The union only carried out a study about the pros and cons of membership with the result that no significant disadvantages for academic employ-ees were identified. This did not, however, prevent affiliated unions from taking a position and a similar division between transnational and national social forces could be observed. The Swedish Association of Graduate Engineers recommended a 'yes' in 1994. Its members often occupied high positions within the transnational sector industry and therefore represented transnational forces. They argued that in case of non-membership many jobs would be lost. The Swedish Association of Graduates in Social Science, Personnel and Public Administration, Economics and Social Work, on the other hand, was rather reluctant. It did not recommend a 'no', but large numbers of its members, who were predominantly employed in the public sector, clearly opposed accession to the EU (Interview 7).

Due to their institutional autonomy, individual unions of the peak organisations campaigned on both sides prior to the referendum, being closely aligned to the two groups of the Swedish Social Democratic Party. The referendum result on 13 November 1994 was very close: 52.7 per cent voted 'yes' versus 47.3 per cent 'no', after the no-side had led from spring 1992 to just shortly before the referendum (Luif, 1996: 214).

Conclusion

In all three countries, the question of EU membership caused a split in the labour movement. Austrian internationally-oriented labour, together with the ÖGB and AK, regarded membership as an economic necessity, since no other strategy would lead to similarly high welfare gains. In Sweden, transnational labour unofficially supported by the peak trade union organisations was behind the drive towards the EU. Considering the restructuring pressures of globalisation and the fact that Swedish TNCs had already become part of the Internal Market via investment, membership was the only way to regain some control over capital lost at the national level. Nationally-oriented labour in Austria and national labour in Sweden, on the other hand, opposed membership. The consequences for employment levels in the protected industrial sectors were feared in Austria, while Swedish trade unions warned against the negative impact of membership on the Swedish Model. Due to the ÖGB's predominant position in the trade union structure, it was almost impossible for Austrian nationally-oriented labour to organise resistance. In Sweden, national trade unions could and did participate on the no-side of the referendum struggle, but here too the outcome was accession to the EU. As in Austria, the Swedish forces opposed to the EU were a minority within the trade unions.

In Norway, by contrast, nationally-oriented labour had the upper hand. Fearing cuts in government spending and a decrease in subsidies to domestic industries, nationally-oriented labour opposed EU membership and campaigned actively against it. Internationally-oriented labour, on the other hand, argued that EU membership would best serve the interests of the export industries. The LO leadership shared the concern of internationally-oriented labour and was clearly in favour of EU membership. At the LO congress, however, arguments against were given more weight, which left the LO leadership unable to campaign in favour of Norwegian accession to the EU.

It is clearly not possible from the discussion of the labour movements in these three countries alone to conclude that the different decisions had a decisive impact on the outcome. Nevertheless, trade unions enjoy a significant role in policy-making through their participation in corporatist institutions. It can, therefore, at least be argued that the overall positive trade union position on EU membership in Austria and Sweden and the negative evaluation in Norway was one of the important reasons for the different results in the referenda.

The findings of this chapter provide some information about trade unions' strategies to counter the negative effects of global structural change. Despite their overall negative position on EU membership, the Norwegian trade unions continue their involvement in European and international labour organisations. This commitment is equally strong in all LO-N affiliated unions regardless of what their positions were in the membership debate. LO-N stresses the importance of using ETUC as a means of gaining influence on EU policies. Several representatives note, however, LO-N's presently weak position in ETUC in comparison to the early 1990s, when Norway was an EU membership candidate (Interviews 14 and 18). Nevertheless, the main emphasis is still placed on the national level, where labour has maintained a strong position. Trade union rights and work standards have not been challenged with the adoption of the EEA agreement. Indeed it is argued that LO-N's political and economic role at the national level has increased significantly in the 1990s (Dølvik, 1998: 137–9). A tripartite income policy framework, known as the 'Solidarity Alternative', took effect in August 1992. Concerned to secure mainland industrial competitiveness, LO-N has ensured wage restraint in Norway despite the booming oil economy (NUO, 1992: 126). In return, LO-N has retained a prominent role in domestic politics and finds itself still recognised as an important partner by industrial capital.

The support of Austrian and Swedish internationally-oriented and transnational labour for EU membership does not indicate that they support neo-liberal restructuring; rather, it is the expression of a desire for greater control over capital and the free market. Both labour movements, first, still put an emphasis on full employment. Austrian trade unions argue that the economic benefits of European integration should be used to achieve full employment, while Swedish labour

wants to subordinate the neo-liberal convergence criteria to the goal of full employment. Second, both emphasise the importance of regulating the free market via further development of the social dimension. The extent to which these strategies are likely to be successful at the European level is, however, unclear. First, employment policies are still of secondary importance. The Commission's White Paper on 'Growth, Competitiveness, Employment' in 1993 put unemployment on the EU agenda. Nevertheless, by linking lower unemployment to the notions of higher competitiveness and labour market flexibility, neo-liberal solutions to the problem were accepted (van Apeldoorn, 1998a: 25–30 see also Chapter 4, this volume: pp. 85–7). The Treaty of Amsterdam in 1997 included a 'Resolution on Growth and Employment', but it still left employment policy within the national domain (Devuyst, 1998: 624).

Some advances for the influence of labour have been made in the social dimension. As Falkner (1998) demonstrates, a corporatist policy community has emerged in EU social policy since the Treaty of Maastricht in 1991. Capital and labour can negotiate collective agreements and then request the Council of Ministers to implement these agreements without discussing their contents. While this procedure has been successfully applied in several instances (e.g., Parental Leave Directive, June 1996; Part Time Directive, December 1997), so far the results of these negotiations are slight in comparison to what trade unions used to achieve at the national level. In sum, there are possibilities at the European level, but the idea of controlling capital currently appears rather optimistic. As van Apeldoorn outlines in Chapter 4 in this volume, while the full-blown neo-liberal project has not gained hegemonic status within the EU, embedded neo-liberalism, successfully established since the mid-1990s, clearly favours the neo-liberal objective of competitiveness over the concerns of the rival neo-mercantilist and social democratic projects. At the same time, however, the accession of Austria and Sweden to the EU implies that new social forces (in the form of Austrian and Swedish labour in favour of the social democratic project) have entered the arena. They may trigger a new challenge to embedded neo-liberalism. In short, the hegemonic status of embedded neo-liberalism continues to be contested and the future shape of the European 'form of state' is still wide open. Importantly, as demonstrated by Bieling in Chapter 5 in this volume, in order to have a chance of success, trade unions need to move from flanking social policies to fundamental policy issues dealing with the macroeconomic co-ordination of the European political-economic system. The co-ordination of trade union strategies in respect of wages, working conditions and social regulation at the transnational level may be a first important target in this respect. An integration of Norwegian labour in these efforts would clearly strengthen the position of those trade unions which operate within the EU.

Interviews

1. Political Adviser, Section for Foreign Trade and Integration, *Arbeiterkammer* (Chamber of Labour, AK); Vienna, 08/05/1995.
2. Political Adviser, Section for National Economy, *Österreichischer Gewerkschaftsbund* (Austrian Federation of Trade Unions, ÖGB); Vienna, 12/05/1995.
3. Central Secretary, *Gewerkschaft Agrar, Nahrung, Genuß* (Trade Union of Food Processing Industry, ANG); Vienna, 22/04/1996.
4. President of the Trade Union for Textile, Clothes and Leather and Head of the ÖGB Integration Committee since 1987, responsible in the Austrian Social Democratic Party (SPÖ) for the drawing up of the coalition agreement of 26/06/1989; Vienna, 23/04/1996.
5. Head of the President's Office, *Gewerkschaft der Privatangestellten* (White Collar Workers' Union, GPA); Vienna, 14/05/1996.
6. International Secretary, *Tjänstemännens Centralorganisation* (Swedish Confederation of Professional Employees, TCO); Stockholm, 11/11/1996.
7. Senior Adviser, *Sveriges Akademikers Centralorganisation* (Swedish Confederation of Professional Associations, SACO); Stockholm, 11/11/1996.
8. Political Adviser, International Department, *Landsorganisationen i Sverige* (Swedish Trade Union Confederation, LO-S); Stockholm, 21/11/1996.
9. International Secretary, *Kommunalarbetare Förbundet* (Municipal Workers' Union, LO-S affiliate), member of the LO Committee on the EU; Stockholm, 26/11/1996.
10. Member of Steering Committee Secretariat, *Landsorganisationen i Sverige* (Swedish Trade Union Confederation, LO-S); Stockholm, 27/11/1996.
11. EU Co-ordinator, Research Department, *Metallindustriarbetareförbundet* (Metal Workers' Union, LO-S affiliate); Stockholm, 29/11/1996.
12. International Secretary, *Fellesforbundet* (Norwegian Industry Workers' Union, FF); Oslo, 17/12/1998.
13. Director of the International Unit, *Landorganisasjonen* (Norwegian Confederation of Trade Unions, LO-N); Oslo, 04/01/1999.
14. Union Representative, *Norsk Nærings- og Nytelsesmiddelarbeiderforbund* (Norwegian Union of Food Producing Workers, NNN); Oslo, 05/01/1999.
15. Vice-President of *Norsk Olje og Petrokjmisk Fagforbund* (Norwegian Oil and Petrochemical Workers' Union, NOPF); Stavanger, 14/09/99.
16. President, *Fellesforbundet* (Norwegian Industry Workers' Union, FF); Oslo, 28/09/1999.
17. Consultant, *Kommuneforbundet* (Norwegian Public Sector Workers' Union, KF); Oslo, 28/09/1999.

18. President, *Norsk   Transportarbeiderforbund*   (Norwegian   Union   of Transportation Workers, NTF); Oslo, 29/09/1999.

Notes

1. For a similar analysis of intra-class divisions, see Swenson's account of the formation of Swedish corporatism (1991a) and his discussion of the limits of the welfare state in Sweden and West Germany in the 1980s (1991b).
2. The line of argument in favour of EU membership resembles closely the position taken by unions of EU member states supporting the Internal Market programme and EMU during discussions within the EU in the 1980s and early 1990s (see Bieling, Chapter 5, this volume).
3. The Norwegian Parliament passed in 1994 a law that allows for an extension of agreements between capital and labour into national regulations. This guards against possible lowering of work standards and undermining of Norwegian labour in competition with European off-shore workers. Nevertheless NOPF maintained its scepticism and continued to argue against EU membership on the grounds of a possible undermining of work standards (Interview 15).

7

Neo-Liberal Regionalism and the Management of People's Mobility[1]

Hélène Pellerin and Henk Overbeek

Introduction

The control of migration flows is generally interpreted either as a function of labour market needs, whereby states respond to pressures from particular economic sectors (e.g., Burawoy, 1976), or as part of a statist logic of defending sovereignty (e.g., Collinson, 1993). The present chapter will differ from these interpretations. It will be suggested that migration controls constitute a series of mechanisms through which particular state forms and processes of economic restructuring are imposed on countries that originate migrants. Important changes contribute to this reflection on migration controls. As such they are integral components of neo-liberal regional integration projects.

First, globalisation involves a process of regionalisation of economic and political activities that also concerns migration policies. Second, migration policies at the regional level are articulated with a particular economic and political project known as neo-liberalism. Third, the migration issue is linked to other forms of mobility[2] (internal, sectoral and social) that are being restructured in regional contexts. The study of mobility, its corollary fixity, and their control, thus provides relevant material for an argument about the neo-liberal nature of the management of migration at the regional level. This will allow the development of an argument about the tight connection between emerging migration control frameworks and measures for labour market restructuring, economic re-localisation and the logic of capital expansion that characterise neo-liberal regional integration processes. Two case-studies will be presented: the relationship between the

EU members and countries of Eastern Europe and then the relationship between North American countries and Central America.

The study of the neo-liberal management of mobility will be presented in the following fashion. In the next section, the general context of re-territorialisation is sketched. Second, we turn to a discussion of the regional dimensions of mobility and the organisation of the economy before outlining the emergence of regional frameworks for the control and management of mobility in Europe and in the Americas. Finally, in a third section, we present an analysis of the significance of these emerging regional mobility frameworks for the process of neo-liberal regionalism/globalisation. As a result we reach the conclusion that these frameworks serve, on the one hand, to project the standards, regimes and specific state–civil society configurations of hegemonic formations into privileged 'semi-peripheries', thus ensuring incorporation into the circuits of metropolitan capital; on the other hand, such frameworks redraw and fortify boundaries between advanced capitalist hegemonic formations and the outlying peripheries.

Globalisation, neo-liberalism and the re-territorialisation of capitalism

Globalisation is often referred to as a process of restructuring, intensifying and deepening capitalist social relations. Three interrelated aspects of this complex process are central to our understanding of globalisation: the commodification of the social existence of people through a relentless expansion of market practices; the guidance of these processes by attempts to bring about coherence and purpose through a neo-liberal concept of control;[3] and changes in the spatial structuration of capitalist production and reproduction affecting territorially defined social relations. These aspects are interrelated insofar as the ascendancy of commodification proceeded through the geographical and social expansion of capitalist social relations, which was itself made possible through the spatial reconfiguring of social forces around transnational historical blocs (see Chapter 1 this volume).[4] With these three aspects in mind, globalisation can be analysed, on the one hand, in terms of geographical and social expansion and, on the other, in terms of regional concentration. These two angles, starting with the global dimension, are discussed below.

The global reach of capitalism

The contemporary phase of capitalist expansion is driven by three distinct processes, namely: (i) the expansion of productive capital through foreign *direct* investment (FDI);[5] (ii) the reconfiguration of *historical blocs* around new spatially defined economic processes; and (iii) the expansion of money capital through the globalisation of financial markets, which is one of the most spectacular manifestations of globalisation.

Regarding the first element, foreign direct investment has consistently grown faster than total world output, world trade or world fixed capital formation. By 1997, the total stock of FDI had reached the level of $3.5 trillion, while sales by foreign subsidiaries reached $9.5 trillion. The share of FDI in world gross fixed capital formation reached the level of 7.4 per cent in 1997 (United Nations Conference on Trade and Development, or UNCTAD, 1998). Through strategic alliances and other non-equity arrangements, transnational corporations (TNCs) moreover control innumerable assets and markets not measured in these statistics.

Another component of the historical bloc that has been transformed is labour. In their path-breaking study of the new international division of labour (NIDL) Fröbel, Heinrichs and Kreye (1977) observed an accelerating relocation of labour-intensive production processes to low wage countries in Asia and Latin America. The three preconditions which made this relocation drive possible were the existence of an inexhaustible reservoir of cheap labour, new developments in production technology making it possible to separate the labour-intensive parts of the production process from the capital-intensive parts, and new developments in transport and communication technology facilitating the co-ordination of dispersed production and assembly establishments. The authors concluded that 'the conjuncture of these three conditions...has created a single world market for labour power, a true world-wide industrial reserve army, and a single world market for production sites' (Fröbel, Heinrichs and Kreye, 1977: 30; our translation).

Subsequent developments have made it abundantly clear that globalisation indeed draws an increasing proportion of the world population directly into capitalist labour markets and increasingly locks the national and regional labour markets into an integrated global labour market (see also Chapter 3 this volume on the 'locking in' of neo-liberal reforms within the EU). This can take place through various forms of commodification of labour power that were not previously bought and sold on 'free' labour markets. We can think of three developments in particular:

1. The incorporation of previously disconnected areas (primarily former 'socialist' economies, but also the remaining pre-capitalist societies on the outskirts of the modern world) into the capitalist world market.

2. The continuing proletarianisation of the world's population through urbanisation and the disintegration of subsistence economies in the Third World and through increasing labour market participation in the industrial economies
3. The commodification, by means of liberalisation and privatisation, of economic activities within capitalist societies previously organised outside the market.

In addition, a further dimension of the process of spatial reconfiguration inherent to globalisation and the rise of a global labour market is the spatial re-allocation of labour that takes place through various forms of migration. The spread of TNCs brings with it increased international mobility for top and intermediate level managers and executives. The internationalisation of services (engineering, advertising, software development) creates increased international mobility for technical and commercial experts. The combination of more restrictive immigration policies and labour market flexibilisation and deregulation in the Organisation for Economic Co-operation and Development (OECD) countries creates increased opportunities for illegal immigration through the intervention of organised crime. Finally, the crisis of the state in many Third World countries and the resulting violent intensification of social and ethnic conflicts swells the ranks of international refugee movements.

Changes in production organisation and location have been accompanied by attempts at the political and ideological levels to create historical blocs that are more transnational in nature. Central among this reconfiguration is the state. State forms and functions are being transformed by the dynamics of globalisation.[6] Global restructuring leads to (or implies) the creation of additional formal and informal structures of authority and sovereignty besides and beyond the state. With globalisation and the progression of the neo-liberal ideology, there has also been a strengthening of (quasi-)authoritarian structures and practices and an assault on established forms of progressive or popular left participation. In the core areas of the world economy this discipline appears in the shape of 'voluntary' programmes of competitive deregulation and austerity which are codified and 'constitutionalised' in such arrangements as the Economic and Monetary Union (EMU) stability pact or the World Trade Organisation (WTO) liberalisation regime (for extended analyses, see Chapters 3 and 9, this volume).

Under the impact of globalisation we can observe that the functions of the state dealing with transnational processes are also increasingly performed transnationally by a variety of state, inter-state and non-state institutions. The state is no longer the proto-typical Westphalian nation-state in which sovereignty and territoriality are exclusively combined. John Ruggie has called this the 'unbundling' of sovereignty and territoriality (Ruggie, 1993: 165). This 'unbundling' provides a useful way of managing mobility and fixity issues, particularly with regard to migration, which becomes at times very politicised and destabilising for governments. It provides a very convenient way for governments to circumvent the need to account for the international agreements they conclude in their own national parliaments. It has also created a greater space for social forces outside the state to become involved in new forms of regulation. The boundaries between public and private regulation and between national and international relations are becoming increasingly blurred. This means that policy formation in international contexts is increasingly *informalised*, opening up channels of governance to non-governmental organisations of various kinds. Such developments require a conceptual framework that can more adequately account for these tendencies rather than solely relying on the increasingly inadequate recipes that are cooked up in International Relations (IR) theory. The following analysis of the regional management of migration issues will aim to elaborate upon central features of an alternative approach (see below).

In sum, globalisation engenders mobility. This mostly includes the mobility of capital, but also of labour, or at least a particular form of labour mobility. The transformation of the labour process has made it possible to use flexible – thus mobile – labour in the most integrated and fixed sectors of the global political economy. Mobility in the globalisation context is being promoted both in terms of the precariousness of work and in terms of the expandable dynamic of commodification in all spheres and locations of the world. From the codification of land for the purpose of assigning an exchange-value, to the commodification of social relations and human beings themselves,[7] mobility is becoming a condition of capitalist integration in the peripheral sectors of the economy as well as in peripheral regions of the world. Neo-liberalism also encourages specific forms of mobility for people: for instance, a greater facility of movement for highly skilled and business people, promoted through intra-company transfers and specific agreements and programmes controlled by states and bilateral arrangements.

Re-territorialisation and regionalisation of capitalism

Globalisation, as highlighted above, is an ambiguous and contradictory process: it produces universalising as well as localising tendencies, and in fact implies 'regionalisation', the re-structuring of the global political economy into macro-regions which can, in turn, encourage micro-regionalism (see Cox, 1992: 34–5). Governments in the core areas of the global economy seek to compensate for their weaker control over the forces of the market by pursuing projects of 'open regionalism': that is, forms of regional integration aimed at combining further liberalisation of the flow of goods and capital with a revival of certain structures of governance of the market. Thus the Internal Market project in Europe, but also the North American Free Trade Agreement (NAFTA), the Asia and Pacific Economic Co-operation (APEC), Mercosur and several other regional free trade initiatives can all be understood as instances of what we call neo-liberal regionalism. This is the combination of 'open regionalism' and neo-liberal economic restructuring.[8]

In order to enhance mobility, fractions of capital require the existence of some fixity – in political and economic terms – in various places. This has been defined as a *spatial fix* (Harvey, 1985). The mobility–fixity nexus, meaning the logic determining both the instances and places of mobility and fixity within global capitalism, tends to become more regional in nature, particularly in key sectors of the economy. While the embedded liberal system of the post-Second World War period was based on a nationally-oriented model of growth that was remarkably fixed (Ruggie, 1982), the globalisation context creates and shifts places of mobility and fixity to both transnational and regional levels. Land, labour and capital thus tend to follow various logics of spatial reconfiguration where new centres of fixity emerge, notably in global cities and in regional centres of excellence specialising in research and development (R&D) for the capital-intensive sectors of the world economy.

The mobility of capital is increasingly structured around regions that slowly emerge as coherent spatial organisations of production. Most activities by TNCs are concentrated more and more in the three core regions of the world: North America (NAFTA), Western Europe (Internal Market) and East Asia. This is true for trade as well as for investment. Two sets of reasons can explain this. In the first place, productive capital in particular is not immediately and limitlessly mobile. This is both because of the 'sunk costs' that accompany any investment in fixed assets and because states compete with each other to lure and secure the location of TNCs in order to provide employment and, concomitantly, a sound fiscal basis and ultimately social stability. Second, the incentive for TNCs to organise their locationally-fixed activities within regional contexts is strong, due to the demands of flexible accumulation, as a consequence of regional integration schemes and in response to the volatility of the global financial system. This has induced transnational corporations to seek protection by trying to develop complete sourcing networks within each of the major currency areas (i.e., the dollar, yen and Euro zones).

Globalisation thus seems to engender a coherent logic for the spatialisation of motion and fixity, at least in terms of capital; but this is only part of the picture. Tensions arise, for instance, between the combination of mobility and fixity of capital required by different industrial sectors or fractions of capital, and tensions also arise between people and capital in the spatial reconfiguration of mobility and fixity. Spatial practices, like temporal ones, contain elements of tension, resistance and crisis that all require some form of regulation. Inter-state and regional arrangements are instruments designed to manage such differences and bring about some coherence.

Neo-liberal regionalism and the control of mobility in the European Union and the Americas

Regional migratory movements

The patterns of regional concentration in the globalisation process simultaneously create and reinforce a framework for the consolidation and intensification of regional migration networks. Movements of people are partly occurring in regional contexts, not just as a reflection of the emerging new production and labour market structures, but also as a result of a series of factors that are migration-specific, such as geographic proximity, cultural affinity, historical linkages and migration chains. This explains the fact that, in most OECD countries, a majority of immigrants (excluding asylum seekers) come not as independent migrants but as relatives or dependents.

In Western Europe more than a third of the foreign residents come from other West European countries, and some 36 per cent come from the Mediterranean countries that were the traditional suppliers of 'guest workers' during the post-Second World War decades. Some 5 per cent come from Central and Eastern Europe, leaving less than one in four who come from further away (Eurostat, 1997: 48–9).

In the case of the USA the twentieth century showed a clear tendency towards regional concentration of immigration: immigrants came from neighbouring regions, first of all Mexico, in increasing proportions, while immigration from Europe declined steadily until the 1990s. Immigration from Asia, while rising after the 1940s, became the largest in the late 1980s (Hamilton, 1994: 75; OECD SOPEMI, 1998: 235). With NAFTA, these trends have been maintained. From 1992 to 1996, the proportion of Asian migrants to the USA declined, from 43 per cent to 33.6 per cent, while the proportion of North Americans (mostly Mexicans) increased from 29.4 per cent to 37.2 per cent (INS statistics).

In the case of Canada, the situation is different, due in large part to the highly selective immigration policy put in place from the 1960s onwards, which made it possible to target particular regions for the supply of labour. While migrants from Central America historically have represented a very small percentage of all migrants, those from Asia have replaced Europeans as the most important group of migrants in the last decade. This situation was maintained in 1997, with 44.1 per cent of all migrants coming from Asia (East and South-East), and only 4.1 per cent of migrants coming from Central America (Citizenship and Immigration Canada, 1998a).

As for Mexico, while most flows are still out-migration to the USA, Mexico has become in the last fifteen years an in-migration country as well. Migrants to Mexico generally come from Central America and belong to three categories: refugees (although their number is decreasing); transit migrants *en route* to the USA; and temporary workers for the agricultural sector (OECD SOPEMI, 1996).

Regionalisation of control frameworks

Since the beginning of the 1990s the number of international migrants, especially forced migrants, has risen dramatically. Although some 80–90 per cent of these migrants move within the Third World, the rapid increase in the numbers arriving in the OECD states has been invoked as proof of a refugee and immigration 'crisis' requiring more active restriction measures. Although the responses differed from one region to the other, developments both in the policy sphere and in terms of actual movements in different regions are interconnected (Zolberg, 1993). This interconnectedness has led to an intensification of co-operation among the OECD member states and the member states of the Council of Europe. Both globally and within other major macro-regions of the global political economy, this has led to convergence in the modes of regulation of migration.[9] For instance, in the increasingly co-ordinated interpretation and application of the Geneva Refugee Convention and in the spreading network of bilateral and multilateral re-admission agreements dealing with the illegal crossing of borders. These developments are especially strong in Europe and (to a lesser degree) in the Americas.

Europe: the Budapest Process

The European Union's policies in the area of migration and asylum have focused on five broad issues: free movement of people within the European Union (EU); the treatment of so-called third-country nationals; harmonisation of asylum policies; harmonisation of visa regulations and requirements; and combating illegal immigration and trafficking of people. In this chapter we will not deal with all aspects of the EU's policies in these areas.[10] We are primarily interested in how the latter three issues affect the relations between the EU and its neighbours.

As for the Mediterranean region, these issues were of central importance in the negotiations over, and final formulation of, the *Euro-Mediterranean Partnership* in Barcelona in November 1995.[11] The Treaty's main objectives were the promotion of peace and stability, the creation of a Free Trade Zone, and the stimulation of social, cultural and human partnerships. The partners undertake specific obligations to diminish the migratory pressures in the region and to combat illegal migration and international crime. The North African states will receive financial and technical aid in order to enable them to honour their obligations in this respect (e.g., through improving their border controls: see Euromed Agreement, 1995, Title VI, 'Co-operation in Social and Cultural Matters').

In the case of Central and Eastern Europe, a similar development started a few years earlier, with the collapse of the socialist regimes. In the initial years, similar deals with regard to re-admission of illegal migrants, assistance for the improvement of border controls and so on were undertaken in bi-lateral agreements, often initiated by Germany as the main recipient of migrants from the East. In addition, these agreements also contained provisions regarding cross-border seasonal labour, short-term labour contracts and job training programmes, and long-term labour migration. Subsequently, these agreements were multilateralised and incorporated into the *Europe Agreements* (see Europe Agreement, 1994; Niessen and Mochel, 1999). Furthermore, the European states (East and West) have developed a parallel system of informal consultations, the so-called Budapest Process, to deal with a number of these issues.

The origins of the Budapest Process go back to the events leading up to the fall of the Berlin Wall in 1989 and the disintegration of the Soviet Union. The EU member state most directly affected by increased flows of irregular migrants and asylum seekers from Eastern and Central Europe – Germany – convened a Ministerial Conference in Berlin in October 1991. To this meeting all Ministers of the Interior of

EU member states were invited, plus representatives from Switzerland as well as thirteen Central and East European states. The primary objective of the conference was to discuss 'measures for checking illegal migration from and through Central and Eastern Europe'. Much emphasis was placed on the need to strengthen the surveillance of borders, the conclusion of re-admission agreements and the harmonisation of visa policies. Technological and financial aid was promised. During follow-up meetings, the themes that would dominate subsequent conferences became clear: criminalisation of trafficking and improvement of police forces and border controls; imposition of carrier sanctions on airlines; exchange of information; conclusion of re-admission agreements; and financial assistance to the Central and East European countries who were in reality the targets of these measures, given their deficient or totally absent legislation and policies (Budapest Group, 1993). The *Statutory Meeting of the Budapest Group* (December 1993) reconfirmed these objectives and decided that the Group would consist of senior officials from all participating states, making the Budapest Group into the only pan-European discussion forum for these issues.[12]

After agreement, in principle, on a joint visa regime for the EU – this was foreseen in the Treaty on European Union which came into force in 1993 – and after the abolition of border controls and the adoption of common visa requirements following the entering into effect of the Schengen Area in March 1995, after many years of delay, the EU member states used the channels of the Budapest Group to introduce visa harmonisation as a new objective. They repeatedly put pressure on the Central and East European states to adapt their own visa regimes to the EU/Schengen system. The issue of *visa 'approximation'* was taken up again at a special meeting in Portoroz (Slovenia) in September 1998 (International Centre for Migration Policy Development, or ICMPD, 1998a). The harmonisation of visa policies was thus to be achieved by the Central and East European states aligning their policies with those of the EU member states (ibid.: 1–2). The report refers to the strategy adopted by the European Council meeting in December 1994 to prepare for the future accession of the Central and East European states and, in reference to the Portoroz meeting, signals 'the complementary role of this informal process with regard to the more formal structures of EU/Schengen' (ibid.: 43). In recent years the Budapest Group has also set up an elaborate monitoring system to keep track of progress with the implementation of agreed measures, thus acquiring a very real influence over national policy-making (cf. Budapest Group, 1998).

America: the Puebla Process

In the Americas most of the regional integration processes ignore or side-track the question of the movement of people. This is the case with Mercosur as well as with NAFTA and the series of bilateral treaties on free trade in the region. There had been precedents in the form of regional agreements such as the Punto Arenas agreement of 1990 which sought to elaborate a regional migration policy (Berglund, 1993), or NAFTA and its clause on professionals, but they had been limited in scope and effect. Yet, despite limited state regulations, labour migration represented a significant dimension of transborder economic activities, controlled mostly by the respective private sectors. This has been the case in South America, where labour transfers had been organised by employers, particularly in Mercosur economies. In the Central and North American cases, employers and business are also increasingly capable of conceiving and implementing migration schemes as part of their production.

The Puebla Process, which started in 1996 under the name Regional Conference on Migration (RCM), marks a significant step in the regionalisation trend in migration control.[13] Officially the direct trigger of the RCM was the Population Conference in Cairo in 1994 where countries had been invited to propose regional solutions to population problems. But it would be very short-sighted to not mention the influence of the Miami process or the Free Trade Area of the Americas (FTAA). This latter process, which can be seen as an extension of NAFTA in terms of its content (Deblock and Brunelle, 1998), seeks to extend the liberalisation of national economies to Central and South America (also see Payne, 1996, 1998, 2000). Differing from earlier regional initiatives that aimed to strengthen the economies of the region in a more closed or even protectionist manner, the Free Trade Area of the Americas constitutes an *open* form of integration, as one specialist has called it, in order to emphasise the opening towards trade and capital from the rest of the world (Grinspun, 1998). The immediate initiative for the Puebla Process came from Mexico, a country facing important pressures from both its Northern partners, particularly the USA, to control the flows of people crossing the border, and from its southern neighbours in the form of transit migration.

The RCM's Plan of Action, adopted in 1997 during its second annual meeting in Panama, set out very broad objectives. The Plan of Action introduced the need for annual meetings at the rank of vice-ministers, as well as expert meetings on a more frequent basis to implement parts of the Plan. Its focus has been on information gathering as well as on five areas of activities: (i) the formulation of migration policies (both emigration and immigration) that would respond to the commitments of the Conference; (ii) migration and development; (iii) combating migrant trafficking; (iv) collaboration for the return of extra-regional migrants; and (v) human rights (Citizenship and Immigration Canada, 1998b). Most of the work of the RCM has been devoted, since then, to the combating of migrant trafficking while the area of activity that received the least attention was the formulation of harmonised migration policies. Yet, paradoxically, some form of co-ordination of these policies does take place, albeit indirectly, notably through the promotion by the RCM of transborder and labour market co-operation schemes (FOCAL, 1998; RCM, 1999).

There is a clear affinity between the Puebla Process and the Budapest Process in terms of which issues are central to their work. They share an emphasis on the co-ordination of visa and migration policy and, especially, stress both combating illegal trafficking and promoting a system of re-admission agreements. The Puebla emphasis on the interface between migration and development reflects the North–South dimension that is lacking in the Budapest Process (but is clearly present in the Euromed agreements). In addition, the above outline provides us with a clear insight into the functions of these flexible and informal frameworks, which are set out below:

1. *Communication*: they serve as channels for communication between policy-makers, experts and interested third parties. This is especially important for those countries (e.g., several of the CIS countries) whose officials have little or no direct contact with their counterparts in the OECD world.
2. *Socialisation*: they further serve to socialise the officials, experts and policy-makers of peripheral states into the existing epistemic communities in the migration field within the OECD.
3. *Institutionalisation*: they help to moor the policy reforms desired by the OECD partners within the associated states. Migration policies deemed desirable by the OECD partners are thus locked in within the dependent states.
4. *Integration*: in the case of the relationship between the EU and a number of the Central and East European states involved, the Budapest Process is clearly complementary to the on-going accession process and prepares the ground, in the area of the regulation of people's mobility, for ultimate full membership of the EU.

Whilst these observations tell us something about the mechanisms involved in the process of migration policy co-ordination, they teach us little about the substance and the underlying broader significance of the policies that are being co-ordinated. This is the question we will address in the following section.

Restructuring people's mobility under neo-liberal regionalism

The significance of the Budapest and Puebla processes is not so much grasped by the IR neo-realist discourse, in terms of the domination of one state over others, or by the notion of American or German imperialism, or by the discourse of most mainstream theories of international integration, whether intergovernmentalist or neo-liberal institutionalist (see Chapter 1 this volume); the significance lies rather in what a neo-Gramscian perspective would conceive as the attempts by hegemonic formations to project their standards and political forms onto and into their surrounding peripheries, for the purpose of managing the mobility– fixity nexus of globalisation.[14] These hegemonic struggles take place in the context of regional integration and globalisation: first, in the relationship between the regulation of migration, in the narrow sense, and the broader process of promoting and locking in a programme of neo-liberal politico-economic reforms in the participating (semi-)peripheral states; second, in the restructuring of the geopolitical hierarchies of the regions in question involving, among other issues, the selective criminalisation of migration.

Promotion and lock-in of neo-liberal reforms

The idea of mobility is often associated with, in an age of globalisation, the dynamic of capital expansion, perhaps even more so than that of people. Indeed, an increased mobility of capital implies transformations of national economies in the sense of liberalisation and harmonisation so that the movement of capital is facilitated.

In the Americas, some 20 bilateral agreements have been signed since 1990 that serve to liberalise trade and investment between South, Central and North American countries. In Europe, the significance of arrangements facilitating the mobility of capital within the region (primarily the completion of the Internal Market) has overshadowed the number of initiatives that European capital developed in peripheral economies. Nevertheless, in the framework of increasing co-operation and economic aid, the EU has signed a series of Association Agreements with countries in Central and Eastern Europe, with the Mediterranean countries, and with the remaining states of the former Soviet Union. These agreements all have in common a number of regulations with respect to the freedom of movement of people insofar as this movement is connected to capital mobility. Common factors include: freedom of establishment, freedom to migrate in order to set up business as self-employed individuals, and non-discrimination (national treatment) of legally established firms, workers, and their families (cf. Niessen and Mochel, 1999). These rules about national treatment for investments and labour tend to have repercussions on labour markets, on industrial policies and on judicial systems. One can find these preliminary measures harmonising state–society relations, through the imposition of particular forms of fixity, in two ways.

The circulation of capital can, first, fundamentally challenge the ways in which land, production facilities and urban settings – to name just a few ways of organising space – are structured, thus encouraging the movement of people, whether voluntarily or not. Second, the movement of capital requires some mobility of people as well, for labour market purposes, but also for access to land and to markets. Especially relevant here is the movement of professionals and business people whose professions are related to trade in services. Their movement is encoded in bilateral or trilateral treaties, regional agreements (e.g., NAFTA, European Economic Area), and global agreements (e.g., General Agreement on Trade-in-Services: cf. OECD SOPEMI, 1998: 55, 185 ff.; see also Ghosh, 1997).

In the North, Central and South American contexts of neo-liberalism, large corporations favour the reduction of trade barriers, the freer flow of capital, and a harmonisation of some of the internal and external regulations of states regarding the movement of people. This suggests that the mobility of capital has priority over that of people and that political efforts at the regional level seek to legalise such a hierarchy of mobility. The emphasis being given within the EU to specific sectors of co-operation, notably in R&D activities and in infrastructure, also suggests a similar set of priorities (on the role of transnational business in formulating these priorities, see van Apeldoorn, 1998b and Chapter 4 this volume). In the Americas, the position of the Regional Conference on Migration, on the question of mobility, seems to be quite clear: to encourage some migration and mobility on condition that it is orderly. This was the position adopted in Cairo during the International Conference on Population and Development. The RCM has endorsed the principles of ordered migration and mobility promoted by the International Organisation for Migration (IOM) and the Economic Commission for Latin America and the Caribbean (ECLAC). To cite the outlook of such institutions directly:

> Viewing the situation realistically, then, what is proposed here, in the context of the relationships between migration and development, is that the governments of the region, rather than preparing for a slackening off of migration, should be planning ways of imposing some order on future flows and adapting them to national and regional development needs. (IOM, ECLAC, 1998: 6)

A more mobile population allows for the removal of some rigidities in the use and management of space, production and distribution. A population that can be made easily mobile is a population that is more flexible in its relation to space or, perhaps, a population that is in a permanent state of uprootedness. At the same time, the creation of fixed spaces of capitalist development is encouraged in particular places. Two mechanisms provide for the ordered mobility of people, namely the subordination of the migration of people to the needs of capital and the integration of flexibility into labour market practices. In terms of reflecting different state–civil society configurations, the first mechanism is primarily promoted in the American situation, whereas the latter has been emphasised within the European scene (cf. various contributions to Holman, Overbeek and Ryner, 1998).

Ordered mobility refers, in general, to the manageability of migration flows – the circulation of people – in order to serve a specific goal. But ordered mobility also refers to the ability to make mobile some fixed practices that have become too rigid for the purpose of competitiveness. Deregulation of labour market practices, in this sense, constitutes forms of ordered mobility. Such practices have been encouraged in both regions, especially in Europe. Because of its emphasis on capital deepening rather than capital widening as a strategy of capital accumulation, which has been maintained in the era of neo-liberal regionalism, the conditions of fixity have been more steadily addressed compared with those of mobility, especially within the capitalist industrial heartland. Accordingly, the mobility that has been promoted was closely related to conditions of flexibility, more so than to real territorial movements. Measures of labour market deregulation were promoted, both within the EU and its outskirts, in order to create propitious conditions for capital innovation and formation. As mentioned before, the agreements between the EU and Central and East European as well as

Mediterranean countries did include specific conditions regarding labour markets (cf. OECD SOPEMI, 1999; see also Niessen and Mochel, 1999).

In the Americas, the RCM has not dealt directly with these issues but it endorsed the work of other organisations committed to the same principles of flexibility, productivity and competitiveness. The Inter-American Conference of labour ministers, the International Organisation for Migration and the Organisation of American States, all closely associated to the Puebla Process, support the idea of modernising and deregulating labour market practices in the name of enhanced competitiveness. This follows the same direction of the only existing labour agreement in the region, the North American Agreement on Labour Co-operation (NAALC), which states in its preamble the prevalence of competitiveness rather than labour rights: mutual prosperity, it is argued, depends upon the promotion of competition based on innovation and rising levels of productivity (FOCAL, 1998).

American organised labour has played a prominent role in the regionalisation of the Americas. Unlike some South American countries, such as Argentina (and also in most of Europe) where labour played a central role in a model of growth based on corporatist structures, labour movements are relatively weak in most Central American states. North American labour movements, particularly in the USA, have been more important. In fact, rather like what happened in the NAFTA negotiations, the American Federation of Labour–Congress of Industrial Organisations (AFL–CIO) seems to have influenced the content of some of the co-ordination measures of neo-liberal integration in the Americas, in the sense of reproducing the American model of industrial relations and corporatism. Within the USA, the side agreement on labour within NAFTA, the NAALC, was the product of intense negotiations between governments and the AFL-CIO (Stevis and Boswell, 1998). North American non-governmental organisations too, through their emphasis on *individual* 'human rights' based on access to education for migrant children and rights for detained migrants (*IOM News*, 1998), but not on *social* rights, have contributed to isolating the issue of migration from the politics of neo-liberalism and regional integration, and thus to promoting the North American model of liberalism.

It is reasonable to suggest that the neo-liberal forms of mobility control discussed above will not disappear with political changes, at least in those countries on the receiving end of such policies. Because of their inclusion into regional frameworks of integration, these mechanisms become *locked in* and it would be extremely costly, both economically and politically, not to respect them (see Chapter 3 this volume). Accordingly, states become more accountable to external rather than internal forces. States are made responsible for maintaining the direction or the orientation of the regional alliance and for upholding the principles or social purpose of the agreements signed. Both 'processes' have developed mechanisms to strengthen these tendencies and to monitor the compliance of the participating states. The recognition of this externally imposed discipline brings us to the second dimension of the overall process: that is, the restructuring of regional hierarchies involving the selective criminalisation of migration.

Re-constituting regional hierarchies

The new articulation between mobility and fixity that neo-liberal restructuring requires is slowly being constructed at the state and regional levels, notably by de-politicising the question of migration in at least two ways. First, by locking in migration policies, objectives and specific instruments in informal regional frameworks, states contribute to removing the question of migration from public debates at the national level. The second way of de-politicising migration is by emphasising the technical, criminal or humanitarian aspects of the question. In this way, the larger issues related to the spatial consequences of migration, or of the mobility of capital and the migration effects of integration, are not dealt with, or are dealt with separately.

In the Puebla Process, it is possible to see the influence of the USA in this process, as their own internal political division of power makes any decisions on migration quite difficult to reach, unless phrased in terms of combating crime. The approach of the US Congress to defining migration issues mostly in criminal terms was notably reproduced in the Regional Conference on Migration.[15] The Plan of Action adopted at the second annual meeting encouraged other governments to add to their legislation the characterisation of migrant trafficking as a criminal offence (Citizenship and Immigration Canada, 1998b: 3). Such influence can only contribute to isolating migration questions from further public participation, particularly considering that there are few social forces organised around migration issues.

In the Budapest Process the initiating role is more difficult to assign to any one state in particular. This is due to the specific *sui generis* nature of the EU as an emerging polity characterised by a system of 'multi-level governance' in which sub-national, national, intergovernmental and supranational elements all have a place. Nevertheless, it has been Germany, being the country most immediately affected by the post-1989 migratory movements, which has taken the initiative in several cases. The criminalising discourse has become more and more prominent in the Budapest Process over the years: it was expressed in the increasingly complex network of bi- and multi-lateral *re-admission agreements* and it culminated, in 1998, in the commissioning of a report on the connections between trafficking of aliens and international organised crime (cf. ICMPD, 1998b; see also Budapest Process, 1999).

In fact, this selective criminalisation of specific forms of migration and the privileged treatment of other types of mobility is functional not only in the context of proliferating neo-liberal labour market reforms but also in the context of redrawing the boundaries of the regions concerned. Both in the case of the Americas and in the case of Europe, what we can observe happening is a restructuring of regional hierarchies. Within this process certain countries or regions are gradually integrated into the OECD heartland (Mexico, Central Europe and possibly, in the long run, Turkey). These countries are themselves becoming destination countries for migrants from the outer layers of the emerging new regional geo-hierarchies, just as a decade ago the Southern European countries made the transition from being migrant-sending to migrant-receiving countries against the background of their integration into the hegemonic structures of the West. Other countries are recast in the role of dependent (semi-)peripheries. Migrant workers from such regions are admitted to the heartland countries only on the strictest conditions. The burden of policing borders between peripheral and core heartland countries also falls on the former, whose people can only enter the latter as illegal migrants and, in decreasing measure, as asylum seekers (cf. van Buuren, 1999).[16]

Conclusion

Immigration policies take place at the intersection of economic and political considerations. Governments are increasingly subject to contradictory forces and tendencies and, as a result, are being called to play many functions. In the context of globalisation, such functions include the management of tensions that arise as a result of a spatial reconfiguration and redefinition of the mobility–fixity nexus. Tensions arise between migrants and non-migrants and between labour and capital in the reconfiguration of the mobility–fixity nexus of neo-liberal restructuring. In addition, another important set of tensions exists between different fractions of capital in the process of reconfiguration.

A neo-Gramscian perspective can help to analyse and directly address some of these issues. It favours the understanding of regionalisation of migration controls in Europe and in the Americas as part of the phenomenon of globalisation and it explores the struggles for hegemony within a regional setting. Accordingly, the regional frameworks on migration did not serve so much to curb migration flows but to contribute to the creation of ordered mobility: that is, a mobility that is on a par with the fixity of the spatial reconfiguration of the economy. Integral to this has been the operation of conditions and hegemonic forms of control – through particular negotiations and agreements – within those state–civil society configurations that originate migrants.

Notes

1. This chapter is based on some of our earlier work: see Overbeek (1998, 1999) and Pellerin (1999).
2. Mobility is a larger notion than migration, insofar as it concerns the movement of all kinds of agents, as well as their relationship with territory. When attributed to persons, the notion of mobility refers to both a movement in space and across sectors and social strata, without necessarily involving changes of residence. The notion of mobility seems more appropriate than the narrower concept of migration to discuss the range of forms of movement, from the not so frequent long-term migration (or settlement) to the shorter-term work contracts and circular migration, to name but a few. Mobility is also a good description of the movement between sectors and places in a given country which can happen as a result of economic restructuring and the adoption of modern (meaning more capital-intensive) techniques in sectors such as agriculture and soft industries.
3. The *comprehensive concept of control* notion was introduced to capture the process of interest aggregation.

   > A concept of control represents a bid for hegemony: a project for the conduct of public affairs and social control that aspires to be a legitimate approximation of the general interest in the eyes of the ruling class and, at the same time, the majority of the population, for at least a specific period. It evolves through a series of compromises in which the fractional, 'special' interests are arbitrated and synthesised. (van der Pijl, 1984: 7)

   For the emergence of neo-liberalism, see Overbeek and van der Pijl (1993).
4. The notion of historical bloc highlights the importance of social forces and state apparatuses in constituting the power and legitimacy of a particular alliance. As Gill describes it, a historical bloc is a coalition of social forces, and not just states, that can create a 'political synthesis of interests and identities' (1998: 11). Also see Rupert (1995: 29–30).
5. Whereas money capital imposes an abstract and indirect discipline on labour, FDI has a much stronger impact on social relations than earlier forms

of internationalisation because it directly reproduces capitalist relations of production *within* the host countries (Poulantzas, 1974).

6. In the era of globalisation, the privatisation of state functions has become important, with the outsourcing of services such as social insurance and prison management, the abolition of state subsidies for the poor, and the lifting of restrictions on capital mobility. These forms of de-statification are all guided by variants of neo-liberal thought, in Western Europe and North America signalling the unravelling of the Keynesian consensus, in the South and the East reflecting the imposition of the IMF's logic of structural adjustment. One can further think of the decisive roles states have had in the emergence of liberalised global financial markets (cf. Helleiner, 1994) and in the spread of FDI, as well as on liberalising labour markets.

7. Commodification reaches into spheres of the social existence of humankind where the market has never penetrated before, including more and more innate qualities and properties of human beings themselves, beginning of course with their labour power but currently including social and individual characteristics such as language, values and interpersonal skills (all being a part now of social and human capital) as well as the genetic properties of living organisms in the form of so-called 'intellectual property rights' (IPRs) (for a critical study of IPRs in the global political economy, see May, 2000).

8. The literature on the new regionalism is by now abundant. Especially useful works would include Gamble and Payne (1996), Grinspun and Cameron (1993), and Hettne and Inotai (1994).

9. The concept of convergence of policies provides a way out of the often invoked 'regulation – no regulation dichotomy' (Thomson, 1992: 197): even when there is no formally institutionalised 'regime', migratory policies of states may still interact in such a way as to form a *de facto* regulatory system in which there is 'a displacement of government functions on to non-governmental or quasi-governmental institutions and criteria for legitimacy' (Sassen, 1996: 24).

10. There is an abundant literature on the general topic of EU migration policy: see, for instance, Brochmann (1993), Butt (1994), Collinson (1993), Favell (1998), Hamilton (1994), Luciani (1993), Sampol (1993), van Selm-Thorburn (1998), Thränhardt (1992).

11. The signatories were the EU, its fifteen member states, and Algeria, Cyprus, Egypt, Israel, Jordan, Lebanon, Malta, Morocco, Syria, Tunisia, Turkey and the Palestinian Authority.

12. By 1997 the Group encompassed 36 European states (including among the republics of the former Soviet Union the three Baltic states, Belarus, Ukraine, Moldova and the Russian Federation), Australia, Canada, the USA, as well as the Central European Initiative, the Council of Europe, the EU Council Secretariat, the European Commission, the Intergovernmental Consultations on Asylum, Refugee and Migration Policies, the International Centre for Migration Policy Development (ICMPD), functioning as the Secretariat of the Budapest Group, the International Organisation for Migration (IOM), Interpol, the United Nations High Commissioner for Refugees (UNHCR), the International Civil Aviation Organisation, and the United Nations Commission on Crime Prevention.

13. The Puebla Process involved the participation of ten countries of Central and North America (Belize, Canada, Costa Rica, El Salvador, Guatemala, Honduras, Mexico, Nicaragua, Panama and the USA). A few countries and international organisations were invited as observers: Colombia, the Dominican Republic, Ecuador, Jamaica and Peru, as well as the Economic Commission for Latin America and the Caribbean (ECLAC), the United Nations High Commissioner for Refugees (UNHCR) and the IOM.

14. Kees van der Pijl (1998: 98–135) refers to such processes as 'hegemonic integration in the Lockean heartland'.

15. Such a balance of forces explains in part why negotiations have so far focused more on criminal issues, and much less on questions of development, despite the insistence by some governments that the question of remittances is central to their economies (*IOM News*, 1996).

16. Of course we must remember (although this takes us beyond the scope of the present chapter) that the process of regional hierarchisation as described here intersects with processes of geo-strategic rivalry which are being played out partly in the same region (such as the intervention in Kosovo and the involvement of several Western interests in the Caucasus).

Part IV

European Integration and the Expansion of Neo-Liberalism beyond the EU

8
The Enlargement of the European Union Towards Central and Eastern Europe: The Role of Supranational and Transnational Actors

Otto Holman

Introduction

In December 1999, the European Union (EU) closed a decade with the umpteenth 'historical summit', held in Helsinki. This time such a euphoric final conclusion was first and foremost inspired by the decision of the European leaders of government and the French head of state to extend the number of candidates for membership to thirteen countries. The particular inclusion of Turkey into this group of privileged states was a true masterpiece of diplomacy.

Everyone seemed happy. In the first place, of course, this included the political elites of the new candidate members. But the geopolitical interests of the fifteen member states also seemed to be better represented: the Scandinavian countries were now assured of the entrance of all three Baltic states; France considered itself fortunate with the inclusion of Romania and Bulgaria; and Greece was hoping for the settlement of a number of long-term conflicts as a result of the Turkish candidacy. 'A better close of the millennium was unthinkable', according to the Dutch Prime Minister, Wim Kok (*NRC Handelsblad*, 13 December 1999).

Now that the smoke of political rhetoric has cleared, it is time for a more critical assessment of the Helsinki decision. Will the prospect of membership and the disciplining nature of the EU's conditions substantially increase stability and security in Central and Eastern Europe as the presidency conclusions suggest? Or is it just a symbolic act with, potentially, destabilising consequences? The many problems with which the candidate members – and the EU itself – are faced leads one to suspect the latter. Thus far the EU and its member states are reluctant to set a clear deadline for enlargement. For instance, the present Intergovernmental Conference (IGC), succeeding the 1996 IGC that resulted in the Treaty of Amsterdam, was organised to deal with a large number of political and institutional issues, in the process effectively delaying enlargement. But even if these problems are solved in the short term, and at least some of the candidate countries can actually enter the EU, stability is by no means the necessary, or even likely, outcome. Three factors will have a decisive impact on future cohesion within an enlarged EU:

1. The enlargement strategy of the EU, and particularly its emphasis on neo-liberal restructuring in Central and Eastern Europe (CEE).
2. The process of restructuring which is taking place within the EU itself, and particularly the introduction of Anglo-Saxon practices under the banner of the 'New Economy' (which in turn affects the enlargement strategy).
3. The course and direction of the so-called double transformation in CEE – that is, from a command economy to a free-market economy and from authoritarian rule to parliamentary democracy – and particularly its primacy of economic liberalisation over social cohesion (which is partly imposed upon the new regimes from the outside, *inter alia* by the conditionality of EU membership).

In this chapter, a widely accepted claim with respect to the first factor (i.e., the pre-accession strategy of the EU) will be contested. In particular, the chapter questions the assumption that this strategy (with its emphasis on economic and legal adjustment to EU standards) will have a positive impact on stability and security in the region of CEE. In doing this, a more comprehensive understanding of the pre-accession strategy of the EU – including the role of foreign direct investment in the double transformation of CEE – will serve as a point of departure.

Taking the enlargement strategy of the EU towards CEE as our starting point, then, some of the basic assumptions of one of the leading theorists in the field of European integration, Andrew Moravcsik, are criticised by referring to the pre-accession strategy of the EU and the agenda-setting role of transnational business. Particular attention is drawn to those companies organised in the European Round Table of Industrialists (ERT).

In his recently published *The Choice for Europe* (1998), Moravcsik offers an explanation of European integration, *inter alia* stressing the primacy of inter-state bargaining, based on prior national preference formation. In developing his own 'liberal intergovernmentalist' per-spective, he strongly rejects a current in European integration theory commonly referred to as neo-functionalism or supranational institu-tionalism. This becomes particularly clear in his assessment of the role of supranational institutions and transnational business. The influence of the former is neglected and the role of the latter is restricted to the national level (see also Chapter 1, this volume).

With a focus on the enlargement strategy of the EU towards CEE, this chapter will point out that the role of supranational officials is far from 'futile or redundant, let alone counter-productive', as Moravcsik (1998: 8) suggests. In fact, it will be argued that the European Commission played a pivotal role in developing the pre-accession strat-egy of the EU, from the early Europe Agreements and the 1995 White Paper to Agenda 2000. An analysis of the ideas of the ERT with respect to the future course and direction of the process of European integra-tion in general and EU enlargement in particular will furthermore show that the impact of transnational business on European decision-making transcends the process of *national* preference formation and, indeed, forms a clear instance of transnational class formation. From a neo-Gramscian perspective, the first section therefore develops a cri-tique of 'liberal intergovernmentalism'. A second section will then review four interrelated components of the post-1989 strategy of the EU – internationalisation of capital, trade liberalisation, financial assis-tance and the actual pre-accession strategy – with a special emphasis on the social consequences of this co-ordinated strategy of neo-liberal economic restructuring and the massive sell-off of former state compa-nies to foreign capital. The lack of strong, self-regulating civil societies in countries such as the Czech Republic, Poland and Hungary is one of the elements explaining the dependent and asymmetrical way in which these countries are in the process of being fully incorporated into the European heartland of transnational production and finance. In the final section it will, in turn, be argued that this may have de-stabilising effects on the (enlarged) EU as a whole.

Liberal intergovernmentalism and a neo-Gramscian critique

The re-launch of European integration in the second half of the 1980s – through the European Commission's White Paper on the completion of the Internal Market (1985) and the signing of the Single European Act (1986) – resulted in a renewed interest in European integration theory.

Two different sets of hypotheses concerning the future direction of European integration dominated the debate in the late 1980s and early 1990s. One, conveniently labelled 'supranational institutionalism', echoed some of the propositions of neo-functionalism. This notably included the (functional, political and geographical) spill-over mechanism supposedly inherent to European integration, the unanticipated or unintended consequences of previous decisions, and the (autonomous, but in any case initiating) role of supranational actors and institutions (cf. Sandholtz and Zysman, 1989). The other, known as 'intergovernmental institutionalism' or 'liberal intergovernmentalism', strongly rejected theories which stressed the *sui generis* nature of European integration and supplemented a particular branch of the emerging discipline of International Political Economy (IPE). Echoing some of the propositions of neo-realism and using the insights of related pluralist theories of complex interdependence, intergovernmental institutionalism emphasised the primacy of inter-state bargaining and the convergence of policy preferences of major member states towards the lowest common denominator (see Moravcsik, 1991, 1993).

In his most recent work, Andrew Moravcsik further develops one of the most sophisticated and consistent theoretical frameworks presently on offer (Moravcsik, 1998). His 'liberal intergovernmentalist' explanation of the post-Second World War process of European integration basically consists of three interrelated aspects:

1. The process of inter-state bargaining is based on prior national preference formation. Moreover, inter-state bargaining is issue-specific and characterised by the primacy of (national) *economic* interests, taking shape in the context of, and responding to, the exigencies of an increasingly interdependent international economic order.
2. Inter-state bargaining outcomes are decisively shaped by the relative power of nation-states (i.e., by patterns of 'asymmetrical interdependence') as well as by rational state choices. Governments have access to all the relevant information and therefore bargain as rational actors. This is why the role of supranational or transnational actors is less important. In fact, while referring to the role of the European Commission, Moravcsik claims that 'the entrepreneurship of supranational officials tends to be futile and redundant, and even sometimes counterproductive' (ibid.: 8). Partly as a result of this, i.e., the absence of a strong supranational authority, the role of (transnational) business is limited to its capacity to influence the process of *national* preference formation.

3. Governments delegate and pool sovereignty in international institutions first and foremost to constrain and control one another:

> Significant pooling and delegation tend to occur, not where ideological conceptions of Europe converge or where governments agree on the need to centralise policy-making in the hands of technocratic planners, but where governments seek to compel compliance by foreign governments (or, in some cases, future domestic governments) with a strong temptation to defect. (ibid.: 9)

In this chapter, I will focus notably on the political influence of the European Commission and European transnational corporations in an emerging system of multi-level governance in the EU. In doing this, I will contest Moravcsik's claim that the role of supranational officials is 'futile and redundant'. Instead of taking the nation-state as an ontological primitive, I will interpret the process of European integration as an instance of transnational class formation. Such an emerging transnational class at the European level recruits from national political elites, from a transnational cadre class composed of European and national civil servants but also, for example, trade union cadres, and from transnational corporate elites.

It is important to note that a neo-Gramscian critique of Moravcsik's liberal intergovernmentalism is not aimed at modifying or complementing his *theory*, in the way mainstream critics would have it. The critique basically boils down to the formulation of a different set of theoretical claims based on different ontological and epistemological premises. To put it in more general terms, a neo-Gramscian perspective on European integration includes at least the following aspects.

First of all it is an integrated approach, combining an historical analysis of the development of social forces, an analysis of the interrelationship of economic, politico-institutional and ideological processes, and an understanding of present neo-liberal restructuring as resulting from (and strengthening) transnational social forces. It therefore transcends traditional state-centric perspectives and the related dichotomy between internal and external determination. A neo-Gramscian perspective is thus concerned with transnational social forces and transnational class formation. In the context of the subject matter of this chapter (i.e., the eastward expansion of the EU), this means isolating the actors that play a pivotal role in cementing a certain degree of cohesion among the different national, transnational and supranational forces in Europe: that is, those social forces that are *inter alia* manifested in the enlargement strategy of the EU towards CEE, which are connected to transnational class configurations. Although this is the most difficult part of the analysis it is indeed an essential one.

Second, a neo-Gramscian perspective is a *critical* theory inasmuch as it focuses on patterns of exclusion and inequality (see Chapter 1). Again, in mainstream integration theory 'the social dimension' is sporadically treated beyond the level of policy making. In the case of the enlargement strategy of the EU, its impact on the economic transformation in CEE and its social consequences are of particular importance in this respect. Moreover, a neo-Gramscian perspective (and critical theory in general) is concerned with emancipation and patterns of change which the static or system-maintaining recipes of problem-solving theory cannot offer (Cox, 1981). An analysis of the outward expansion of the EU towards CEE should, then, include an analysis of the potential opponents of European integration. This might include those stemming from social exclusion and growing inequality resulting from the extreme influence of foreign capital in domestic industry and banking in CEE, as well the emerging opposition in the EU itself. In essence, this raises the issue of alternative scenarios to the present strategy of neo-liberal restructuring.

A central concept in a neo-Gramscian perspective, then, is the notion of class which nowadays, indeed, is not an uncontested concept (see, for instance, Pakulski and Waters, 1996). In reaction to those who proclaim the 'death of class', Erik Olin Wright distinguishes two conditions for a genuine class society: (i) ownership and control of economically-relevant assets or income-generating productive resources (such as land, capital – including shares, stock options, etc. – skills, information, labour power) by a small minority in society; and (ii) the consequences of this unequal distribution of income-generating assets for the material well being of the majority of people. Or, to put it the other way round: 'the more egalitarian the distribution of assets and the less a person's material wellbeing depends upon their relationship to those assets, the lower the classness of a society' (Wright, 1996: 699).[1]

We have to keep in mind, first, that the income-generating nature of capital assets is anchored in the labour process. Or better, that the level of income inequality (whether or not the result of direct ownership or control of capital assets) is correlated to the level of exploitation of labour power and the price it fetches in the market, like other commodities. In this sense, it can be argued that the post-Second World War period of de-commodification (Esping-Andersen, 1990) came to an end in the course of the 1970s and turned into a period of accelerated commodification in the 1980s and 1990s (see van der Pijl, 1998). In our understanding of the last three decades of neo-liberal restructuring, this is the real meaning and objective of the flexibilisation of labour markets in Europe. Second, we have to realise that both the ownership and control of economically-relevant assets, and the income-generating nature of it, are increasingly transnational phenomena. In Europe, the dominant trend of transnational production and finance and the ever closer integration of capital markets are just two cases in point.

Is this enough ground to speak of transnational class formation? Certainly not. At stake is the difference between class and class *formation*. An important addition is that the structures, which reproduce or even increase the unequal distribution of assets and income at the transnational level, have to be reduced to the agency of transnational actors (in the same way as these and other structures determine the behaviour of transnational actors). In other words, we have to ascend from the abstract level of commodification and exploitation to the concrete level of agenda setting and policy planning. Apart from the institutional context, the level of ideas is of particular importance. How can we present decisions – which have the net effect of increasing the above mentioned inequalities – as the general interest? And which are the politico-institutional points of reference at the national, transnational and supranational level, and which transnational coalitions are possible or necessary in order to translate certain interests into policy making?

In the remainder of this section, I will briefly outline an alternative perspective on European integration, focusing on the role of ideas in cementing a certain degree of cohesion among different political, bureaucratic and social elites at the European level. At the end of this section and the start of the next one, I will then introduce a particular group of European transnational corporations, organised in the ERT, as a particularly influential source of ideas. Its agenda-setting role – and its role at the level of discourse production – will be illustrated by referring to the EU's enlargement strategy.

Concepts of control and European integration

One particularly weak point in the analysis of Moravcsik is his argument that national economic interests are directly translated into national preferences. Starting from a pluralist account of interest politics, he argues that different actors – producers, consumers, taxpayers, environmental organisations, organised public interest groups – play a role in issue-specific preference formation at the national level. Different national preferences with respect to different issues reflect different power configurations of national economic interest groups. This argument can be contested on three different grounds. First, economic interests do shape ideas or preferences, but the reverse is equally true: ideas may provide 'the framework in which economic interests are constructed' (Dietz, 1999: 361). Ideas play an important role in shaping or structuring economic and, indeed, political interests. Second, economic interests and ideas are generally formulated in a more comprehensive and consistent way than the 'issue-specific interest politics' approach suggests. Third, both economic interests and ideas are not confined within national borders and may transcend national state–civil society configurations (see Chapter 1) and, in the process, modify or constrain inter-state bargaining. To fully understand the implications of this threefold critique, it is useful to introduce the notion of comprehensive 'concepts of control'.

Concepts of control are comprehensive frameworks of thought and action which demarcate the 'limits of the possible' of a given configuration of capitalist society. Dealing in an integrated way with such areas as labour relations, socio-economic policies and the international socio-economic and political order, a concept of control simultaneously serves to organise and safeguard the particular interests of specific social groups or classes. However, the rise to hegemony of a particular concept, and its success in representing the specific interests related to it, can be achieved only if these particular interests are presented as the 'general interest' (see van der Pijl, 1984: ch. 1). Hegemony in this sense refers not so much to the extent to which a class or class fraction 'is able to impose a uniform conception of the world on the rest of society, but to the extent that it can articulate different visions of the world in such a way that their potential antagonism is neutralised' (Laclau, 1977: 161). Hegemonic concepts of control are expressions of both the structural and behavioural power of capital, reflecting what Gramsci has called a historical bloc (see Chapter 1). Originating in socio-economic relationships between different fractions of the bourgeoisie, and between (fractions of) the bourgeoisie and (parts of) the working class, concepts of control must be translated into domestic and foreign policy at the state level to become effective.

The state forms the organisational framework within which the elaboration, reproduction and transformation of specific, ideal-typical concepts of control can take place. Apart from this function as a political platform on which particular concepts can be articulated, the state has to organise and safeguard the interests and hegemony of the bourgeoisie as a whole. The state can accomplish this only when it can take a stand as an autonomous subject *vis-à-vis* the separate fractions of the bourgeoisie. This is why, to be hegemonic, a concept of control has to be presented as expressing the general interest, which it partly achieves by incorporating or neutralising competing visions of the world. However, the role of the state is not confined to its strict, national character as a political platform. From the moment that the functional forms of capital become internationalised (i.e., when international movements of circulating and productive capital come into being) the material basis will exist for the realisation of the political articulation of internationalised concepts of control at the national level. Both the internationalisation and internalisation of specific concepts of control depend on the pre-existence of historically determined national socio-economic and political structures. As Gramsci (1971: 241; emphasis added) put it:

> It is in the concept of hegemony that those exigencies which are national in character are knotted together ... *A class that is international in character has* – in as much as it guides social strata which are narrowly national (intellectuals), and indeed frequently even less than national: particularistic and muncipalistic (the peasants) – *to 'nationalise' itself in a certain sense.*

In this sense the state forms the political framework within which internationally operating concepts of control can be synthesised with particular national political cultures, attitudes, constitutional arrangements and so on, or, conversely, the very medium through which hegemonic concepts of control can transcend national frontiers.

According to Robert Cox, the emergence of what he refers to as 'world hegemony' results from a combination of social power and state power: that is, the leading social forces within a state or group of states establish a world order based on consensus rather than on coercion, functioning according to general principles that guarantee the continuing hegemony of both the state and their leading social classes by imposing a uniform conception of the world on an increasingly global society, thereby incorporating or neutralising subordinate states and social classes by offering them particular rewards (or at least the prospect of them):

> In such an order, production in particular countries becomes connected through the mechanisms of a world economy and linked

into world systems of production. The social classes of the dominant country find allies in classes within other countries. The historic[al] blocs underpinning particular states become connected through the mutual interests and ideological perspectives of social classes in different countries, and global classes begin to form (Cox, 1987: 7).

Essential in this process of 'global' or transnational class formation is the development of what Gramsci identified as the most universal and political form of class consciousness (Gramsci, 1971: 181–2). It is within the moment of class *formation* that particularistic economic interests are integrated in more comprehensive world views, in which new balances of class forces are both manifested and constituted through new, hegemonic formulations of the general interest, and in which the process of agenda-setting and policy planning transcends the economic or corporate level. In other words, it is the final stage of class formation in which the economic, the social and the political (in terms of structure *and* actor) come together in an 'organic' way, marking 'the decisive passage from the structure to the sphere of complex superstructures' (ibid.: 181). It is also the final stage in which – at a very concrete level – the (re)formulation of the 'best' economic policy is intrinsically linked to issues of social, educational and foreign policy.

However, as Stephen Gill says, such a process of class formation does not take place spontaneously: 'it needs leadership and action based on a highly developed political consciousness within the dominant social class' (Gill, 1990: 45). And it needs a constant stream of ideas which – synthesised in long-term strategies (i.e., in comprehensive concepts of control) – provide the framework in which economic and political interests are constructed (or made explicit), and their potential antagonisms neutralised. Returning to our critique of Moravscik's liberal intergovernmentalist approach (and to our claim that the process of European integration must be understood as an instance of transnational class formation), it is *inter alia* at the level of ideas that we can question this basically state-centric view of European integration. The EU is increasingly functioning as a 'quasi-state' structure, characterised by a complex system of multi-level decision making in which national (and sub-national) governments, bureaucracies and business elites develop converging ideas about, and related interests in, a New European political economy. Elsewhere I have argued that the ERT has been (and still is) a particularly influential actor when it comes to shaping the socio-economic contours of such a new form of bourgeois domination at the European transnational level (Holman, 1992, 1996, 1999; see also Chapter 4 above). By this, I did not mean to imply that economic interests were (and are) the only thing that count, or that the ERT is the only (or primary) actor in the field of discourse production at the European level. I did suggest, however, that in a world of on-going commodification and accelerated deregulation and flexibilisation, transnational business opinions played a privileged role in mobilising economic interests, governments and Union institutions. The ERT is clearly *primus inter pares* in the European landscape of think tanks, agenda-setting and policy planning groups, for instance.

Choosing the fittest: transnational business and the European Commission at work

Perhaps it is now time to modify this position slightly. It still can be argued – and documented – that the ERT is a privileged agenda-setting and policy planning group, privileged in its access to European institutions and member state governments and in its capacity to influence the European agenda. It certainly plays a central role in existing networks at the European and global level. We find members of the ERT prominently figuring in transnational networks such as the Transatlantic Business Dialogue, the World Economic Forum, the International Chamber of Commerce and the Competitiveness Advisory Group (CAG, see below), and also in propagating notions such as the 'Third Way'.[2] But in stressing the importance of the ERT, I downplayed the role of the European Commission, *de facto* reducing it to the political mainstay and executive of the pro-active ERT at the European level. This implicit picture of an omnipotent ERT and a weak and subordinated Commission has to be modified.

In reality the European Commission is much more important – particularly in its policy planning capacity and in its role as the *Guardian of the Treaties* – and operates on a much more equal footing with the ERT than previously envisaged. The relationship between the two can best be described as a 'symmetrical interdependent' one: the Commission and the ERT need each other in the realisation of their respective goals. This is increasingly the case as a result of the convergence of their views and agendas in the course of the 1990s (after a period of estrangement during the second Delors Commission).

In the early years of its existence, it was a member of the Delors cabinet who referred to the ERT in the following way: 'We see this group as a very useful bunch of people. These men are very powerful and very dynamic. They seed us with ideas. And when necessary, they can ring up their own Prime Ministers and make their case' (quoted in Merritt, 1986: 22). In other words, the Commission could (and can) use the members of the ERT in its attempt to strengthen its position *vis-à-vis* the member states, both in its policy initiating and innovating capacity. On the other hand, the ERT needs the Commission because of its role as executive and co-legislature at the European level. The fact that the Commission has 'a quasi-monopoly of policy initiation and innovation inside the [EU]' (Church and Phinnemore, 1994: 271) makes it the very political addressee of numerous interest groups. Again, among these interest groups the ERT is *primus inter pares*. This is particularly because the ERT is exceptionally well equipped – in terms of 'infrastructure', status and comprehensiveness – to formulate and organically integrate the various ingredients of potentially hegemonic concepts of control, especially in the era of neo-liberal restructuring. In the words of the former chairman of the ERT, Jerome Monod: 'Perhaps more than in the past, business opinions today express a comprehensive world-wide vision of modern society and its problems, a vision which may in some ways go beyond the ideas of our political leaders' (ERT, 1991: 2). Needless to say it is *big* business that counts most in this respect.

Almost ten years later, the above quotation is even more illuminating. Perhaps more than in the past, business decisions today determine to a large extent the way political leaders *react* and anticipate similar future business decisions. Recent cross-border mergers in the banking and telecommunications sectors in Europe have shown the capacity of European capital to impose an Anglo-Saxon vision of modern society on (only rhetorically resisting) 'political leaders'. In this process, the European Commission plays a very important supportive role.

This is not to plea for a 'supranational intergovernmentalist' interpretation of European integration and a relapse into the theoretical 'trench warfare' of the late 1980s and early 1990s. My argument here is that the EU is increasingly dominated by what I refer to as the New Trias Politica: the European Commission, in close co-operation with organised business, the European Court of Justice (ECJ), and the Council of Ministers. The ECJ is first and foremost the European institution which guarantees a fair economic playing field or – in less neutral terms – ensures the free movement of market forces in the de-regulated Internal Market. It does not have substantial jurisdiction outside the first pillar of the Maastricht Treaty, but it does play a central role in compelling compliance by member state governments with respect to the Union's *acquis communautaire* (which in turn is mainly concerned with the completion of the Internal

Market, and its institutional underpinnings). The Council of Ministers is the ultimate decision-maker and legislature (together with the European Parliament, since the introduction of the co-decision procedure) and controls – that is, checks and restrains – the Commission. Its role as the guardian of member states' interests has been effectively – and voluntarily – eroded since the ratification of the Single European Act in 1987 (again primarily in the first pillar). The Council of Ministers and the European Council have not been the political voice of culturally and historically distinct constituencies at the member state level, whose primary aim is to avoid integrational steps which run counter to the 'general interest' of the respective peoples. Instead, since the mid-1980s, they have increasingly become, *par excellence*, the European institutions that defend and legitimise the on-going process of negative integration. This has also involved positive integration in selected areas, supportive of the all-dominating process of market integration, and the concomitant processes of capital concentration and centralisation, economic deregulation/privatisation and labour market flexibilisation, while upholding the illusion of national sovereignty in important other areas. This is the real meaning of popular concepts such as subsidiarity and benchmarking or best practice. The rhetorical language of national governments – to promote European decisions (or non-decisions) as the ultimate guarantee that national interests, values, identities and peculiarities will continue to be defended ('the European rescue of the nation-state') – can best be described as the 'New Populism'. In practice, however, a new system of multi-level decision making is unfolding, an emergent and novel form of bourgeois domination at the European level, which supports and strengthens a genuine transnational European class society in which an increasingly cohesive, transnational class of capital owners – embedded in a transnational structure of political elites, bureaucracies and think tanks – is faced with little opposition as a result of the (sub-) national and sectoral dispersion of subordinated social groupings.[3]

Returning, then, to the enlargement strategy of the EU, the quasi-constitutional separation of powers we just outlined (which is as much about co-operation as it is about separation), and the dominant role of the Commission/ERT in the field of policy initiation and innovation – *and in giving ideological direction to the overall process of European integration* – can be illustrated by looking more closely at the different components of this strategy. In doing this, we will concentrate on the convergence and synchronisation of ideas and strategies as developed by the ERT and the Commission. We will first look at the role of the ERT in pushing for market liberalisation in the candidate member states and at the impact of foreign direct investment (FDI) in CEE. We then turn to the pre-accession strategy of the European Commission, its emphasis on opening up markets in CEE and its lack of social content.

Foreign direct investment in CEE and the role of the ERT

Immediately after the 1989 revolutions in CEE, the ERT published a number of reports in which it called for immediate action in response to 'the new challenge' and 'the window of opportunity' offered by 'the astonishing developments in Eastern Europe' (ERT, 1991: *passim*). The same euphoric language was used in a number of subsequent reports, but the tone changed after the June 1997 summit in Amsterdam, where the EU political leaders were unable to agree on the internal reforms (the so-called 'deepening' process) necessary for enlargement. In a *Message to all 15 EU Heads of State and Government* on 1 December 1997, the ERT proposed a comprehensive action plan with respect to EU enlargement. The reason for sending this message was quite clear. The members of the ERT 'would like to express their conviction that enlargement offers a golden opportunity to raise the competitiveness and prosperity of the whole European economy (existing EU members and new candidates alike) provided that it is done on the basis of sound economic principles, free competition and open markets' (ERT, 1997). The ERT asked the European Council to give the accession negotiations the political impetus they required, because European business:

> is concerned that the hesitations shown by some political leaders risk to discourage our partners, to discourage new investors and to delay integration. The economic advantages are widely underestimated. We believe that the radical economic transformation within the candidate countries will increase their ability to export, raise their living standards and give a tremendous impetus to their imports and to investment from the west (ibid.).

Widening, then, should be one of the main priorities of the member states. But the ERT hastened to say that deepening is a prerequisite to widening. Deepening is equated with (and restricted to) the completion of the Internal Market and with deregulation and flexibilisation, both in economic and politico-institutional terms:

> To facilitate negotiations there is a responsibility on the EU to deal with its own unfinished business. The [Internal] Market must be

completed, for there are too many obstacles to free movement of goods even among the current members. Regulations should be further simplified. Institutions and their decision-making procedures should be improved to ensure that a Union of 25 members can be managed effectively (ibid.).

It was of course no coincidence that the letter was published just before the European Council meeting in Luxemburg in December 1997. It was during that summit that the 'comprehensive action plan' of the European Commission – the *Agenda 2000* report from July 1997 – had to be approved by the member states and a decision on opening the accession negotiations (in 1998) had to be made. *Agenda 2000* was accepted and the Commission received a green light to start negotiations. Without suggesting a direct causal link between the ERT's letter and the decision making in Luxemburg, the orchestrated action of the ERT in support of the Commission's action plan was manifested, as was the convergence and synchronisation of their respective ideas and strategies, with respect to eastward enlargement (see the next section).

In 1999, the ERT published a report which exclusively dealt with EU enlargement and the role of European business. The main tenet of this report is that – under the right conditions – enlargement is a 'win–win' process. More specifically, the report argues that companies and economies on both sides of the former iron curtain can reap the benefits from EU foreign direct investment in CEE. This conclusion is based on the experience of EU companies (and ERT members) in CEE. But these companies have also encountered some 'obstacles': ineffective public administration and an inadequate regulatory framework; poor staff skills and attitudes to work; uncompetitive local suppliers and poor infrastructure; and out-dated social attitudes (ERT, 1999: 25). In order 'to overcome these obstacles and to secure the full benefits from enlargement' the report *inter alia* makes the following recommendations:

1. Both the EU and the candidate members should maintain the momentum in the accession negotiations and the preparations for membership. In concrete terms, this means that the EU should no longer delay negotiations and set a clear timetable, while the candidate members should make an effort to implement 'the most important aspects of the *acquis communautaire*' (ibid.), and particularly those aspects related to the proper functioning of the Internal Market.
2. The experiences of the ERT companies in CEE should be used as benchmarks 'to measure the progress made to date and to set goals

for improvements in the most critical areas' (ibid.), such as taxation, banking and infrastructure.

3. An 'East–West Training and Skills Programme' should be established in which EU and CEE governments and companies work together 'to improve the range of skills and attitudes to work needed in the new, more competitive free-market economies of CEE' (ibid.).

4. EU and CEE policy-makers should support the initiative of the ERT to create so-called Business Enlargement Councils (BECs) consisting of representatives from the head offices of ERT companies and senior management representatives of the local operating companies, senior government officials and senior officials of the European Commission. The Hungarian BEC, which was established by a number of ERT members, is supposed to 'discuss critical EU accession issues with the Hungarian government, channel appropriate information to the EU, [and] assure multiple communication channels among the company members of the BEC, and senior officials of the European Commission and the Hungarian government' (ibid.: 23). The establishment of similar BECs in other CEE countries is under consideration.

Unsurprisingly, the report is one big apologia for FDI in CEE, claiming that the benefits of the free and unrestricted movement of capital will be optimal as long as the proper economic, social, political and knowledge infrastructure is created. Indeed, from a theoretical point of view, it is easy to assume the positive impact of FDI in CEE. Potential advantages and expectations include the contribution of FDI to the recovery of output, improved skills in the workforce, the introduction and application of modern technologies and new forms of industrial organisation, the creation of new jobs, and so on. A closer look at the experiences of the CEE countries with FDI thus far suggests, however, a different reality. Many of these would-be advantages have not been realised yet. The improvement of the quality of labour has been quite limited so far, and restricted to technical and managerial staff. The same applies to the impact of new technologies. The positive impact of greenfield investments on job creation has also been more than counterbalanced by the negative effects of rationalisation (read: labour shedding) in companies which have been privatised to foreign capital (Simai, 1998a, 1998b).

Moreover, if we look at the broader social and political consequences of FDI in CEE, three different but related issues have to be raised. First, it has been argued that the double transformation in CEE boils down to the introduction of 'capitalism without capitalists'. The emerging social structure in the post-1989 period is characterised by 'the absence of a capitalist class' or the lack of an 'organised group of major capitalists'. In fact: 'The new power elite of post-communism is not composed of owners, but rather of the technocratic-managerial elite together with the new politocracy which constitute its dominant fraction, and elite humanistic and social science intellectuals which form its dominated fraction' (Eyal, Szelényi and Townsley, 1997: 61). Contrary to this rather state-centric idea of a new power elite which does not face 'competition from a propertied bourgeoisie', it is our belief that all the elements of our definition of *class* and *class formation* (see above) can be applied to the new situation in CEE. It is foreign capital – and the quasi-state structures and cadres at the supranational level organically related to it – which plays an essential role in the process of *transnational* class formation in CEE. The ownership and control of economically-relevant assets, and the income-generating nature of it, are increasingly transnational phenomena, while the growing inequality in the distribution of these assets is defended – that is, presented as the 'general interest' – by the 'new power elite'. This link between national power elites and transnational classes can be the result of mutual interests and consent, the behavioural and structural power of transnational capital (Gill, 1990: 112ff), and/or overt pressure from the EU.

Second, FDI in CEE is first and foremost directed to the most attractive and often strategically important industries and services such as banking, telecommunications or utilities. One could argue that in times of globalisation the concept of 'strategic sectors' has become obsolete. Strength and competitiveness should be emphasised, rather than nationality. This may be true, however, in societies where globalisation does not pose new economic security threats (for instance, because inward flows of goods and capital are more than counter-balanced by outward flows). But in CEE, the massive sell-off of the so-called diamonds of the former state sector has increased foreign dependence and has unilaterally moved strategic decision-making power to the head offices of foreign companies. This in turn has had (and still has) an important impact on employment and social cohesion.

Third, the crucial importance of FDI in transforming the economies of CEE is reflected in savage 'regime competition' among the respective governments, resulting in the excessive political influence of transnational capital (see also Chapter 5 above). In other words, national governments in CEE are constrained by the policies of other governments and by the investment decisions of transnational capital.

Here the notion of the internationalisation of the state becomes of particular importance (see Chapter 1). If we accept that this is 'the global process whereby national policies and practices have been adjusted to the exigencies of the world economy of international production' (Cox, 1987: 253), we may recall what was said above about the notion of comprehensive concepts of control. In order to become effective, concepts of control not only have to transcend their origin at the level of fractions of the bourgeoisie in such a way that their potential antagonism is neutralised (i.e., the condition of hegemony), but they must also be translated into state policy. In this sense, the 'internationalisation of the state' can be explained both from 'external' pressures related to the world economy and the 'internal' articulation of hegemonic concepts of control, its mediating force being the process of capitalist transnationalisation, and its vehicle the internationalised state institutions at the national and supranational level. The pre-accession strategy of the European Commission – which reflects the interests of transnational capital and is *internalised* by the new power elites in CEE – forms a paradigmatic example of this phenomenon. It is this strategy that we will consider next.

Enlarging the Union: a multi-speed restructuring race

In reaction to the 1989 revolutions in CEE, the EU unfolded a strategy which basically consisted of three elements: the gradual liberalisation of interregional trade; a financial assistance programme; and preparatory steps to absorb (some of) the CEE countries as full members. Elsewhere I have argued that the first two elements of this strategy respectively boiled down to a form of 'managed multilateralism', introducing free trade while continuing the protection of vital EU interests, and symbolic financial assistance presented as an 'incentive to self-help' (Holman, 1998). The third element (i.e., the prospect of integration into the EU) has proved to be the most effective weapon of the EU in disciplining the governments of the candidate members.

In June 1993, the Copenhagen European Council formulated – in extremely broad terms – the political and economic conditions for accession:

1. Stability of institutions guaranteeing democracy, the rule of law, human rights, and respect for and protection of minorities.
2. Existence of a functioning market economy, as well as the capacity to cope with competitive pressure and market forces within the Union.

3. An ability to take on the obligations of membership, including adherence to the aims of political, economic and monetary union.

In addition, it was stated that 'the Union's capacity to absorb new members, while maintaining the momentum of European integration, is ... an important consideration in the general interest of both the Union and the candidate countries' (quoted in Dinan, 1994: 479–80). In other words, an eastward enlargement of the EU could take place only after the process of consolidating and deepening the Union was completed.

This was reaffirmed at the Essen Summit in December 1994. In its conclusions, the European Council stipulated that the reform of the institutional structure of the EU would have to be completed before negotiations between the Commission and the prospective associates could start. Two initiatives were launched at the Essen Summit: a structured dialogue between the EU members and the associated countries and a strategy to prepare the latter countries for their future incorporation into the Internal Market. To this end, a Commission White Paper was published in May 1995. The main objective was 'to provide a guide to assist the associated countries in preparing themselves for operating under the requirements of the EU's internal market' (European Commission, 1995a). The Paper identifies:

> the key measures in each sector of the Internal Market and suggests a sequence in which the approximation of legislation should be tackled. However a merely formal transposition of legislation will not be enough to achieve the desired economic impact or to ensure that the Internal Market functions effectively after further enlargement. Accordingly, equal importance is attached to the establishment of adequate structures for implementation and enforcement, which may be the more difficult task (ibid.).

A next step in the EU's strategy of rapprochement towards CEE was the publication of the Commission's *Agenda 2000* report in July 1997. In three parts, the report deals with the development of the internal policies of the Union, the challenge of enlargement and the new financial framework for the period 2000–6. It also contains opinions on each applicant country. These opinions were prepared by the Commission at the request of the Council on the basis of the aforementioned Copenhagen criteria. With respect to the political criteria, the Commission concluded that only one applicant country – Slovakia – did not satisfy the political conditions laid down in Copenhagen. As for the economic criteria – a functioning market economy and the capacity to withstand competitive pressure – Hungary and Poland were considered closest, with the Czech Republic and Slovenia lagging not far behind. Finally, only three countries – Hungary, Poland and the Czech Republic – should be able, in the medium term, to take on the major part of the *acquis communautaire* and to establish the administrative structure to apply it (European Commission, 1997b). On the basis of these individual opinions, the Commission suggested that accession negotiations should be opened with only five CEE countries: Hungary, Poland, the Czech Republic, Slovenia and, surprisingly, Estonia. As we saw above, this proposal was adopted at the Luxemburg Council in December 1997.

The same European Council meeting invited the Commission to draw up regular reports on the progress made towards accession by each of the candidate countries. Since then, two series of progress reports have been published which, by and large, confirm the 1997 conclusions (though Slovakia now also fulfils the political criteria). In 1998, negotiations were started with the above-mentioned CEE countries, plus Cyprus. These negotiations are conducted on a bilateral basis but follow an identical procedure. After presenting their negotiating position, the applicant countries may start 'substantive negotiations at ministerial level' on the 31 chapters of the *acquis communautaire*.

Two conclusions can be drawn from the above. First, the Union's strategy of rapprochement developed thus far has necessarily resulted in a differentiation of integration. More concretely, the fact that a final decision about whether the candidate members are suited for full membership will be made on an individual basis (i.e., same conditions, individual testing) makes it possible to exclude countries like Bulgaria and Romania because of their poor economic performance and Turkey because of its bad human rights record. To put it in other words, only those countries that have been able or willing to adjust their economic and political structures in line with the requirements of the EU will be in the first wave of the next round of enlargement.

Second, a closer look at the Commission's 1997 opinions and its subsequent progress reports clearly shows the primacy of economic criteria over political ones. More concretely, the existence of a functioning, competitive market economy and the ability to take on the obligations of membership are the two criteria on which most of the attention is concentrated. Of particular importance in this respect is the adjustment of administrative structures in the applicant countries so that EU legislation can be implemented effectively. Since most of this legislation is related to the single market and its 'four freedoms', it is no exaggeration to conclude that the Commission's pre-accession strategy is basically about disciplining the candidate members in terms of free market integration. If we then return to the issues raised in the previous section, our claim that the strategies of the Commission and the ERT *vis-à-vis* CEE converged in the course of the 1990s can be further substantiated by concluding that both strategies are primarily directed at preparing the countries in CEE for incorporation into the Internal Market. This basically boils down to opening up the emerging markets of CEE to the benefit of, first and foremost, West European business.

If we look at the flows of FDI into CEE, a clear correlation can be established between the ability of the applicant 'to assume the obligations of membership by satisfying the economic conditions required' and the amount of accumulated FDI flows (see Table 8.1). It turns out that the three economies that perform best in terms of the Copenhagen economic criteria – that is, Hungary, Poland and, to a lesser extent the Czech Republic – are also the most attractive host economies to foreign capital. This may come as no surprise, since FDI is flowing to those countries in CEE which have the most friendly business environment. A survey conducted by the United Nations Conference on Trade and Development (UNCTAD) among investment-promotion agencies in the region showed that the factors enhancing inward FDI included labour cost, labour skills, integration prospects, macroeconomic stability and favourable privatisation strategies (UNCTAD, 1998: 286). It is this ideal combination of low labour costs, relatively high labour skills, macroeconomic stability at the expense of social security arrangements, privatisation of the most attractive parts of the former state sector, and the

Table 8.1   FDI inward stock by host economy in Central and Eastern Europe

Host economy	1990	1995	1996	1997
Bulgaria	4	337	446	943
Czech Republic	59	5923	7061	6763
Estonia	–	736	886	1148
Hungary	648	11919	14690	15882
Latvia	–	511	679	901
Lithuania	–	495	647	1041
Poland	109	7843	11463	16463
Romania	–	978	1243	2467
Slovakia	81	950	1109	1293

Source: UNCTAD (1998), 376–7.

disciplining effect of (the prospect of) international integration, that determines the rating of the candidate members.

Widening versus cohesion: Helsinki's missing link

It is from this perspective that we can understand the decision of the Helsinki European Council to increase the number of applicant states from six to thirteen. At first sight this seems a rather risky enterprise, since it implies the candidature of a group of countries with an enormous development gap *vis-à-vis* the present Union. If the EU were to grow from 15 to 28 member states, the EU population would increase by 45 per cent but total GDP by only 7 per cent. GDP per capita of the candidate members ranges from 23 per cent (Bulgaria) to 68 per cent (Slovenia) of the EU average. Growth rates of industrial production have been negative in some countries (Bulgaria and Romania) since 1995, and in most of these countries are below the EU average. Economic activity rates in the candidate members are all below the EU15 rate of 67.5 per cent, whereas unemployment rates are above the EU15 rate of 10 per cent in five countries. Finally, all the applicants have high inflation rates (with the exception of Malta and Cyprus), with Turkey having the highest rate of inflation in 1998 at 84.6 per cent, coupled also with large structural trade deficits (Eurostat, 1999).[4]

These are, however, the statistics of 'today'. The official reasoning of the EU is that the very prospect of membership – and the related criteria – will have a disciplining effect on the respective governments. Indeed, this is the very rationale behind the Helsinki decision. If these governments are successful in transforming their economies and adjusting their legal structures to the exigencies of the *acquis communautaire*, European business will profit from the widening of the Internal Market. If these governments are unsuccessful, the EU can indefinitely postpone their entrance. In short, the EU cannot lose, and one can only wonder why the EU did not take this decision at an earlier stage.

Let us assume for the sake of argument that the externally imposed discipline on CEE will be successful, that public deficits and inflation rates can be curtailed and that nominal growth rates can be restored or increased; what then will be the social consequences of such an adjustment strategy? At present, there is much talk in the EU about the so-called *European Social Model*, which should be at the heart of the integration process. It is unclear, however, which model the European decision-makers have in mind. Recent developments in Germany and France suggest the creeping erosion of the continental or Rhineland model, and the triumph of the Anglo-Saxon model of shareholder capitalism. It seems very unlikely that the burgeoning civil societies in CEE will be able to prevent their countries from following the same road.

This brings us to an answer to the following question. If it is true that the pre-accession strategy of the European Commission is contributing to greater social polarisation in CEE – and hence greater instability in the region – why is it, then, that the member states of the EU are unwilling to develop a more active enlargement strategy towards CEE, aimed at unequivocally supporting the double transformation beyond political and economic liberalisation? Part of the answer is to be found in the response to a further question. Why is it that the member states of the EU are reluctant – and since the early 1990s increasingly so, despite rising unemployment rates and growing social unrest – to develop an active social and employment policy at the European level? Both questions are inextricably linked. The lack of any substantial assistance from the EU to the countries in CEE is the result of neo-liberal restructuring within the EU itself since the late 1980s. This in turn is reflected in the neo-liberal discipline that is imposed upon the countries in CEE through the accession strategy of the EU.

To make things even more complicated, eastern enlargement will be premised upon the successful completion of the EU's institutional reform. The European Council of Amsterdam did not result in concrete solutions, but postponed any final decision to a later date. Next to this, another problematic issue has still to be resolved: the future of the Common Agricultural Policy and the role of structural funds. Until now, the process of European integration, and public support for it, has been based on the principle of financial solidarity: that is, solidarity with farmers and with less developed member states and regions. It is this redistributive nature of the Union's budget that is under attack at present (cf. Holman, 1997: 52ff). It may well turn out that the countries of CEE will eventually enter into an EU that pays only lip service to the objectives of economic convergence and social cohesion.

Notes

1. In the case of the USA, 'the inegalitarian distribution of capital assets is clearly consequential'. In 1990, more than 50 per cent of the average family income of the top 1 per cent of income earners in the USA – i.e., $278 000 out of a total of $549 000 – came directly from capital assets. At the other extreme of American society, less than 10 per cent of the average family income of the bottom 90 per cent – $2400 out of a total of $29 000 – came from capital assets (Olin Wright, 1996: 706). This puts the notion of 'popular

capitalism' in perspective. One can assume that this unequal distribution of assets, and its effect on income differences, has resulted in more rather than less inequality in the USA and in Europe in the course of the 1990s. In the case of the EU, however, we do not have access to similar statistics on the distribution of income-generating capital assets, due to a lack of transparency in the member states. We assume that a similar trend can be discerned as that in the USA, although perhaps less pronounced.

2. For a more detailed account of the issues raised in this section, see Holman (forthcoming).

3. Indeed, a reactionary form of opposition that might potentially threaten vested transnational interests is the one stemming from an alternative strand of the 'new populism', that is the extreme right-wing movements in the different member states; especially when these movements turn against 'globalisation' and the (whether real or perceived) concomitant migration flows. Returning to the subject matter of this chapter, the rise of the Austrian Freedom Party (FPÖ) and its opposition to an Eastward enlargement of the EU – mainly because of the feared influx of immigrants from the new member states – is a case in point.

4. These Eurostat statistics are all 1998 data.

9
What Happened to the European Option for Eastern Europe?

Kees van der Pijl[1]

In this chapter I discuss some key areas of strategic rivalry within the Atlantic ruling and governing classes on the issue of reintegrating Eastern Europe into the western orbit from around 1980 onwards. In line with the general theme of this volume, I will identify the different class fractions, national and transnational, which may be seen as having supported rival strategies in this field.

At the time the Reagan administration took office in the USA under a programme of militant confrontation with the Soviet bloc and the left generally, one author saw the potential for reintegrating Eastern Europe arising from a 'reduction of Soviet cultural presence in Eastern Europe' and developing along two axes: a 'Europeanisation of Eastern Europe', and an 'Americanisation of Europe' (Zimmerman, 1981: 100). However, the thesis of this chapter is that the 'Europeanisation of Eastern Europe', whenever it seemed to crystallise at all, was promptly and unfailingly sidelined by a strategy of Americanisation of Europe in its entirety. This latter strategy was effective not just because it was tied to US/North Atlantic Treaty Organisation geopolitical power, but also to a considerable degree because it rallied social forces across a broad transnational, Atlantic spectrum, whereas such transnational unity within the European setting was much more defensive and usually short-lived.

The structural divisions within the Atlantic and European ruling classes, which underlie the ascendancy of 'Americanisation' over any rival project, also transpire in the fact that European integration as such has historically developed along two axes as well (Holman, 1992). Through crisis and compromise, the option in which Western Europe was to integrate into a relatively closed, supranational quasi-state (the original federalist idea was initially hegemonic in the European Movement, traces of which may still be detected in the European Coal and Steel Community, for instance), has step by step been diluted into a 'functionalist' trajectory prioritising free trade and capital movements, although (from the mid-1980s re-launch of the integration process onwards) various intergovernmental aspects have been retained or reintroduced. Clearly, the Americanisation of Europe in response to Soviet decline implies a loose, free trade interpretation of European integration leaving state sovereignty intact. On the other hand, anything even faintly moving in the direction of the Europeanisation of Eastern Europe would have to be grafted on to a supranational integration tendency. The dominance of such a tendency would obviously be a precondition for any pattern of pan-European coalescence in which the USA is not automatically involved. But supranationalism is on the wane and, with the collapse of the bipolar bloc structure of the Cold War and the restoration of sovereignty to a reunified Germany, it seems less probable than ever.

However, the deeper cause of the failure of a European strategy for Eastern Europe to really take shape in the more recent period is that this 'strategy' itself is already largely determined by structure and is less a matter of choice than the term suggests. A structural divide revealed itself in the course of the 1980s, I would argue, between two stages in the imposition of capitalist discipline on different state–civil societies. The first involved corporate liberalism, which took shape in the New Deal in the USA and in the Marshall Plan in Western Europe, and in which capital accumulation was guided by the requirements of productive capital and industrial class compromise. Against this, a newly ascendant neo-liberalism in the course of the 1980s and 1990s gradually worked to dislodge the structures in which corporate liberalism was embodied, forcing its constituent social forces on to the defensive. Neo-liberalism, anchored in the exploitative netherworld of a 24-hour economy, widens the discipline of capital to include all aspects of work, daily life, humanity and nature, while the short-term profitability prioritised by a footloose international money capital defines the parameters of capital accumulation.

The hegemony of neo-liberalism and the social forces constituting it has propelled the Americanisation of Europe forward, including the liberal intergovernmental option for European integration. This was particularly the case whenever attempts were made to develop a specifically 'European' policy for Eastern Europe. This ascendancy of Americanisation was possible precisely because the social forces embodying the underlying neo-liberal drive were growing stronger and more numerous with every defeat of the organised working class, related managerial cadre and state socialism. By contrast, the forces on which a European option had to rely, grafted on to corporate liberalism with its structures of social protection, crumbled and became disorganised in the process.

The argument supporting this thesis will take three steps. First, there will be an account of the rise of neo-liberalism; second, the crystallisation of a European challenge in the late 1980s and the US resumption of a geopolitical offensive will be discussed; and finally, features related to the triumph of neo-liberal Americanisation will be outlined. Of course, these three steps are interrelated. By attempting to theoretically reconstruct historical development a dialectic unfolds between, following Marx's method in *Grundrisse*, the 'concrete-real' and the 'thought-concrete' in which all elements determine each other within an evolving material totality embodied in the configuration of classes and class fractions (Marx, 1973: 100–8).

Neo-liberalism over corporate liberalism

Capital historically imposes its discipline over society through a definite configuration of classes unified around a common definition of the general interest which demarcates the 'limits of the possible' for society at large. When we use the term 'comprehensive concept of control' for such a formula of the general interest (Overbeek, 1993), 'control' has both a managerial and a power connotation. Indeed, the sense that the particular structure of society has organically evolved into what it is allows a concept of control to remain largely implicit, as everything which is 'programmatic' about it is already in place and largely self-evident. Rival concepts, by contrast, seem willed and artificial because the objective confluence of ascendant social forces and the structural coherence of the particular mode of accumulation, which lends the hegemonic quality to the dominant concept, is lacking. They are therefore broadly seen as expressions of 'specific interests', outdated and outlandish 'constructions', instead of as the straight translation of reality. History is certainly the history of class struggle here. Since every concept of control ultimately centres on a particular mode of extraction of the social surplus, it crystallises in a situation defined by the outcomes of social struggles and by the possibilities contained in the level of development of the productive forces.

Corporate liberalism, then, was the ascendant hegemonic concept of mid-century capitalist development. It took shape when American capital in the New Deal was restructured from an earlier railway and heavy industry configuration to a mass-production system exploiting the opportunities for raising surplus extraction offered by Fordist assembly line production and the application of electrical machinery. Simultaneously, by opening the free trade window, New Deal economic policies, through several steps, restored the momentum of the internationalisation of capital while avoiding a corporatist deadlock with labour. In the Marshall Plan, the foundations for an adjustment to New Deal-style corporate liberalism were laid in Western Europe. Indeed, the time-lag allowed American capital to re-deploy and, through foreign direct investment, exploit the ample labour supply of Western Europe at (initially) a fraction of the US wage rate (van der Pijl, 1984: chs 4–6).

The strategic core of the corporate liberal ruling class configuration is in 'finance capital', combinations of big banks interlocked with big industrial corporations. It relies on protective state intervention and a class compromise with organised labour. The productive-capital orientation of corporate liberalism implies an emphasis on the material aspect of the capital circuit. In combination with a managerial perspective, this concept is typically shaped by its topography of 'corporate' units (business firms, states, trade unions) which are internally organised as bureaucracies to the point where, in their mutual relations, the 'liberal' (market, free-contractual) component tends to be crowded out. Class compromise is another structural factor. Although state intervention and the welfare state may have been important in obtaining the consent of organised labour, agriculture and various state bureaucracies for a liberal world market strategy, they can be seen as the building blocks of a merely national architecture of class compromise.

Neo-liberalism crystallised in the attack on the corporate 'fortresses' – trade unions and welfare states first, business firms next – which had formed in the three decades of hegemonic corporate liberalism and had become a fetter on the rate of exploitation of labour. Expressing the microeconomic, *rentier* perspective of money capital and benefiting from an economic orthodoxy with a long academic pedigree, neo-liberalism surfaced in tax revolts against the welfare state and in attacks on organised labour and socialist or socialist-inspired political forces. Within the ruling class, neo-liberalism was spearheaded by investment banks catering to the newly emancipated capital markets (as well as by auxiliary forces in the accountancy, management consultancy, and credit rating professions). US commercial banks, too, joined the hunt for short-term profits in privatisation and take-over activities as they lost their role in finance capital structures in the 1980s (Albert, 1993: 66).

Most importantly, neo-liberalism permits a flight forwards out of a deadlock between a reformist labour movement and capital and between democracy and political authority in particular national settings. It also promises to overcome the inadequacy of the corporate liberal configuration to deal with new productive-technological possibilities. By exposing all the elements of production, social reproduction and nature directly to capital, neo-liberalism has multiplied the productive forces but, at the same time, it threatens to exhaust the capacity of society and nature to support capitalist discipline (van der Pijl, 1998: 43–9).

Now corporate liberalism and neo-liberalism, or Rhineland and neo-American capitalism in Albert's classification, are not 'strategies' in the sense that they can be adopted at will. Concepts of control are expressions of objective configurations. By labelling them according to geographical terms, Albert may actually obscure the fact that both corporate liberalism and neo-liberalism have spread within a geopolitics of capital in which the English-speaking world, with the USA at its centre, continues to represent the most advanced stage of capitalist discipline over society. Hence in the 1980s, the USA once again acted as the spearhead of the newest form of capitalism (with Britain ideologically prominent if materially confined to the financial and militarist aspects of neo-liberalism: cf. James, 1996). Continental Europe, on the other hand, like Japan and South Korea, remained entrenched in a corporate liberal configuration of forces, not least because of the continuing (defensive) strength of organised labour.

In particular, this applies to Germany, the industrial core of the continent. Germany is still strong in the industries related to corporate liberalism (automobile, engineering and chemical industries), while the USA has moved to strengthen involvement in industries of the future, on which neo-liberalism is grafted, such as the information and bio-genetics industries. In the mid-1990s, world trade shares in the former sector were 21 per cent for Germany and 12 per cent for the USA; whereas, in the new industries, they were 14 per cent for Germany and 28 per cent for the USA (Lipp, 1997: 58). Two-thirds of global profits made in the electronics and data processing industries between 1989 and 1994 went to American corporations (van der Pijl, 1998: 60, Table 2.4). This sectoral transition in the USA has been accompanied by a rising share of money capital in the profit distribution process to 58 per cent of the total in 1990 (from 48 per cent in 1975, before declining again as neo-liberal industrial capital came into its own in the 1990s), whereas in (West) Germany, the share of money capital was only 30.9 per cent in 1975, 36 per cent in 1990, but was still increasing thereafter (ibid.: Table 2.5).

Taking European capital as a whole, orientations vary around this German pattern. We may distinguish here between firms with a strong, mobile capital base relative to productive engagement, which can exploit labour and/or compete at the world market level directly (and hence are inclined to take their place in the configuration of forces expressed by the neo-liberal concept of control) and firms relying more heavily on productive capital outlays, state support, regional cohesion, and other elements in the productive equations underpinning the corporate liberal concept. Elsewhere Otto Holman and I have compared European corporations in terms of straight world market, as well as active (export-competing) and passive (import-competing) regional European orientation (Holman and van der Pijl, 1996). Taking the top 15 rankings by assets and by employment as a cue (for 1992), I use these rankings to obtain an initial division into three categories, which for present purposes can be labelled: the Global (straight world market competitors); Euro-Global (internationally assertive from a secure European base); and Euro ('Fortress Europe') blocs of European capital (see Table 9.1). In case of double rankings, I have placed each firm according to its highest ranking.

The biggest firms in terms of assets are notably British firms, as can be seen in the left-hand column, 'Global capital'. German firms are concentrated in the central column, 'Euro-Global capital', while most French firms are in the 'Euro-capital' column. This differentiation would underpin the plausible assumption that, within Europe, corporate

Table 9.1   Three orientations in European capital, 1992
(15 largest companies in Europe ranked by assets and by employment)

Global capital (first 8, assets)	Euro-global capital (second 7, assets) (first 8, employment)		Euro-capital (second 7, employment)
Royal Dutch		Daimler-Benz	ABB Asea
Shell		Siemens	Alcatel Alstom
British Telecom	Hanson	Fiat	Gén des Eaux
Glaxo	Deutsche Bank	Unilever	Hoechst
BP	Elf Aquitaine	Philips	Bayer
Allianz	Guinness	Volkswagen	Peugeot
British Gas			
Nestlé			
		BAT Industries	

Source: adapted from Holman and van der Pijl (1996: 68, Table 3.4).

liberalism retains its main stronghold in France, neo-liberalism is strongest in Britain, while Germany is somewhere in between. While this is brought out fairly clearly in each country's economic policy, there is of course also a geopolitical aspect which modulates economic interests and influences different perceptions of such interests.

One channel through which company orientations become part of a wider class perspective is the international network of joint directorates. Such networks can be interpreted as a structure of communication and strategy formulation because the actual links are also usually made not by managers but by so-called network specialists, or 'big linkers' (Fennema, 1982: 208). It is they who also often participate in informal planning councils, such as the Bilderberg Conferences, the Trilateral Commission or the World Economic Forum. These, in turn, play a key role, as collective 'organic intellectuals' (see Chapter 1), in forging the consensus underpinning the comprehensive concept of control (cf. Gill, 1990: ch. 6). They do so not so much by secretly conspiring on strategies for world government, but by first of all understanding the trends in the development of the productive forces and discussing the real and potential challenges in the sphere of their profitable exploitation. Every late January one may read in the papers how, at the World Economic Forum's Davos meeting, economic statesmen discuss, say, genetic engineering, climate change and fashion trends in addition to the topics directly pertinent to stockholders' interests.

Taking the definition of Mattera (1992), the network of joint directorates of the 100 most global corporations broadly confirms the picture suggested in Table 9.1. Indeed, when drawing the connecting lines between corporations, one finds that only British and Swiss firms are part of the Atlantic core of the most densely connected corporations and banks. When one looks at the eight most central firms in the network, Unilever and Crédit Suisse Holding are the European firms closest to Citicorp, GM, AT&T, IBM, 3M and Hewlett-Packard of the USA. When one looks at clusters of firms connected by two or more joint directors and to the remaining firms connected by two or more joint directorates to the groups thus obtained, one similarly gets the impression that only Unilever and Royal Dutch Shell – in addition to the combination of Swiss firms around CS Holdings, Nestlé and Ciba-Geigy – are linked to the central US core (configured again around Citicorp). Other European firms listed by Mattera with two or more links (Deutsche Bank, Bayer, Daimler-Benz, Alcatel Alstom and FIAT) are not connected into the larger network at this level of multiplicity (van der Pijl, 1998: 61, Table 2.6, and 1999: 8, Diagram 1). The early 1990s pattern actually brings out a shift away from the situation prevailing during the 1970s, when German banks such as Deutsche and Dresdner, and firms such as Volkswagen, were still part of the core network (Fennema, 1982: 117, 191).

Let me now try and link the different European corporate profiles to government policies. The most straightforward articulation of a Euro-capital perspective into an overall strategy would then seem to have been represented by the Socialist-led government in France elected in 1981. The Socialists initially attempted to entrench a position within a defensive corporate liberalism, which soon proved impossible to sustain. The introduction of administrative import restrictions by the Mauroy government, to ward off the disruptive effect of Japanese imports on Keynesian demand management, ran into fierce opposition also from neo-liberal elements in the Socialist Party itself, organised in the Fondation Saint-Simon. This strategy was then given a second try at the European level when Jacques Delors, a cabinet member under Mauroy, was appointed to head the European Commission (Deppe, 1992: 64–6). But at that level the strategy had to adjust to a German alternative strategy which sought to articulate the perspective of Euro-Global capital.

Indeed, as Richard van der Wurff (1993) has shown in a seminal article, in West Germany there developed a tentative transformation towards a synthesis. This absorbed elements of the neo-liberal emphasis on the market, instead of state regulation, and the incorporation of a post-materialist ideology into a state-led reconfiguration of German export industries. This reconfiguration, while retaining high wage and high taxation levels, was aimed at orienting technological progress to new fields such as ecologically sustainable development. The harbingers of this new concept striving for hegemony were Oskar Lafontaine in the Social Democratic Party (SPD) and Lothar Späth in the Christian Democrat Union (CDU). The CDU had been helped to power when the leader of the smaller liberal party, Count Lambsdorff, switched sides in 1982 but, as with earlier shifts in policy, the ascendant concept animated the two big popular parties alike.

However, before this modernised and adaptive version of corporate liberalism could link up at the European Union (EU) level with its French counterpart under Delors, Franco–German alignment crystallised out of concern over the risks involved in the aggressive North Atlantic Treaty Organisation (NATO) posture driven by the Reagan administration. Far from inspiring an Atlanticist, neo-liberal fraction of the European ruling class, the Reagan offensive mainly caused concern in Europe because of its nativist-populist dynamic, its anchoring in the arms industry and independent finance, and its apparently disconnected status from the established centres of international capital. However, the demonstrative celebration between Chancellor Kohl and French President Mitterrand, in October 1982, of the 1963 Franco–German friendship treaty did not stop the unveiling of Reagan's Strategic Defence Initiative (SDI) a year later. SDI combined a deficit-financed, high-technology research programme which put European research and development (R&D) at a distance and led to a qualitative acceleration of the arms race which, more than anything else, served to demoralise the Soviet military and party-state leaderships (Garthoff, 1994: *passim*; Junne, 1985). When Gorbachev came to power in 1985 on a programme of renovating Soviet state socialism, which soon came to include giving up the arms race, different currents within the broader Atlantic ruling class were already at loggerheads over the issue of Soviet–Western co-operation. Conservatism in the West even allowed the new Soviet leadership to briefly capture the initiative, while the Atlantic divide now opened wide.

The Lafontaine/Späth concept taking shape in the later 1980s, and referred to above, did adapt to neo-liberalism in its labour market, trade and agricultural policies, but simultaneously included a new emphasis on European political unity in combination with East–West economic co-operation (van der Wurff, 1993: 180). In 1983, the European Round Table of Industrialists (ERT) actually constituted a forum set in the image of the American example (see also Chapter 4 above). The ERT initially set its sights on reinforcing the infrastructure of the European economy but it also displayed a tendency to shield the EU economy from foreign competition. When Delors assumed the presidency of the European Commission, the modernised corporate liberal strategy gained further cohesiveness. The Single European Act of 1986, aiming for 'Europe 1992', sought to restore European competitiveness by an active industrial policy rather than straight liberalisation, a strategy that temporarily united Euro-Global and Euro-capital (Holman, 1992).

While a number of mainly British firms walked out of the ERT in an obvious rejection of this policy from a perspective of 'global' capital (van Tulder and Junne, 1988: 215), the remaining ones, connected by the bank and finance capital structures, clearly began to converge on the European option, that of a 'Europeanisation of Eastern Europe'. This not only reinforced mutual links through, for example, the 1986 acquisition of the Libyan participation in FIAT by the Deutsche Bank and AEG by Daimler, to name one example, but the infrastructure for an independent West German/European defence industry also seemed to crystallise. This occurred when the Deutsche Bank group, the historic centre of autonomous, innovative German capital, succeeded in welding a number of defence-related companies into a single bloc while its rival, Atlanticist network centred around the Dresdner Bank failed to do so (*Newsweek*, 11 December 1989; *NRC Handelsblad*, 13 November 1985).

These developments were accompanied by various initiatives to exploit opportunities in Eastern Europe and the USSR created by *perestroika*, in which, again, the Deutsche Bank and its group companies such as Mannesmann were prominent (van der Pijl, 1997a). By thus reciprocating Gorbachev's theme 'Europe, our common Home' and the broad social democratic framework in which he envisaged an East–West rapprochement, West Germany, along with France and Italy, seemed well on the way to leading the EU to relative autonomy based on 'Euro-Global' capital and away from the Atlantic mainstream. This was seemingly in combination with a Europeanisation of Eastern Europe (which also, of course, entailed the promise of German reunification). The Lafontaine/Delors/Späth combination seemed to hold all the main options by providing political cohesion to this development, almost irrespective of electoral outcomes.

Resuming the American geopolitical offensive

In the course of 1989, spokesmen in the UK and the USA began voicing fear about a new 'Rapallo', the 1922 economic agreement between Weimar Germany and revolutionary Russia. Former State Department planner, Hugh de Santis, on the eve of the opening of the Berlin Wall, viewed the problem as one of a German locomotive heading for the East and possibly pulling Western Europe behind it. At a Bilderberg conference in May which brought together Atlantic statesmen, Anglo–American investment bankers, European politicians and the NATO commander in Europe, Timothy Garton Ash warned that there were 'profound differences of approach between the Ostpolitik of the Federal Republic of Germany, on the one hand, and the East European policy(ies) of the United States of America on the other', with the UK supporting the American position, Austria that of West Germany, and other states somewhere in between. Noting that in Germany itself there was talk of a 'Europeanisation of *Ostpolitik*', Ash proposed that, instead, the strategy should be one of 'Westernisation of *Ostpolitik*' to keep German ambitions in check, because 'Europeanisation can also mean de-Americanisation' (Ash, 1989: 5).

This straight juxtaposition of an Americanisation of Europe option versus the Europeanisation of Eastern Europe was not just confined to intellectual debate. The forces working for a European strategy at this juncture were certainly crippled when several of their key protagonists, such as Deutsche Bank head Herrhausen, the SPD candidate for Chancellor, Lafontaine, and the head of the privatisation trust for East Germany, Rohwedder, became the victims of terrorists (cf. Wisnewski, Landgraeber and Sieker, 1993: 236–8; on the attempt at Lafontaine's life, see Lafontaine, 1999: 23–7). At any rate, the Lafontaine/Delors/Späth concept was effectively beheaded (Späth was later removed by a scandal), leaving the forces supporting it without leadership at a crucial juncture.

In the meantime, the reunification of Germany also strengthened, on the one hand, centrifugal forces within Europe, as the Thatcher government as well as President Mitterrand were suspicious of the restoration of a more powerful Germany. On the other, neo-liberalism was strengthened as Germany, through a high-interest rate policy, tried to contain the inflationary effects of reunification. France therefore sought to gain a voice for the EU in monetary policy in order to steer clear of further deflationary interventions by the Bundesbank, which it obtained through the Maastricht Treaty for Economic and Monetary Union (EMU) in December 1991 (Lafontaine, 1999: 180). But the concept underlying the EMU project had already been reformulated towards neo-liberalism to such an extent that one author, in a perceptive article on the issue, uses the term 'compensatory neo-liberalism' to denote it (Ryner, 1998). This highlights the thin line still separating neo-liberalism in the EU from 'orthodox' neo-liberalism. Significantly, though, the dissenting British and Anglo–Dutch former member firms had re-joined the ERT (cf. Holman, 1992; and see Chapter 4 above).

At this stage, European countries as well as the USA seemed incapable of developing a coherent strategy in order to fill the void opening up in Eastern Europe as a result of the collapse of the Soviet bloc, the subsequent break-up of the USSR and the unfolding crisis in Yugoslavia. In the circumstances, it would seem that the option of Europeanisation would, in the absence of an active, overt American involvement, become a reality. The Bush administration was preoccupied with (nuclear) stability, even though it did assist the Yeltsin forces against the coup attempt of August 1991, which precipitated the disintegration of the USSR (Hersh, 1994: 84–6).

In fact, I would argue that at this point, 'national interests' (i.e., concerns in and of the individual European states) gave at best a semblance of Europeanisation. This, again, concerned Germany first. Apart from reunification, the theme of restoring a *Mitteleuropa* as the cultural heart of the sub-continent which it had been until 1914, inspired key social forces in Germany and the former Dual Monarchy, as well as the Vatican, to begin thinking again in terms of cultural spheres-of-influence that historically had been connected to either the Catholic Church or the Austro–Hungarian and German empires. Indeed the decision by a reunified Germany to precipitate the dissolution of Yugoslavia by recognising, ahead of the EU, the secessions of Slovenia (originally part of the Austrian half of the Dual Monarchy) and Croatia (formerly of the Hungarian half), was primarily driven by the *Mitteleuropa* mood whipped up in Catholic German-speaking society by the church and some parts of the media (notably, the *Frankfurter Allgemeine Zeitung*: see Woodward, 1995: 148–9).

This move was a departure from Atlantic as well as European consensus, which at this point was still largely committed to maintaining Yugoslav integrity in order to ensure the repayment of sovereign debt which, it was hoped, would be enabled by the re-imposition of capitalist discipline (Samary, 1995: 11). Certainly the disintegration of the Soviet bloc and the collapse of the USSR, which removed the threat of Soviet military support for the Yugoslav army, emboldened Western powers considerably (the German action would not have been possible otherwise). But even when full-scale fighting had erupted between Croatian forces and the Yugoslav army, the Serb leadership, for instance, could still hope that the USA, Britain and France, through the UN, would act to contain German involvement. The appointment of former US Secretary of State, Cyrus Vance, as UN emissary seemed to confirm these hopes (Woodward, 1995: 180).

The Americans in fact were active notably in Albania and Bulgaria, where they helped anti-Communist, liberal forces to win the elections, and also in Turkey, which occupied a pivotal position on three axes of Atlantic rivalry: the tottering USSR; Iraq and the Persian Gulf; and the Balkans. So, while Germany seemed to be moving in through the north-west, along with Austria and – in a covert role as an arms supplier – Hungary, all with the Vatican's blessing, the USA was cultivating Serbia's southern neighbours (Woodward, 1995: 159–60; cf. Gervasi, 1996).

Within Western Europe, centrifugal forces were operative as well. In addition to using their influence in the UN as a means to contain German ambitions, Britain and France also revived the idea of common European defence as a means to impose a modicum of control. In a way the original West European Union had served such a purpose in 1954–5. By mid-1991, France actually reactivated the idea of an independent European military force as an alternative to NATO. This plan, at the core of which was to be a Franco–German 'Eurocorps', met with 'immediate and unambiguous opposition' from the USA (Woodward, 1995: 174). The prior attempt at carving out a European sphere-of-influence, crippled of course by the removal of key players, would in this way have obtained the means of coercion that usually constitutes the ultimate ratio of world politics.

Yet the security vacuum that was opened up by the collapse of Soviet power would not in the longer run be filled by the Organisation for Security and Co-operation in Europe (OSCE, established by the 1975 Helsinki Agreements), which enshrined a commitment to preserve the status quo in Europe. Certainly the Carter administration had used humanitarian issues to give an offensive twist to the Agreements and, under Reagan, the post-war borders had openly been challenged as 'artificial' (US Department of State, 1984). But under Bush, the USA had become more cautious, prioritising oil and geopolitical interests in the Gulf. However, the establishment of the North Atlantic Co-operation Council, in November 1991, indicated that, as far as the USA was concerned, the OSCE was not the ticket on which they aspired to a European role.

The Clinton administration, taking over in January 1993, among other things expressed the rise of social forces committed to a more activist state role. First, Clinton relied on a segment of the investment bank community in Wall Street (Goldman Sachs, Lehman Bros, and others). Indeed Clinton had been subjected to what the *New York Times* later called a 'job interview' by future cabinet members Robert Rubin, Roger Altman, and other prominent investment bankers in June 1991. Also, Clinton was well groomed in the ascendant concept of neo-liberalism as a member of the Trilateral Commission (*International Herald Tribune*, 16 February 1999). The offensive foray of speculative money capital into 'emerging markets' would require, at some point, an activist foreign policy and security strategy. The other pole of ruling class support for Clinton, the telecommunications and computer industries and research-intensive export industries, were also dependent on an activist state (Ferguson, 1995: 291, 297–301).

As several of the initial policy initiatives of the new administration backfired (most notably, health reform), foreign policy became a focal point of attention. Thus 'reform' was projected abroad now that its achievement at home was obviously too divisive. In the background, the restructuring of the American arms industry also contributed to increasing a critical mass behind an offensive policy. In late 1993, the heads of the US strategic arms manufacturing sector were urged by the Defence Department to engage seriously in reorganising corporate assets. In a parallel move, the decision was taken to abandon caution and expand NATO into former Warsaw Pact territory. Geopolitically, expansion was based on the idea that Soviet collapse had opened a 'window of opportunity' that should not be left unused (Achcar, 1998). Through NATO, the USA after all could ensure that it retained a decisive voice in the shaping of the new, undivided Europe as well as even Russia and Central Asia.

However, there was also the need to provide the US defense industries, engaged in the process of rapid consolidation from 1994 onwards (Lockheed/Martin-Marietta, Boeing/Rockwell/McDonnell-Douglas, Raytheon/Hughes), with new markets. Consolidation in Europe was indeed seen as 'a formidable offensive operation, aimed at the development of a tool to conquer the rest of the world and, in the first place, European industry' (*Context Newsletter* 37, Jan./Feb. 2000: 4). In their merger movement, the strategic arms producers had to rely more strongly on Wall Street, cementing an offensive coalition between them and the investment bankers prominent in the Clinton administration. One of these, Assistant Secretary of State Richard Holbrooke (who was himself actively engaged in Eastern European ventures upon his move from Lehman Bros to Crédit Suisse First Boston), in early 1995, concluded that 'the West must expand to central Europe as fast as possible in fact as well as in spirit, and the United States is ready to lead the way'. NATO would be the 'central security pillar' of the new European architecture (Holbrooke, 1995: 42).

The third component of the capital fraction behind the turn to a geopolitical, 'Americanisation' strategy, in addition to the arms industry and the investment bankers, were the oil companies. While the president declared himself in favour of increased defence spending after the disastrous congressional election of 1994, he soon afterwards also began cultivating the leaderships of former Soviet republics such as Azerbaijan with their important oil reserves (Ferguson, 1996: 63).

After the re-election, the cautious Secretary of State, Warren Christopher, was replaced by Czech émigré Madeleine Albright, while Samuel Berger, former adviser of *Solidarnosč* and of the first non-Communist government in Poland, was appointed National Security Adviser. By that time, Holbrooke's diplomacy in former Yugoslavia had resulted in NATO air attacks on the Bosnian Serbs and the Dayton

Agreement of 1995. This agreement stabilised the Bosnian situation with the consent of Tudjman of Croatia, Izetbegovic of Bosnia, and Milosevic of rump-Yugoslavia.

The triumph of Americanisation

In Western Europe, meanwhile, the period coinciding with the second Clinton term in the USA was unexpectedly characterised by mounting social protest against the neo-liberal hollowing out of corporate liberal, welfare state capitalism. This was the platform of a mass movement in France that brought the country to a standstill in the winter of 1995–6 and ousted the Juppé government after Chirac had called an early election. This mood was not confined to France either. Even upon the election of the Blair 'New Labour' government in Britain in 1997, Samuel Brittan in the *Financial Times* of 3–4 May 1997 noted that, given the depth of the mood for change, 'Labour could have won the election on a much more anti-capitalist platform.' Blair, however, sought to normalise neo-liberal discipline instead, by strengthening its orientation towards Europe. Thus Lord Simon, prominent in the ERT and former head of BP (the major investor, with its US partner Amoco, in Azerbaijan's Caspian oil venture), received the portfolio to improve neo-liberal European 'competitiveness' (*Financial Times*, 24 March 1998, and 15–16 May 1999). Militarisation, rampant under Thatcher, was re-framed into a moral imperialism whilst retaining the same high defence budget (Edgerton, 1998).

However, the nominally leftward drift evolved into a potentially real challenge to Atlantic unity when, in 1998, after the general election in Germany, Gerhard Schröder, at the head of an SPD/Green government, replaced Chancellor Kohl. The resurrected Oskar Lafontaine also came to lead a reinforced Ministry of Finance and was committed to the 'compensatory neo-liberalism' which had survived the earlier, modernised corporate liberalism (Ryner, 1998; cf. van der Wurff, 1993). While the myth of the emerging markets was exploded during the Asian crisis and the crisis of Russian finances led to the suspension of foreign debt payments, the Lafontaine platform of working hours reduction, job creation in the depressed welfare sector, and a package directed at the young (proposed by the Jospin government at the European employment summit in Luxemburg in November 1997) seemed to herald a real shift away from neo-liberalism. Its industrial orientation more specifically transpired in the proposal for an intercontinental financial architecture with fixed exchange rates to be agreed between the USA, the EU and Japan to allow productive capital a longer time horizon and to crowd out speculative money capital.

Although the 'European' dimension at this stage centred on a Franco–German axis, the French Socialists were remarkably reticent as Lafontaine was bashed in the financial press and subjected to all kinds of abuse and ridicule. This was particularly notable in the British tabloids belonging to the Murdoch group which had supported the Blair candidacy. *The Sun* at one point dubbed Lafontaine 'the most dangerous man in Europe'. The earlier French defeat in the struggle over the presidency of the new European Central Bank is also relevant here. Now Lafontaine found himself confronted with the neo-liberal Dutch bank president, Duisenberg, who refused, with hardly concealed disdain, to follow Lafontaine's recommendation for lower interest rates in order to trigger new economic activity.

At this point, the USA once again imposed a solution in an area of on-going European discord. With NATO's 50-year anniversary coming up in April 1999, at the beginning of the year Secretary Albright was urged by the White House to solve the Kosovo crisis before the celebrations in order to reaffirm NATO as the prime 'European power' (E. Rouleau in *Le Monde diplomatique*, December 1999: 7). The continental European allies were then compelled to join the Kosovo operation in spite of the lack of a UN mandate. In both Germany and France, parliamentary procedures, cabinet-level rules and (in the German case) the constitution were violated to allow the military to take part in the war (Lafontaine, 1999: 242–5; E. Rouleau in *Le Monde diplomatique*, December 1999). The Rambouillet agreement, negotations over which had begun in January 1999, would have turned not only Kosovo but all of rump-Yugoslavia into a NATO protectorate (Kosovo Agreement, 1999). This would build on the US presence already established in Albania and Macedonia, and of course on NATO links with its allies, Turkey and Greece.

As Gilbert Achcar has shown, the US defence strategy, by 1997, had developed to the point where arms expenditures were tailored to provide for two 'theatre wars', one challenging Russia on its own periphery (e.g., in the Balkans or on the Black Sea) and one directed against China by also challenging it, say, in North Korea or over Taiwan or Tibet (Achcar, 1998: 104). In Europe, NATO expansion proceeded formally by including the new members Poland, the Czech Republic and Hungary, and informally by rallying to the Atlantic cause a series of Balkan states and Ukraine. This tends to widen the projected area of European integration to include states whose membership

would exacerbate migratory pressures already causing political problems in several states. The forming of a conservative/right-wing pop-
ulist government in Austria in February 2000 is one expression of this
and in this light one should also perhaps reflect on the active role of
President Clinton in encouraging the Euro–Turkish agreement on
future EU membership (*Financial Times*, 12 December 1999). Certainly
the NATO advance creates a US presence before any comparable
European one on the same level, effectively turning the USA into the
doorman for European dealings with Russia. As Peter Gowan (1999:
301) writes:

> for American policy planners, Poland is only one part of the neces-
> sary geopolitical wedge between Germany and Russia. In many
> ways, Ukraine is an even more important prize. A combined
> Polish–Ukrainian corridor under US leadership would decisively
> split 'Europe' from Russia, exclude Russia also from the Balkans, go a
> long way towards securing the Black Sea for the USA, link up with
> America's Turkish bastion, and provide a very important base for the
> 'Great Game', for the energy and mineral resources of the Caspian
> and the Asian Republics of the former USSR.

There still remained, though, especially after the Dayton Agreement
stabilised the Balkan situation, one key traffic link and political corridor which offered Germany and Austria a potential share in any 'Great
Game'. This was the Danube River and the recently opened Main–
Danube canal (near Regensburg), linking the Black Sea to the Rhine
and the North Sea. The mere prospect of this connection in the 1970s
led to intense debates about the possibility of Soviet penetration into
Europe's waterways (*Frankfurter Allgemeine Zeitung*, 30 June 1977). It
also influenced Germany's sudden reticence after its initial recognition
of Slovenia and Croatia. Any isolation of rump-Yugoslavia might jeop-
ardise the Balkan corridor and Danube link, which was vital to the
Austrian and German economies (Gervasi, 1996: 72; Woodward, 1995:
195–6).

Indeed, following Dayton and the lifting of the embargo against
Serbia, it was observed that all the littoral Danube states could once
again expect to profit from 'the growing importance of the Black Sea
region as a transit route for Russian gas and central Asian oil' (*Financial
Times*, 26 April 1996). However, in combination with the oil and gas
pipelines run by Gazprom, Bulgarian Topenergy and other regional
players, the old fear of Russian penetration revived. Indeed, as the

Financial Times noted in the same article, 'The danger in this is that Russia…could re-establish a stronghold in the Balkans. This could limit Bulgarian independence and cause nervousness among several NATO countries, not least Turkey.'

In the air war against Yugoslavia, launched in late March 1999, the bridges over the Danube at Novi Sad were among the targets hit. This resulted in interrupting the traffic of ores and minerals from Ukraine to the Austrian and central European metallurgical industry and the transport of wheat, amongst other things (*Financial Times*, 8 December 1999). Bombing targets during the war were set by NATO on the basis of US intelligence ('all but one', if we are to believe the *Financial Times*, 5–6 June 1999, the one supposedly being the Chinese embassy). Targets were then politically cleared by telephone with Atlantic leaders and foreign ministers, and of these the continental Europeans, notably the French President, Chirac, often resisted escalation. At one point France even threatened to not attend the NATO anniversary celebrations (*Washington Post*, 20 September 1999). The suspicion that the USA and Britain may have allowed geopolitical considerations of the sort referred to by Gowan (preventing a German/Russian economic link-up) to influence military action here also seems warranted. This is because Britain, at the time of writing, continues to block, 'on political grounds', the clearing of the debris of the three bombed bridges, for which the EU has reserved 25 million European currency units and which is strongly advocated by Germany and France (*Financial Times*, 8 December 1999).

On the positive side for Britain and the USA, on the other hand, was the establishment, at NATO's fiftieth anniversary celebration in Washington, of GUUAM, named after Georgia, Ukraine, Uzbekistan, Azerbaijan, and Moldova (adding Uzbekistan to the year-old link already established by the other four). Following prior joint Black Sea naval manoeuvres, including landings on the Ukrainian coast, the sponsors of GUUAM (Turkey, Britain and the USA) could thus provide security cover for these countries through which oil transport from the Caspian (but outside Russian or Iranian control) could pass (*Financial Times*, 6 May 1999; Reuters dispatch on www.russiatoday.com, 4 May 1999).

NATO was now manoeuvred into the position of defining the eastern limits of European integration, and hence of precluding a more restrained, 'supranational' expansion strategy. The latter could leave the complex redistributive and balancing mechanisms of the EU intact, yet the transnational forces committed to neo-liberalism effectively blocked the way of those social democrats who might have preferred to follow the path of 'compensatory neo-liberalism'. Also under the influence of incessant attacks from the Bonn Chancellery, Oskar Lafontaine, the key representative of this concept, had already resigned from all his functions before the war was launched. Lafontaine was strongly opposed to a NATO war that ignored the UN, but in his memoirs he specifically relates how the experience of the earlier assassination attempt came back to haunt him, as personal attacks became more vicious (Lafontaine, 1999).

The war did coincide with a mounting offensive to bring European governments in line with the neo-liberal, Americanisation option in its entirety. As the *Financial Times* ominously put it on 16 April 1999, 'the battle for European capitalism has begun in earnest', meaning the struggle between the 'Anglo–American model' based on the 'rules of risk and return' against a 'stakeholder capitalism which aims to balance the interests of employees, shareholders, suppliers and the wider community'. A week before, Assistant Secretary of the Treasury, Edwin Truman, according to the same newspaper (*Financial Times*, 7 April 1999), 'used the strongest language heard from the US administration' concerning lagging neo-liberal reforms which threatened to turn EMU into an industrial export bloc rather than a freely accessible part of the open world economy desired by global capital.

Within the EU, the responsiveness to neo-liberalism resulted in a manifest displacement of the earlier Franco–German axis previously embodied by Lafontaine and the Economics and Finance Minister, Strauss-Kahn (later removed by a financial scandal), in favour of a British–German one. Indeed, at the employment summit of the European Council in Cologne in June 1999, when the Kosovo war was in its final stages, the 'French' orientation – 'a co-ordinated employment strategy' – was safely sandwiched between a commitment to close co-ordination between wage policies and financial and monetary policy, on the one hand, and structural reforms to foster competitiveness and the operation of markets, on the other (Wolf and Dräger, 1999: 783–4). Four days later, on 8 June, with peace talks in progress thanks to the mediation of the Finnish President Ahtisaari acting for the EU, and Gazprom head Chernomyrdin, Chancellor Schröder, on the occasion of the impending elections for the European Parliament, co-signed a manifesto with Tony Blair (Jospin, although invited, refused to co-sign it). This manifesto redefined the goal of European Social Democracy as one of gaining the support of the 'new Centre' for a Social Democracy of the 'Third Way'. At least in rhetoric, this marked an overt turn to neo-liberalism for the German government.

However, as indicated above, the mandate of the European Social Democratic governments at least partly had its roots in the resistance to neo-liberal capitalist discipline and a resurgence of democratic aspirations after a long, often numbing, conservative period of government in several countries. It need not therefore come as a surprise that the ensuing elections for the European Parliament were not only a crushing defeat in terms of voter turnout, but also a defeat more particularly for the Social Democrats. As John Grahl (1999: 909) comments on this first of a longer line of electoral defeats for the Third Way Socialists, 'the leaders of New Labour and the SPD now got what they deserved – a Right majority in the European Parliament. National elections in the last few years had offered a real chance to give the European project a new direction. This chance was missed.'

This sums up how the democratic impulse of the 1995–6 social movements was sidelined along with the European option for Eastern Europe. While the conclusion of the war over Kosovo was certainly not a triumph as regards NATO's original terms, the EU and Russia – which eventually had to save NATO's face – were profoundly and negatively affected by the war having been waged and by the eastward shift of the co-ordinates of NATO jurisdiction and influence.

Note

1. I wish to thank Karin Waringo for detailed criticism of an earlier version of this chapter, notably for emphasising that the 'European option' never really materialised in the cases discussed. Of course she bears no responsibility for any remaining misinterpretations or errors.

Part V
Concluding Remarks

10
Conclusion: Thinking about Future European Social Relations

Andreas Bieler and Adam David Morton

In a lead article entitled 'European Revolution', Romano Prodi, President of the European Commission, recently declared:

> A consensus...is beginning to emerge on the shape of economic reform. Europe is no longer crudely divided between corporatists and free-marketeers, between the Anglo-Saxon or continental model, or between advocates and opponents of the welfare state. Few are any longer in denial over the need for tough structural reform (*The Guardian*, 21 March 2000).

The contributions to this book clearly contest this construction of European restructuring. The aim of the book was to develop a study of the politics of European integration and economic restructuring, 'understood as a body of practical rules and research and of detailed observations useful for awakening an interest in effective reality and for stimulating more rigorous and more vigorous political insights (Gramsci, 1971: 175–6). In line with Morton's argument in Chapter 2, it is argued that a series of related but diverse neo-Gramscian perspectives, rather than one 'correct' perspective or an '-ism', capture the processes of struggle between social forces that are constitutive of the 'New Europe'. All the perspectives, despite differences of emphasis, have concentrated on social forces as the main actors engendered by the production process. This makes it possible to overcome shortcomings evident in established integration theories, such as the inability to explain structural change or the problem of determinism. First of all, it becomes possible to incorporate the transnational restructuring of social relations, referred to in Chapter 1 as globalisation, in the explanation of instances of European integration. Second, a deterministic account is avoided because of the emphasis on the continuous struggle between social forces propagating different projects vying for hegemony. Hence the nature of European integration is understood as an open-ended process. Importantly, neo-Gramscian perspectives also include an analysis of the social purpose behind different historically specific stages of European integration. This questioning of existing structures and 'common sense' assumptions establishes neo-Gramscian perspectives as a 'critical theory'. It is therefore possible to analyse how European integration has developed, as well as discuss future possible scenarios and developments including the opportunities for resistance against dominant hegemonic projects. Whilst the future is necessarily indeterminate, attention is directed in this conclusion towards understanding shifts in power relations related to European integration. The method of understanding historical processes put forward by neo-Gramscian perspectives is suitably disposed to consider possible outcomes or alternative directions of historical change within the nascent order whilst thinking about the future (Cox, 1976/1996). In the next section, an assessment of the current situation in the EU is attempted, drawing on the contributions to this volume, before we investigate the potential for counter-hegemonic forces in the final section.

Neo-liberalism as a hegemonic project within the EU

In order to assess the current situation in the EU, we proceed in two steps: first, we assess which project is currently hegemonic and, second, we attempt to identify the social forces supporting it. Van der Pijl identifies two rival projects in Chapter 9. The European project is based on corporate liberalism and its structure of social protection, which was originally adopted from the USA in the wake of the Marshall Plan after the Second World War. It had a productive capital orientation with finance capital subordinated to the requirements of industrial capital and it was based on a class compromise. This provided trade unions with the opportunity to participate in decision making and it provided workers with access to mass consumption and a generous welfare state. If European integration followed this 'European option' it would take place within a supranational quasi-state, transferring a vast range of responsibilities and national sovereignty to central institutions. From the mid-1980s onwards, however, European integration proceeded along a path of neo-liberal Americanisation, based on a new hierarchy of social relations of production and capital accumulation. This new project has included an attack on trade unions and the welfare state and widened the discipline of capital by extending exploitation to all aspects of work and daily life, including the sphere of social reproduction. As a result, finance capital came to dominate over industrial capital. European integration, in this view, has been driven by a functionalist rationale concentrating on free trade and capital mobility combined with intergovernmental decision-making.

While van der Pijl's analysis provides a good first account of rival projects within European integration, van Apeldoorn's account in Chapter 4 allows us to further refine the picture. He distinguishes three different projects: first, a neo-liberal project that closely resembles van der Pijl's Americanisation drive. This concentrates on negative integration, emphasising market-led integration and a drastic reduction in state intervention. Such a project attempts to subordinate European integration to the 'beneficial' forces of globalisation. Then, second, a neo-mercantilist project is outlined. The loss of international competitiveness was considered to be less the result of labour market rigidity and extensive welfare states than the fragmentation of the European market. The establishment of the Internal Market, in combination with an active industrial policy by the EU, centred around European technology programmes and infrastructure projects, and also common tariff walls, supporting the position of European champion companies, was regarded as the best way forward in the mid-1980s. Finally, van Apeldoorn outlines a social democratic project for Europe. Pro-European social democrats, with the then President of the Commission Jacques Delors as their most prominent exponent, looked at the EU as a way of retaining and protecting a European model of society. This was based on a mixed economy and extensive social protection against the onslaught of the destructive forces of globalisation. The outcome of the struggle between these three rival projects was not simply a straightforward success for neo-liberalism, and neither was it a straightforward process of consensus formation, as Romano Prodi would indicate. Instead, it was a result of compromise and social struggle between all three rival projects, which van Apeldoorn labels 'embedded neo-liberalism'.

The content of this hegemonic project is clearly dominated by neo-liberalism and its emphasis on deregulation, flexibilisation and the free market. The concept of competitiveness can be regarded as the core of 'embedded neo-liberalism'. By incorporating some concepts of the other two rival projects, it promotes an expression of neo-liberalism in a way that neutralises opposition. It includes aspects of the neo-mercantilist project, in that it favours some degree of industrial policy at the European level to obtain the conditions for competitiveness, and it includes aspects of the social democratic project, in the form of the watered-down social chapter of the Maastricht Treaty, in order to achieve some degree of social consensus.

The increased degree of competition within the European Union (EU) due to the Internal Market and Economic and Monetary Union (EMU), according to Bieling in Chapter 5, has two main consequences. First, the single currency intensifies the pressure on trade unions towards further deregulation of industrial relations systems. Due to more visible and, therefore, comparable wage costs, national bargaining systems are more exposed to the dynamics of 'regime competition'. Second, EMU compels governments to adopt austerity budgets. They are forced to cut back the welfare state and other measures of social protection. At the same time, neo-liberalism is protected from any further demands by neo-mercantilist or social democratic forces. As Gill outlined in Chapter 3, the new constitutionalism of neo-liberalism, involving the construction of governance devices to insulate economic institutions from democratic accountability, has been established within the European monetary and economic field. By entrusting an independent European Central Bank (ECB) with monetary policies along neo-liberal lines, focusing on low inflation and price stability, these policies have been removed from political accountability and, thereby, future possible questioning. As Gill notes, however, the constitutionalising of neo-liberalism creates new obligations for the state and takes place through the state rather than simply bypassing the state. This is not only reflected in the World Bank's 1997 *World Development Report: The State in a Changing World*, advocating the need for a strong state, to which Gill refers; it is also evident, for example, in a recent International Monetary Fund (IMF) working paper stressing that, as globalisation will affect social protection offered by states, 'the power of the state to *effectively* and *efficiently* regulate private activities would need to be enhanced' (Tanzi, 2000: 20; original emphasis). Moreover, as Pellerin and Overbeek have pointed out in Chapter 7, the new neo-liberal regime of accumulation, even within the compromise of 'embedded neo-liberalism', also requires a specific management of mobility in relation to the supply of labour. The role of an EU framework on migration is not necessarily the prevention of immigration, as such, but the creation of a system of ordered mobility in accordance with the demands for labour in Europe. The state clearly still plays a role in these processes of constitutionalising neo-liberalism and controlling peoples' mobility.

The hegemonic project of 'embedded neo-liberalism' is supported by a highly complex alliance of different social forces, which together form a concrete historical bloc. Van Apeldoorn identifies, firstly, a globalist fraction of capital – sub-divided by van der Pijl into Global and Euro-Global fractions of capital – engendered by financial institutions and industrial players, which are integrated into global finance and production networks. Originally, such social forces had been opposed by a Europeanist fraction of capital, engendered by transnational production within Europe and mainly serving the European market, which supported a more neo-mercantilist project. Towards the end of the 1980s and early 1990s, the Europeanist fraction had lost ground. This was partly due to an ineffective European industrial policy and the unwillingness of core EU members to contemplate protectionism (e.g., Germany, the UK and the Netherlands). It was also partly due to the fact that companies within the Europeanist fraction had themselves become more globalist as a result of intensifying globalisation processes. The outcome of this struggle, so van Apeldoorn argues, was 'embedded neo-liberalism' with its dominant neo-liberal core, which is now supported by both the globalist and Europeanist fractions of capital. Importantly, however, for the success of this hegemonic project, significant fractions of labour, located mainly in the export-oriented sectors of different countries' production structures, also lent their support and formed part of this historical bloc.

Bieling has identified three main reasons why trade unions supported the Internal Market. First, it was accepted that intensified competition via liberalisation and deregulation within the EU would lead to economic benefits. The important issue for trade unions was, therefore, to ensure the 'just' distribution of these gains and to include social concerns within the Internal Market. In a way, this also indicated that labour had accepted, to some extent, the neo-liberal economic ideology. Second, the more optimistic fractions of labour even regarded the Internal Market as a first step towards political and eventual social union. Finally, it was Jacques Delors himself and his concern for social issues who helped to convince trade unions that neo-liberalism would not rule supreme within the Internal Market. Nevertheless, EMU proved to be more difficult for trade unions to accept. In the end, against the background of labour's weakness and the small but none the less real social measures of the Maastricht Treaty, many trade unions were convinced that support for European integration – in combination with backing from social democratic governments and the Commission – would be the only way of retaining some influence on policy-making within Europe. From the Commission's point of view, as well as that of business leaders, it was accepted that some social aspects and flexible forms of European regulation had to be adopted for a smoothly functioning accumulation regime. The result, again, was 'embedded neo-liberalism' which included some measures of the social democratic project. This process of assimilation thus resulted in an extremely attractive and powerful project which became the basis for expansion towards Central and Eastern Europe, including the new states of the former Soviet Union (see Chapters 8 and 9).

It would be incorrect to identify this particular bloc with Europe itself. While it concentrated its efforts on aspects of European integration, neo-liberal predominance and the lead set by transnational capital fractions indicates the close integration of these forces within the wider restructuring processes of globalisation. As argued by Gill in Chapter 3, the revival of European integration since the mid-1980s has reconciled regional integration with globalisation. The same transnational fractions of capital that are behind the current drive of European integration are part of a wider transnational historical bloc, working within high profile fora such as the G-7 meetings and including private organisations such as the Trilateral Commission and the European Round Table of Industrialists (ERT). It is this bloc which has generated the ideas, institutions and material capabilities for a global shift towards more neo-liberal forms of state and which crucially influenced the development of European integration in a way compatible with, not opposed to, globalisation.

Nevertheless, historical blocs are never static, but always fluid. Hegemony constantly needs to be reasserted and is open to contestation. Social forces from outside the historical bloc, but also from the margins within, may develop rival projects, challenging the hegemonic bloc and, in some instances, breaking it apart. In short, history is the result of constant struggle between social forces and is, therefore, constantly subject to change. European integration is no exception to this. Hence, while 'embedded neo-liberalism' is hegemonic at present, this does not imply that it will also be so in the future. Highlighting the possibility of change is the first step towards ensuring actual change. The second step is an analysis of the potential forces and projects behind a counter-hegemonic bloc.

Possibilities for a counter-hegemonic project

As indicated in Chapter 1, neo-Gramscian perspectives as a critical theory are also interested in social and political transformation. In this section, we will analyse the possibilities for a successful counter-hegemonic project immanent within the current configuration of social forces in Europe set against the background of globalisation.

Essentially there was a differentiation by Gramsci between counter-hegemonic strategies of resistance based on a 'war of manoeuvre' and a 'war of position'. Although these two extremes should not be regarded as mutually exclusive, the former could be effective where the administrative and coercive apparatus of the state was well developed but civil society was rather weak. Revolutionary upheaval targeted directly towards attaining state power would therefore reflect a war of manoeuvre analogous to the situation in Russia during the revolution led by Lenin and the Bolsheviks. Alternatively, the war of position involved a struggle on the cultural front of civil society, to ascertain the lines of least resistance, in an attempt to penetrate and subvert the mechanisms of ideological diffusion: 'In the East [i.e. Russia] the state was everything, civil society was primordial and gelatinous; in the West, there was a proper relation between state and civil society, and when the state trembled a sturdy structure of civil society was at once revealed' (Gramsci, 1971: 238). Hence a 'war of position' was required, 'which slowly builds up the strength of the social foundations of a new state' (Cox, 1983: 165). The high development of civil society and close links to the political state apparatus in Western European countries makes Gramsci's analysis about the impossibility of a 'war of movement' even more valid in today's context. A counter-hegemonic historical bloc must be prepared and established within civil society before any assault on the state can be successful. Importantly, this has to occur from the bottom up, since if it happens from the top down the hegemonic forces 'influence the development of [the] current version of civil society towards making it an agency for stabilising the social and political status quo' (Cox, 1999: 11).

The location for such a bottom-up strategy, however, is not exactly clear. Murphy, for example, speaks about an international civil society, which he identifies as public and private institutions such as governmental and non-governmental international organisations (Murphy, 1994: 14). This would indicate that a counter-hegemonic 'war of position' at the international level could be feasible. Germain and Kenny, however, point out that Gramsci's concept of civil society was closely linked to the state and, since there is no international state, there can be no international civil society (Germain and Kenny, 1998: 14–17). It is consequently correct to agree with Cox that 'the task of changing world order begins with the long laborious effort to build new historical blocs within national boundaries' (Cox, 1983: 174). Nevertheless, the EU can be perceived as an enduring structure of governance, a macro-region within the capitalist world economy with its specific, histori-cally-determined socio-economic and political structures, where supranational institutions such as the European Parliament and the Commission adopt similar roles to their counterparts within states, and complex policy-making processes link a host of interest groups to decision-making (van Apeldoorn, 1996: 19; Caporaso, 1996: 33; see also Chapter 8). As a result, the EU is increasingly considered to be a political system in its own right (e.g., Hix, 1994, 1999). A counter-hegemonic movement could, therefore, also be developed at the EU level from within European civil society.

In Chapter 5 Bieling noted that the current chances of overcoming neo-liberalism are slim, although this should not be read as an endorse-ment of the slogan of 'there is no alternative' (TINA). Yet rather than new patterns, supportive of a move away from the discipline of capital, a new synthesis has seemingly been established across different state–civil societies in Europe around the concept of a 'Third Way'. It is clearly open to question whether this reflects a rival orientation to the neo-liberal organisation of social relations or merely constitutes a mod-ernisation of capitalist social relations of production and the reconsti-tution of social cohesion rather than transformation. Therefore, despite trade union mobilisation against austerity in the mid-1990s (e.g., in France), and the victory of social democratic parties in Britain, France and Germany, the hegemonic project of 'embedded neo-liberalism' has been hardly challenged. To cite Perry Anderson (2000: 11), 'one might say that, by definition, TINA only acquires full force once an alterna-tive regime demonstrates that there truly are no alternative policies.' A recent exception was the short-lived opposition represented by Oskar Lafontaine and like-minded people in 1998 and early 1999 (see Chapter 9). To be successful, then, counter-hegemonic forces must go beyond flanking social policies. Attempting to mitigate the accepted policies of neo-liberalism will not prove successful.

Counter-hegemonic social forces must concentrate on core issues of macroeconomic policy in order to obtain tangible results. According to Bieling, a first step could be intensified co-operation between trade unions within Europe, including the sectoral level, with an emphasis on co-ordination in respect of wages, working conditions and social reg-ulation. This could be complemented by the much closer co-ordination of national economic and social policies, going beyond neo-liberal solutions. The convergence criteria could also be less tight, the revenue base of the EU could be enhanced and used for employment-creating measures, the approach to cuts in working time could be more flexible and social redistribution could be reversed away from profits and the interests of high income groups. In short, increased integration in economic policy based on a social purpose different from 'embedded neo-liberalism' could be regarded as a possible way forward. Moreover, Gill, partly following Alain Lipietz, has identified a strengthening of European social policy and a neo-Keynesian programme of European-wide co-ordinated expansion, combined with a promotion of job-sharing and uniform taxation of capital within the EU as a way forward in the short- to medium-term. Eventually, finance and money will need to be controlled and subordinated to democratic accountability, possibly through re-regulation at the European level. These suggestions most closely resemble the social democratic project, as identified by van Apeldoorn.

The supporting social forces would come mainly from trade unions, organised at the European level, and those social democratic parties which might return to their traditional policies. Also significant would be the participation of social movements that have a shared resentment against the logic of capitalist exploitation. This would include the variety of identity and social movements (ethnic, nationalist, religious, gender, environmental) that have a common material basis and thus a potentially wide social basis. In terms of labour, the accession to the EU by Austria and Sweden implied a strengthening of social forces which supported the social democratic project. As Bieler and Torjesen have outlined in Chapter 6, the fact that transnational Swedish and internationally-oriented Austrian (but also Norwegian) labour supported EU membership did not imply that these forces supported neo-liberalism; rather, they regarded the European level as a chance to regain some control over capital lost at the national level. As Bieling has rightly argued, European bargaining on economic issues is still not complete, which opens up the possibility for new struggles in new directions. Especially in times of economic recession, it will be important for these counter-forces to put forward a coherent strategy, capable of rivalling 'embedded neo-liberalism'. This issue is crucial because the collective will of a counter-hegemonic movement, that lacks an internal logic and social basis, could become dispersed and scattered into an infinity of individual wills or identities reduced to separate and conflicting paths (Gramsci, 1971: 128–9).

Hence, two notes of caution are necessary. The rationale of support by Austrian internationally-oriented and Swedish transnational labour for membership closely resembles the acceptance by trade unions of the Internal Market and EMU. They too regarded the neo-liberal revival of European integration as the best way of generating economic wealth and ended up stressing the distribution of these gains. In other words, they too accepted the neo-liberal economic logic to a large extent. Only once trade unions fundamentally question neo-liberalism and completely reject 'embedded neo-liberalism', and thus link up with more diverse social movements, can a true alternative be conceived. Severe economic recessions may become a catalyst in this respect. Second, the social democratic project tends to look back to the apparently golden first two, or three, post-Second World War decades in Europe, when trade unions participated in decision making and individual workers achieved significant material and non-material gains. To some extent, workers were protected against the adverse impact of market forces and labour was, thus, partially decommodified: that is, people's standard of living was sustained independently of the market. The social democratic project attempts to establish institutional power within the EU, which would allow the continuation of these policies at the European level. However, in this respect, Lacher has made two crucial observations. First, the partial decommodification of individual labour was only possible because general commodification as such was internationalised, drawing outlying regions of Europe into capitalist accumulation, and extended into the sphere of social reproduction including the exploitation of the environment. Second, the limits imposed by protective measures 'on the commodification of labour and money were undermined by the fact that they were limited by their failure to challenge the commodity form as such' (Lacher, 1999: 357). As a result, it was relatively easy for neo-liberalism to dismantle these protective measures of the post-Second World War Keynesian welfare state. The lesson is clear. For a successful challenge, a counter-hegemonic project cannot go back to the post-war situation. The social democratic option may not offer what its supporters expect.

In order to identify possible forces able and willing to challenge 'embedded neo-liberalism' more fundamentally, van der Pijl's distinction of three separate stages of capitalist exploitation is useful. First, 'original accumulation' imposes the commodity form on social relations. During the second stage, through increased control in the work place over production, the production process itself is subsumed under the power of capital. Finally, the sphere of social reproduction, consisting of human beings' daily life (as distinguished from work) and the environment, is subordinated to the requirements of capital accumulation (van der Pijl, 1998: 36–49). It is this third level of capitalist exploitation which has been particularly pushed forward by neo-liberalism in tandem with globalisation. Nevertheless, capitalist exploitation always leads to resistance. This exploitation of the sphere of reproduction may result in either a nationalist, reactionary response led by extreme-right parties such as the Austrian Freedom Party, or a progressive internationalist response as indicated in the programmes of Green parties and a broad array of social movements (Bieler, 2000: 159; van der Pijl, 1998: 47–8). Recent demonstrations during the 'Carnival Against Capitalism' (London, June 1999) as well as mobilisation against the World Trade Organisation (Seattle, November 1999) and the World Bank and International Monetary Fund (Washington, April 2000; Prague, September 2000) would indicate the latter. Across Europe, then, what is required is the formation of a counter-hegemonic project, which goes beyond the logic of growth and consumerism and includes an increased emphasis on the limits of growth; the need for redistribution; fair trade with the developing world; democratic participation in decision making at all levels; and an understanding of security which goes beyond a military rationale and includes issues of social justice and human rights, responsibility and democracy. Such a project could then provide a basis for new forms of political organisation from below, capable of challenging current social and power relationships within the EU as well the wider world order.

Bibliography

Achcar, G. (1998) 'The Strategic Triad: The United States, Russia and China', *New Left Review* (I), 228 (March–April): 91–127.

Agnew, J. and S. Corbridge (1995) *Mastering Space: Hegemony, Territory and International Political Economy* (London: Routledge).

AK (1989) *Europa Stellungnahme des Österreichischen Arbeiterkammertages* (Vienna: AK).

Albert, M. (1993) *Capitalism vs. Capitalism* (New York: Four Walls Eight Windows).

Altvater, E. and B. Mahnkopf (1993) *Gewerkschaften vor der europäischen Herausforderung. Tarifpolitik nach Mauer und Maastricht* (Münster: Westfälisches Dampfboot).

Anderson, P. (2000) 'Renewals', *New Left Review* (II), 1 (Jan.–Feb.): 5–24.

Andersson, T., T. Fredriksson and R. Svensson (1996) *Multinational Restructuring, Internationalisation and Small Economies: The Swedish Case* (London: Routledge).

van Apeldoorn, B. (1996) 'The Political Economy of Conflicting Capitalisms in the European Integration Process: A Transnational Perspective', *RIES Research Paper*, 31 (November).

—— (1997a) 'Transnationalisation and European Transformation: Contending Social Forces in the Construction of "Embedded Neoliberalism"', mimeo, Paper prepared for the workshop *Globalisation, Myth or Reality?*, 23 April (Robert Schuman Centre, European University Institute, Florence).

—— (1997b) 'Structure and Agency in the Construction of European Order: Gramscian Transnationalism as an Approach to the Study of European Integration', Paper prepared for the 22nd annual British International Studies Association conference, 15–17 December (Leeds).

—— (1998a) 'European Unemployment and Transnational Capitalist Class Strategy: The Rise of the Neoliberal Competitiveness Discourse', Paper prepared for the workshop *The Political Economy of European Unemployment*, 23–27 March, ECPR Joint Sessions of Workshops (University of Warwick).

—— (1998b) 'Transnationalisation and the Restructuring of Europe's Socio-Economic Order', *International Journal of Political Economy*, 28(1): 12–53.

—— (1999) 'Transnational Capitalism and the Struggle over European Order' (Unpublished PhD thesis, European University Institute).

—— (2000) 'Transnational Class Agency and European Governance: the Case of the European Round Table of Industrialists', *New Political Economy*, 5(2): 157–81.

Ash, T. G. (1989) 'Domestic Developments in Eastern Europe: Policy Implications for the West', *Thirty-Seventh Bilderberg Meeting*; Gran Hotel La Toja, Spain, (12–14 May).

Ashley, R. K. (1989) 'Living on Border Lines: Man, Poststructuralism and War', in J. Der Derian and M. Shapiro (eds) *International/Intertextual Relations: Postmodern Readings of World Politics* (Toronto: Lexington Books).

Augelli, E. and C. N. Murphy (1988) *America's Quest for Supremacy and the Third World: A Gramscian Analysis* (London: Pinter).
—— (1997) 'Consciousness, Myth and Collective Action: Gramsci, Sorel and the Ethical State', in S. Gill and J. H. Mittelman (eds) *Innovation and Transformation in International Studies* (Cambridge: Cambridge University Press).
Baker, A. (1999) '*Nébuleuse* and the "internationalisation of the state" in the UK? The Case of HM Treasury and the Bank of England', *Review of International Political Economy*, 6(1): 79–100.
Bellamy, R. (1987) *Modern Italian Social Theory: Ideology and Politics from Pareto to the Present* (Cambridge: Polity Press).
—— (1990) 'Gramsci, Croce and the Italian Political Tradition', *History of Political Thought*, 9(2): 313–37.
—— (1992) 'Gramsci for the Italians', *Times Literary Supplement*, 14 August: 5.
—— (1994) 'Introduction', in Antonio Gramsci, *Pre-Prison Writings*, trs. V. Cox (Cambridge: Cambridge University Press).
—— and D. Schecter (1993) *Gramsci and the Italian State* (Manchester: Manchester University Press).
Berglund, S. (1993) 'Las Migraciones en el Proceso de Integracion de las Americas Seminario Internacional', *International Migration Review*, 27(1): 182–90.
Bieler, A. (1996) 'Neo-Gramscian Approaches to IR Theory and the Role of Ideas: A Response to Open Marxism', mimeo, Paper prepared for the 21st annual British International Studies Association conference, 16–18 December (Durham).
—— (2000) *Globalisation and Enlargement of the EU: Austrian and Swedish Social Forces in the Struggle over Membership* (London: Routledge).
—— (2001) 'Questioning Cognitivism and Constructivism in IR Theory: Reflections on the Material Structure of Ideas', *Politics*, 21(2): 93–100.
Bieler, A. and A. D. Morton (2001) 'The Gordian Knot of Agency–Structure in International Relations: A Neo-Gramscian Perspective', *European Journal of International Relations*, 7(1): 5–35.
Bieling, Hans-Jürgen and F. Deppe (1999) 'Europäische Integration und industrielle Beziehungen – Zur Kritik des Konzeptes des "Wettbewerbskorporatismus"', in H. Schmitthenner and Hans-Jürgen Urban (eds) *Sozialstaat als Reformprojekt. Optionen für eine andere Politik* (Hamburg: VSA-Verlag).
Bilgin, P., K. Booth and R. W. Jones (1998) 'Security Studies: The Next Stage?', *Nação e Defesa*, 84: 131–57.
Birchfield, V. (1999) 'Contesting the Hegemony of Market Ideology: Gramsci's "Good Sense" and Polanyi's Double Movement', *Review of International Political Economy*, 6(1): 27–54.
Bonefeld, W., R. Gunn and K. Psychopedis (eds) (1992a) *Open Marxism: Dialectics and History* (London: Pluto Press).
—— (eds) (1992b) *Open Marxism: Theory and Practice* (London: Pluto Press).
Bonefeld, W., R. Gunn, J. Holloway and K. Psychopedis (eds) (1995) *Open Marxism: Emancipating Marx* (London: Pluto Press).
Booth, K. (1995) 'Human Wrongs and International Relations', *International Affairs*, 71(1): 103–26.
Boothman, D. (1995) 'General Introduction' in A. Gramsci, *Further Selections from the Prison Notebooks*, ed. and trs. Derek Boothman (London: Lawrence & Wishart).

Braunerhjelm, P., K. Ekholm, L. Grundberg and P. Karpaty (1996) 'Swedish Multinational Corporations: Recent Trends in Foreign Activities', *The Industrial Institute for Economic and Social Research: Working Paper 462.*

Breit, J. and D. Rössl, (1992) 'Internationalisierung der Klein- und Mittelbetriebe', in W. Clement (ed.) *Neue Entwicklungen – neue Formen – neue Herausforderungen. Internationalisierung Band VI* (Vienna: Signum Verlag).

Brochman, G. (1993) '"Fortress Europe": A European Immigration Regime in the Making?', in Sampol, 'Migration: The Politics of Contemporary Population Movements' mimeo, Papers prepared for the Sampol Conference, 1993 (Bergen, University of Bergen): 117–32.

Buci-Glucksmann, C. (1980) *Gramsci and the State*, trs. David Fernbach (London: Lawrence & Wishart).

Budapest Group (1993) *Budapest Conference to Prevent Uncontrolled Migration: Recommendations* (Budapest, February 1993).

—— (1998) *General Overview of the Implementation of the Recommendations of the Ministerial Conference on the Prevention of Illegal Migration*, held in Prague (October 1997). A report presented to the 6th Meeting of the Budapest Group in Warsaw (7–8 December 1998) (Oslo/Vienna: November).

Budapest Process (1999) *Overview of the Activities of the Budapest Process, 1991–1999* (December).

Bulmer, S. (1983) 'Domestic Politics and European Community Policy-Making', *Journal of Common Market Studies*, 21(4): 349–63.

Burawoy, M. (1976) 'The Functions and Reproduction of Migrant Labour: Comparative Material from Southern Africa and the United States', *American Journal of Sociology*, 81(5): 1050–87.

Burke, P. (1990) *The French Historical Revolution: The Annales School, 1929–1989* (Oxford: Basil Blackwell).

Burley, A.-M. and W. Mattli (1993) 'Europe Before the Court: A Political Theory of Legal Integration', *International Organisation*, 41(1): 41–76.

Burnham, P. (1991) 'Neo-Gramscian Hegemony and International Order', *Capital & Class*, 45 (Autumn): 73–93.

—— (1994) 'Open Marxism and Vulgar International Political Economy', *Review of International Political Economy*, 1(2): 221–31.

—— (1997) 'Globalisation: States, Markets and Class Relations', *Historical Materialism*, 1 (Autumn): 150–60.

—— (1999) 'The Politics of Economic Management in the 1990s', *New Political Economy*, 4(1): 37–54.

Busch, K. (1994) *Europäische Integration und Tarifpolitik: lohnpolitische Konsequenzen der Wirtschafts- und Währungsunion* (Cologne: Bund-Verlag).

Butt, P. A. (1994) 'European Union Immigration Policy: Phantom, Phantasy or Fact?', *West European Politics*, 17(2): 168–91.

Buttigieg, J. A. (1982) 'The Exemplary Worldliness of Antonio Gramsci's Literary Criticism', *Boundary 2*, 11(1–2): 21–39.

Van Buuren, J.(1999) 'Quand l'Union européenne s'entoure d'un cordon sanitaire', *Le Monde Diplomatique* (6–7 January).

Cafruny, A. W. (1990) 'A Gramscian Concept of Declining Hegemony: Stages of US Power and the Evolution of International Economic Relations', in D. P. Rapkin (ed.) *World Leadership and Hegemony* (Boulder, CO: Lynne Rienner).

Cameron, D. R. (1992) 'The 1992 Initiative: Causes and Consequences', in A. M. Sbragia (ed.) *Euro-Politics: Institutions and Policymaking in the "New" European Community* (Washington, DC: The Brookings Institute).

—— (1998) 'Creating Supranational Authority in Monetary and Exchange-Rate Policy: The Sources and Effects of EMU', in W. Sandholtz and A. Stone Sweet (eds) *European Integration and Supranational Governance* (Oxford: Oxford University Press).

Cammack, P. (1999) 'Interpreting ASEM: Interregionalism and the New Materialism', *Journal of the Asia Pacific Economy*, 4(1): 13–32.

Campbell, D. (1998) 'The Disciplinary Politics of Theorising Identity', in D. Campbell, *Writing Security: United States Foreign Policy and the Politics of Identity*, 2nd edn (Manchester: Manchester University Press).

Caporaso. J. (1996) 'The European Union and Forms of State: Westphalian, Regulatory or Post-Modern?', *Journal of Common Market Studies*, 34(1): 29–52.

Cappelen, A., J. Fagerberg, L. Mjøset and B. Sofus Tranøy (1994) 'Changing the model', in P. Anderson and P. Camiller (eds) *Mapping the West European Left* (London: Verso).

Church, C. H. and D. Phinnemore (1994) *European Union and European Community: A Handbook and Commentary on the Post-Maastricht Treaties* (London: Harvester Wheatsheaf).

Citizenship and Immigration Canada (1998a) *Citizenship and Immigration Canada: Permanent Residents. Country of Last Permanent Residence by Class;* various years.

—— (1998b) 'Conclusion of the 3rd Regional Conference on Migration', *News Release*, Ottawa (February).

Clark, I. (1999) *Globalisation and International Relations Theory* (Oxford: Oxford University Press).

Coates, D. (2000) *Models of Capitalism: Growth and Stagnation in the Modern Era* (Cambridge: Polity).

Cockfield, Lord A. (1990) 'The Real Significance of 1992', in C. Crouch and D. Marquand (eds) *The Politics of 1992. Beyond the Single European Market* (Oxford: Basil Blackwell).

Collinson, S. (1993) *Europe and International Migration* (London: RIIA/Pinter).

Cooper, R. (1994) 'Yes to European Monetary Unification, but no to the Maastricht Treaty', in A. Steinherr (ed.) *Thirty Years of European Monetary Integration* (London: Longman).

Cowles, M. Green (1994) 'The Politics of Big Business in the European Community: Setting the Agenda for a New Europe' (Unpublished PhD thesis, The American University).

—— (1995) 'Setting the Agenda for a New Europe: the ERT and EC 1992', *Journal of Common Market Studies*, 33(4): 501–26.

—— (1997) 'Organising Industrial Coalitions: A Challenge for the Future?', in H. Wallace and A. R. Young (eds) *Participation and Policy-Making in the European Union* (Oxford: Clarendon Press).

Cox, M. (1998) 'Rebels Without a Cause? Radical Theorists and the World System After the Cold War', *New Political Economy*, 3(3): 445–60.

Cox, R. W. (1976/1996) 'On Thinking About Future World Order' in R. W. Cox with T. J. Sinclair, *Approaches to World Order* (Cambridge: Cambridge University Press).

—— (1981) 'Social Forces, States and World Order: Beyond International Relations Theory', *Millennium*, 10(2): 126–55.

—— (1983) 'Gramsci, Hegemony, and International Relations: An Essay in Method', *Millennium*, 12(2): 162–75.

—— (1987) *Production, Power, and World Order: Social Forces in the Making of History* (New York: Columbia University Press).

—— (1992) 'Global *Perestroika*', in R. Miliband and L. Panitch (eds) *The Socialist Register: New World Order?* (London: Merlin Press).

—— (1992/1996) ' "Take Six Eggs": Theory, Finance and the Real Economy in the Work of Susan Strange', in R. W. Cox with T. J. Sinclair, *Approaches to World Order* (Cambridge: Cambridge University Press).

—— (1993) 'Structural Issues of Global Governance: Implications for Europe', in S. Gill (ed.) *Gramsci, Historical Materialism and International Relations* (Cambridge: Cambridge University Press).

—— (1995) 'Civilisations: Encounters and Transformations', *Studies in Political Economy*, 47: 7–31.

—— (1999) 'Civil Society at the Turn of the Millennium: Prospects for an Alternative World Order', *Review of International Studies*, 25(1): 3–28.

—— with T. J. Sinclair (1996) *Approaches to World Order* (Cambridge: Cambridge University Press).

Cressey, P. *et al.* (1998) 'Industrial Relations and Social Europe: A Review', in B. Towers and M. Terry (eds) *Industrial Relations Journal: European Annual Review 1997* (Oxford: Basil Blackwell).

Crouch, C. (1997) 'The Terms of the Neo-Liberal Consensus', *The Political Quarterly*, 68(4): 352–78.

—— and A. Menon (1997) 'Organised Interests and the State', in M. Rhodes, P. Heywood and V. Wright (eds) *Developments in West European Politics* (New York: St. Martin's Press).

Davidson, A. (1974), 'Gramsci and Lenin, 1917–1922', in R. Miliband and J. Saville (eds) *The Socialist Register: A Survey of Movements and Ideas* (London: Merlin Press).

Davies, M. (1999) *International Political Economy and Mass Communication in Chile: National Intellectuals and Transnational Hegemony* (London: Macmillan – now Palgrave).

Deblock, C. and D. Brunelle (1998) 'Les États-Unis et le Régionalisme économique dans les Amériques', *Études Internationales*, 29(2): 287–330.

Dekker, W. (1989) 'Europe's Economic Power – Potential and Perspectives', in Schweizerisches Institut für Auslandsforschung (ed.) *The European Challenge* (Grüsch: Verlag Rügger).

Delors, J. (1992) *Our Europe* (London: Verso).

Deppe, F. (1992) 'The Future of the European Community: A Power Perspective', *International Journal of Political Economy*, 22(1): 63–82.

Devuyst, Y. (1998) 'Treaty Reform in the EU: the Amsterdam Process', *Journal of European Public Policy*, 5(4): 615–31.

Dietz, T. (1999) 'Riding the AM-track through Europe; or, The Pitfalls of a Rationalist Journey Through European Integration', *Millennium*, 28(2): 355–69.

Dinan, D. (1994) *Ever Closer Union? An Introduction to the European Community* (London: Macmillan – now Palgrave).

Dølvik, J. E. (1998) *Norwegian Trade Unionism Between Traditionalism and Modernisation* (Oslo: Fafo).
—— (1999) *Die Spitze des Eisbergs? Der EGB und die Entwicklung eines Euro-Korporatismus* (Münster: Westfälisches Dampfboot).
—— and T. A. Stokke (1998) 'Norway: The Revival of Centralised Concertation' in Anthony Ferner and Richard Hyman (eds) *Changing Industrial Relations in Europe*, 2nd edn (Oxford: Basil Blackwell).
Dombroski, R. (1982–3) 'Antonio Gramsci and the Politics of Literature: A Critical Introduction', *Italian Quarterly*, 25(1–2): 41–55.
Dörre, K. (1999) 'Industrielle Beziehungen im Spannungsfeld von Globalisierung und europäischer Mehrebenen-Regulation', in W. Müller-Jentsch (ed.) *Konfliktpartnerschaft. Akteure und Institutionen der industriellen Beziehungen*, 3rd edn (Munich and Mering: Rainer Hampp Verlag).
Drainville, André (1994) 'International Political Economy in an Age of Open Marxism', *Review of International Political Economy*, 1(1): 105–32.
Dunne, T. (1998) *Inventing International Society: A History of the English School* (London: Macmillan – now Palgrave).
Dyson, K. (1999) 'Benign or Malevolent Leviathan? Social Democratic Governments in a Neo-Liberal Euro Area', *The Political Quarterly*, 70(2): 195–209.
Edgerton, D. (1998) 'Tony Blair's Warfare State', *New Left Review* (I), 230 (July–August): 123–30.
EFTA (1991) *EFTA Trade 1990* (Geneva: European Free Trade Area).
Esping-Andersen, G. (1990) *The Three Worlds of Welfare Capitalism* (Princeton, NJ: Princeton University Press).
Euromed Agreement (1995) *Euro-Mediterranean Agreement*, establishing an association between the European Communities and their Member States, of the one part, and the Republic of Tunisia, of the other part, *Official Journal*, L 132/98.
Europe Agreement (1994) *Europe Agreement*, establishing an association between the European Communities and their Member States, of the one part, and the Czech Republic, of the other part, *Official Journal*, L 360/94.
European Commission (1994) *Growth, Competitiveness, Employment: The Challenges and Ways Forward into the 21st Century. White Paper* (Luxemburg: Office for Official Publications of the European Communities).
—— (1995a) *White Paper: Preparation of the Associated Countries of Central and Eastern Europe for Integration into the Internal Market of the Union*, Com(95) 163 final, Brussels (3 May).
—— (1995b) *On the Practical Arrangements for the Introduction of the Single Currency*, Green Paper, Com (95) 333 (Brussels: European Commission).
—— (1996) *Benchmarking the Competitiveness of European Industry* (Brussels: Com (96) 436 final, 9 October).
—— (1997a) *Benchmarking: Implementation of an Instrument Available to Economic Actors and Public Authorities* (Brussels: Com (97) 153(2), 16 April).
—— (1997b) *Agenda 2000: For a Stronger and Wider Union*, Com(97) 2000 final, Brussels (15 July).
—— (1997c) *The Competitiveness of European Industry* (Luxemburg: Office for Official Publications of the European Communities).
European Roundtable of Industrialists (1983) 'Foundations for the Future of European Industry' (Memorandum to EC Commissioner Davignon, mimeo).

European Roundtable of Industrialists (1991) *Reshaping Europe: A Report from the European Round Table of Industrialists* (Brussels: European Round Table of Industrialists).

—— (1993a) *Beating the Crisis: A Charter for Europe's Industrial Future* (Brussels: European Round Table of Industrialists).

—— (1993b) *European Labour Markets: An Update on Perspectives and Requirements for Job Generation in the Second Half of the 1990s* (Brussels: European Round Table of Industrialists).

—— (1994) *European Competitiveness: The Way to Growth and Jobs* (Brussels: European Round Table of Industrialists).

—— (1996) *Benchmarking for Policy-Makers: The Way to Competitiveness, Growth and Job Creation* (Brussels: European Round Table of Industrialists).

—— (1997) *Message to all 15 EU Heads of State and Government* (Brussels: European Round Table of Industrialists).

—— (1999) *The East–West Win–Win Business Experience* (Brussels: European Round Table of Industrialists).

Eurostat (1997) *Demographic Statistics 1997* (Luxemburg).

—— (1999) 'EU Enlargement: Key Data on Candidate Countries', *Memo*, 10/99, 7 December.

Eyal, G., I. Szelényi and E. Townsley (1997) 'The Theory of Post-Communist Managerialism', *New Left Review* (I), 222 (March/April): 60–92.

Fagbladet (1994) *No.14* (Oslo: Landsorganisasjonen).

Falkner, G. (1998) *EU Social Policy in the 1990s: Towards a Corporatist Policy Community* (London: Routledge).

Favell, A. (1998) 'The Europeanisation of Immigration Politics', *European Integration online Papers* (EIop), 2(10): http://eipo.or.at/eiop/texte/1998.

Femia, J. V. (1981a) *Gramsci's Political Thought: Hegemony, Consciousness and the Revolutionary Process* (Oxford: Clarendon Press).

—— (1981b) 'An Historicist Critique of "Revisionist" Methods for Studying the History of Ideas', *History and Theory*, 20(2): 113–34.

—— (1998) *The Machiavellian Legacy: Essays in Italian Political Thought* (London: Macmillan – now Palgrave).

Fennema, M. (1982) *International Networks of Banks and Industry* (The Hague: Nijhoff).

Ferguson, T. (1995) *Golden Rule: The Investment Theory of Party Competition and the Logic of Money-Driven Political Systems* (Chicago: Chicago University Press).

—— (1996) 'Bill's Big Backers', *Mother Jones* (November/ December): 60–6.

Ferner, A. and R. Hyman (eds) (1998) *Changing Industrial Relations in Europe*. 2nd edn, (Oxford: Basil Blackwell).

FF (1994) *Uttalelse om Norsk Medlemskap i EU*, Møtereferat 22–4 November 1994.

Fischer, S. (1996) 'Maintaining Price Stability', *Finance and Development*, 33(4): 34–7.

FOCAL (1998) 'Labour Mobility, Workers' Rights and Labour Standards in Mercosur, NAFTA, the Caribbean and the FTAA', mimeo, Workshop organised by FOCAL (Ottawa, Canada).

Food Processing Trade Union (1988) 'Hintergrund: Die österreichische Nahrungsmittelindustrie und die europäische Gemeinschaft', *Der Lebensmittelarbeiter* 4.

Forgacs, D. (1989) 'Gramsci and Marxism in Britain', *New Left Review* (I), 176 (July–August): 70–88.

Frank, A. G. (1997) 'Orienting International Studies', *Millennium*, 26(2): 471–7.

Freeman, R. B. (1997) 'Are Norway's Solidaristic and Welfare State Policies Viable in the Modern Global Economy?', in J. E. Dølvik and A. H. Steen (eds) *Making Solidarity Work: The Norwegian Labour Market in Transition* (Oslo: Scandinavian University Press).

Frieden, J. (1998) 'The Euro: Who Wins? Who Loses?', *Foreign Policy*, 112 (Fall): 25–40.

Fritz Haug, W. (1999) 'Rethinking Gramsci's Philosophy of Praxis From One Century to the Next', *Boundary 2*, 26(2): 101–17.

Fröbel, F., J. Heinrichs and O. Kreye (1977) *Die neue internationale Arbeitsteilung. Strukturelle Arbeitslosigkeit in den Industrieländern und die Industrialisierung der Entwicklungsländer* (Hamburg: Rowohlt).

Gale, F. (1998) 'Cave "Cave! Hic dragones": A neo-Gramscian Deconstruction and Reconstruction of International Regime Theory', *Review of International Political Economy*, 5(2): 252–83.

Gamble, A. and A. Payne (eds) (1996) *Regionalism and World Order* (London: Macmillan – now Palgrave).

Gardner, J. N. (1991) *Effective Lobbying in the European Community* (Deventer: Kluwer).

Gareau, F. A. (1993) 'A Gramscian Analysis of Social Science Disciplines', *International Social Science Journal*, 45(136): 301–10.

Garthoff, R. (1994) *The Great Transition: American–Soviet Relations and the End of the Cold War* (Washington, DC: The Brookings Institute).

George, S. (1996) *Politics and Policy in the European Community*, 3rd edn (Oxford: Oxford University Press).

Germain, R. D. and M. Kenny (1998) 'Engaging Gramsci: International Relations Theory and the New Gramscians', *Review of International Studies*, 24(1): 3–21.

Gervasi, S. (1996) 'Waarom is de NAVO in Joegoslavia', in S. Flounders and S. Gervasi (eds) *De tragedie van Bosnia: De rol van de VS en de NAVO*, trs. W. Peters (Amsterdam: Global Reflexion).

Ghosh, B. (1997) *Gains from Global Linkages: Trade in Services and Movements of Persons* (New York: St Martin's Press).

Gill, S. (1990) *American Hegemony and the Trilateral Commission* (Cambridge: Cambridge University Press).

—— (1992) 'The Emerging World Order and European Change: The Political Economy of European Union', in R. Miliband and L. Panitch (eds) *The Socialist Register 1992: New World Order?* (London: Merlin).

—— (ed.) (1993) *Gramsci, Historical Materialism and International Relations* (Cambridge: Cambridge University Press).

—— (1994) 'Political Economy and Structural Change: Globalising Elites in the Emerging World Order', in Y. Sakamoto (ed.) *Global Transformation: Challenges to the State System* (Tokyo: United Nations University Press).

—— (1995a) 'Globalisation, Market Civilisation and Disciplinary Neoliberalism', *Millennium*, 24(3): 399–423.

Gill, S. (1995b) 'Theorising the Interregnum: The Double Movement and Global Politics in the 1990s', in B. Hette (ed.) *International Political Economy: Understanding Global Disorder* (London: Zed Books).

—— (1997) 'The Question Is ...', *Millennium*, 26(2): 483–5.

—— (1998) 'European Governance and New Constitutionalism: Economic and Monetary Union and Alternatives to Disciplinary Neoliberalism in Europe', *New Political Economy*, 3(1): 5–26.

—— and D. Law (1988) *The Global Political Economy: Perspectives, Problems and Policies* (Brighton: Wheatsheaf).

—— (1993) 'Global Hegemony and the Structural Power of Capital', in S. Gill (ed.) *Gramsci, Historical Materialism and International Relations* (Cambridge: Cambridge University Press).

Gill, S. and J. H. Mittelman (eds) (1997) *Innovation and Transformation in International Studies* (Cambridge: Cambridge University Press).

Gilpin, R. (1981) *War and Change in World Politics* (Cambridge: Cambridge University Press).

Gourevitch, P. (1986) *Politics in Hard Times* (Ithaca, NY: Cornell University Press).

Gowan, P. (1999) *The Global Gamble: Washington's Faustian Bid for World Dominance* (London: Verso).

Grahl, J. (1999) 'Aufholjagd im Rückwärtsgang', *Blätter für deutsche und internationale Politik*, 44(8): 907–10.

—— and P. Teague (1989) 'The Cost of Neo-Liberal Europe', *New Left Review* (I), 174 (March–April): 33–50.

—— (1990) *The Big Market: The Future of the European Community* (London: Lawrence & Wishart).

Gramsci, A. (1971) *Selections from the Prison Notebooks*, ed. and trs. Q. Hoare and G. Nowell-Smith (London: Lawrence & Wishart).

—— (1977) *Selections from Political Writings 1910–1920*, ed. Q. Hoare, trs. John Matthews (London: Lawrence & Wishart).

—— (1985) *Selections from Cultural Writings*, ed. D. Forgacs and G. Nowell-Smith, trs. William Boelhower (London: Lawrence & Wishart).

—— (1992) *Prison Notebooks*, Vol. 1, ed. and intro. J. A. Buttigieg, trs. J. A. Buttigieg and A. Callari (New York: Columbia University Press).

—— (1994c) *Letters from Prison*, Vol. 2, ed. F. Rosengarten, trs. R. Rosenthal (New York: Columbia University Press).

—— (1995) *Further Selections from the Prison Notebooks*, ed. and trs. D. Boothman (London: Lawrence & Wishart).

—— (1996), *Prison Notebooks*, Vol. 2, ed. and trs. J. A. Buttigieg (New York: Columbia University Press).

Grant, C. (1994) *Delors: Inside the House that Jacques Built* (London: Nicholas Brealey).

Greenwood, J. (1997) *Representing Interests in the European Union* (London: Macmillan – now Palgrave).

Grinspun, R. (1998) 'Regionalism and Neo-liberal Restructuring in Latin America', mimeo, Paper Prepared for the Workshop on Labour Mobility, Workers' Rights and Labour Standards in Mercosur, NAFTA, the Caribbean and the FTAA (Ottawa, Canada).

—— and M. A. Cameron (1993) *The Political Economy of North American Free Trade* (New York: St Martin's Press).

Gstöhl, S. (1996) 'The Nordic Countries and the European Economic Area (EEA)', in L. Miles (ed.) *The European Union and the Nordic Countries* (London: Routledge).

Haas, E. B. (1958) *The Uniting of Europe: Political, Social and Economic Forces, 1950–1957* (Stanford, CA: Stanford University Press).

Haas, P. M. (ed.) (1992) 'Knowledge, Power and International Policy Coordination', Special Issue of *International Organisation*, 46(1).

Hall, P. A. (ed.) (1987) 'European Labour in the 1980s', *International Journal of Political Economy*, 17(3).

Hall, S. (1986) 'Gramsci's Relevance for the Study of Race and Ethnicity', *Journal of Communication Inquiry*, 10(2): 5–27.

—— (1988a) *The Hard Road to Renewal: Thatcherism and the Crisis of the Left* (London: Verso).

—— (1988b) 'The Toad in the Garden: Thatcherism Among the Theorists', in C. Nelson and L. Grossberg (eds) *Marxism and the Interpretation of Culture* (Chicago: University of Illinois Press).

—— (1991) 'Introductory Essay: Reading Gramsci', in R. Simon, *Gramsci's Political Thought: An Introduction*. rev. edn (London: Lawrence & Wishart).

—— (1997) 'Culture and Power', interview with P. Osbourne, *Radical Philosophy*, 86 (November/December): 24–41.

Hamilton, K. A. (ed.) (1994) *Migration and the New Europe* (Washington, DC: Centre for Strategic and International Studies).

Hansen, S. Olav (1999) 'Utenlandske Direkte Investeringer i Norge til og med 1998', *Penger og Kreditt*, 4: 572–4.

Hanson, B. (1998) 'What Happened to Fortress Europe? External Trade Policy Liberalisation in the European Union', *International Organisation*, 52(1): 55–85.

Harris, J. (1992) *From Class Struggle to the Politics of Pleasure: The Effects of Gramscianism on Cultural Studies* (London: Routledge).

Harvey, D. (1985) 'The Geopolitics of Capitalism', in D. Gregory and J. Urry (eds) *Social Relations and Spatial Structures* (London: Macmillan – now Palgrave).

Hassel, A. (1998) 'Soziale Pakte in Europa', *Gewerkschaftliche Monatshefte*, 49(10): 626–38.

Helleiner, E. (1994) *States and the Reemergence of Global Finance: From Bretton Woods to the 1990s* (Ithaca, NY: Cornell University Press).

Hersh, S.M. (1994) 'The Wild East', *The Atlantic Monthly*, 273(6): 61–86.

Hettne, B. and A. Inotai (1994) *The New Regionalism: Implications for Global Development and International Security* (Helsinki: UNU World Institute for Development Economics Research).

Higgott, R. and S. Reich (1998) 'Globalisation and Sites of Conflict: Towards Definition and Taxonomy', *CSGR Working Paper*, 01/98.

High Level Group on Benchmarking (1999) 'First Report by the High Level Group on Benchmarking', *Benchmarking Paper*, 2 (European Commission, Directorate General III).

Hirst, P. and Thompson, G. (1996) *Globalisation in Question: The International Economy and the Possibilities of Governance* (Cambridge: Polity Press).

Hix, S. (1994) 'The Study of the European Community: The Challenge to Comparative Politics', *West European Politics*, 17(1): 1–30.

—— (1999) *The Political System of the European Union* (London: Macmillan – now Palgrave).

HK (1994) *Aarsberetningen 1994* (Oslo: Handel og Kontor i Norge).

Hoffman, S. (1966) 'Obstinate or Obsolete? The Fate of the Nation State and the Case of Western Europe', *Daedalus*, 95(3): 862–915.

—— and R. O. Keohane (1991) 'Institutional Change in Europe in the 1980s', in S. Hoffman and R. O. Keohane (eds) *The New European Community: Decision-making and Institutional Change* (Boulder, CO: Westview Press).

Holbrooke, R. (1995) 'America, A European Power', *Foreign Affairs*, 74(2): 38–51.

Holland, S. (1995) 'Squaring the Circle', *European Labour Forum*, Summer, 15: 12–23.

Holloway, J. and S. Picciotto (1977) 'Capital, Crisis and the State', *Capital and Class*, 2: 76–101.

Holman, O. (1992) 'Transnational Class Strategy and the New Europe', *International Journal of Political Economy*, 22(1): 3–22.

—— (1996) *Integrating Southern Europe: EC Expansion and the Transnationalisation of Spain* (London: Routledge).

—— (1997) 'De verborgen agenda: de Intergouvernementele Conferentie van 1996 en de oostwaartse uitbreiding van de Europese Unie', in O. Holman (ed.) *Europese dilemma's aan het einde van de twintigste eeuw. Democratie, Werkgelegenheid, Veiligheid, Immigratie* (Amsterdam: Het Spinhuis).

—— (1998) 'Integrating Eastern Europe: EU Expansion and the Double Transformation in Poland, the Czech Republic, and Hungary', *International Journal of Political Economy*, 28(2): 12–43.

—— (1999) *Neoliberale Restrukturiering, transnationale Wirtschaftsbeziehungen und die Erweiterung der EU nach Mittel- und Osteuropa* (Marburg: Forschungsgruppe Europäische Gemeinschaften, Arbeitspapiere No. 19).

—— (forthcoming) *Competitiveness, Convergence, Cohesion and European Integration* (Amsterdam: Amsterdam International Studies).

—— and K. van der Pijl (1996) 'The Capitalist Class in the European Union', in G. A. Kourvetaris and A. Moschonas (eds) *The Impact of European Integration: Political, Sociological and Economic Changes* (Westport, CT: Praeger).

——, H. Overbeek and M. Ryner (eds) (1998) 'Neoliberal Hegemony and the Political Economy of European Restructuring: Special Issue', *International Journal of Political Economy*, 28(1–2).

Holub, R. (1992) *Antonio Gramsci: Beyond Marxism and Postmodernism* (London: Routledge).

Huldt, B. (1994) 'Sweden and European Community-building 1945–1992', in S. Harden (ed.) *Neutral States and The European Community* (London: Brassey's).

Huysmans, J. (1998) 'Revisiting Copenhagen: Or, On the Creative Development of a Security Studies Agenda in Europe', *European Journal of International Relations*, 4(4): 479–505.

International Centre for Migration Policy Development (1998a) *Towards a Joint European Visa Regime: A Draft Report by the Secretariat of the Budapest Group for the Meeting in Portoroz (Slovenia)*, 17–18 September 1998 (Vienna).

—— (1998b) *Outline of a Draft Study on Linkages between Organised Crime and Trafficking in Aliens to be Prepared for the Budapest Group by the Secretariat*, 16 October 1998 (Vienna).

International Monetary Fund (1997) *World Economic Outlook 1997* (Washington, DC: IMF).

IOM, ECLAC (1998) 'Migration and Development in North and Central America: A Synthetic View', mimeo, Paper for the Seminar on Migration and Development organised by the Regional Conference on Migration (Mexico).

IOM News (1996) 'Emigration Dynamics in Mexico, Central America and the Caribbean', *IOM News 1996*: 2.

—— (1998) 'Migrant Rights Discussed in the Puebla Process', *IOM News 1998*, 12.

INS Statistics, United States Government Immigration and Naturalisation Services: *Statistics*, several years, online: http://www.ins.usdoj.gov/stats/annual.

Jacquemin, A. and D. Wright (1994) 'Corporate Strategies and European Challenges Post 1992', in S. Bulmer and A. Scott (eds) *Economic and Political Integration in Europe: Internal Dynamics and Global Context* (Oxford: Basil Blackwell).

James, G. (1996) *In the Public Interest* (London: Warner Books).

Jerneck, M. (1993) 'Sweden B – the Reluctant European?', in T. Tiilikainen and I.D. Petersen (eds) *The Nordic Countries and the EC* (Copenhagen: Copenhagen Political Studies Press).

Junne, G. (1985) 'Das Amerikanische Rüstungsprogramm: Ein Substitut für Industriepolitik', *Leviathan*, 13(1): 23–37.

Katzenstein, P. J. (1985) *Small States in World Markets: Industrial Policy in Europe* (Ithaca, NY: Cornell University Press).

Keohane, R. O. (1984) *After Hegemony: Cooperation and Discord in the World Political Economy* (Princeton, NJ: Princeton University Press).

Kosovo Agreement (1999) *Interim Agreement for Peace and Self-Government in Kosovo* (23 February 1999), www.monde-diplomatique.fr/dossiers.

Krause, A. (1991) *Inside the New Europe* (New York: Harper Collins).

Kurzer, P. (1993) *Business and Banking: Political Change and Economic Integration in Western Europe* (Ithaca, NY: Cornell University Press).

Lacher, H. (1999) 'Embedded Liberalism, Disembedded Markets: Reconceptualising the Pax Americana', *New Political Economy*, 4(3): 343–60.

Laclau, E. (1977) *Politics and Ideology in Marxist Theory: Capitalism, Fascism, Populism* (London: Verso).

Lafontaine, O. (1999) *Das Herz schlägt links* (Munich: Econ).

Lawner, L. (1979) 'Introduction', in A. Gramsci, *Letters from Prison* (London: Quartet Books).

Lee, K. (1995) 'A Neo-Gramscian Approach to International Organisation: An Expanded Analysis of Current Reforms to UN Development Agencies', in J. Macmillan and A. Linklater (eds) *Boundaries in Question: New Directions in International Relations* (London: Pinter).

Lehmbruch, G. and P. C. Schmitter (eds) (1982) *Patterns of Corporatist Policy-Making* (London: Sage).

Lindberg, L. N. (1963) *The Political Dynamics of European Economic Integration* (Stanford, CA: Stanford University Press).

Ling, L. H. M (1996) 'Hegemony and the Internationalising State: A Post-Colonial Analysis of China's Integration into Asian Corporatism', *Review of International Political Economy*, 3(1): 1–26.

Lipietz, A. (1996) 'Social Europe: The Post-Maastricht Challenge', *Review of International Political Economy*, 3(3): 369–79.

Lipp, E.-M. (1997) 'Auf dem Weg zur transatlantischen Wirtschaftsgemeinschaft', in W. Weidenfeld (ed.) *Partnerschaft gestalten: Die Zukunft der transatlantischen Beziehungen (Bellevue-Gespräche II)* (Gütersloh: Bertelsmann Stiftung).

LO-N (1994) *Referat fra den 4. Ekstraordinære Kongress 22 September 1994* (Oslo: Landsorganisasjonen).

LO-S (1994) *Trade Unions and the EC: The Trade Union Evaluation of the Membership Negotiations* (Stockholm: The Swedish Trade Union Confederation).

Luciani, L. (ed.) (1993) *Migration Policies in Europe and the United States* (The Hague: Kluwer).

Luif, P. (1994) 'Die Beitrittswerber: Grundlegendes zu den Verhandlungen der EFTA-Staaten um Mitgliedschaft bei der EG/EU', *Österreichische Zeitschrift für Politikwissenschaft*, 23(1): 21–36.

—— (1996) *On The Road To Brussels: The Political Dimension of Austria's, Finland's and Sweden's Accession to the European Union* (Vienna: Braumüller).

Majone, G. (1998) 'State, Market, and Regulatory Competition in the European Union: Lessons for the Integrating World Economy', in A. Moravcsik (ed.) *Centralisation or Fragmentation? Europe Facing the Challenges of Deepening, Diversity and Democracy* (New York: Council on Foreign Relations).

Marginson, P. and K. Sisson (1998) 'European Collective Bargaining: A Virtual Prospect', *Journal of Common Market Studies*, 36(4): 505–28.

—— 'The Structure of Transnational Capital in Europe: The Emerging Eurocompany and its Implications for Industrial Relations', in R. Hyman and A. Ferner (eds) *New Frontiers in European Industrial Relations* (Oxford: Basil Blackwell).

Marsh, D. and R. A. W. Rhodes (eds.) (1992) *Policy Networks in British Government* (Oxford: Clarendon Press).

Martin, A. (1996) *European Institutions and the Europeanisation of Trade Unions: Support or Seduction?*, Discussion and working papers 96.04.1 (Brussels: ETUC).

—— and G. Ross (eds) (1999) *The Brave New World of European Labour: European Trade Unions at the Millennium* (New York, Oxford: Berghan Books).

Martin, J. (1998) *Gramsci's Political Analysis: A Critical Introduction* (London: Macmillan – now Palgrave).

Marx, K. (1973) *Grundrisse*, trs. M. Nicholas (Harmondsworth: Penguin).

—— and F. Engels (1998) *The Communist Manifesto: A Modern Edition*, with an introduction by E. Hobsbawm (London: Verso).

Mattera, P. (1992) *World Class Business: A Guide to the 100 Most Powerful Global Corporations* (New York: Henry Holt).

May, C. (2000) *The New Enclosures: A Global Political Economy of IPRs* (London: Routledge).

McNamara, K. R. (1998) *The Currency of Ideas: Monetary Politics in the European Union* (Ithaca, NY: Cornell University Press).

Memorandum of European Economists (1997) *Full Employment, Social Cohesion and Equity for Europe: Alternatives to Competitive Austerity* (no place of publication given).

Merritt, G. (1986) 'Knights of the Roundtable: Can They Move Europe Forward Fast Enough?', *International Management*, 26 July: 22–6.

Milward, A. (1996) 'Approaching Reality: Euro-money and the Left', *New Left Review* (I), 216 (March–April): 55–65.

Mittelman, J. H. (1997) 'Decentring International Studies', *Millennium*, 26(2): 479–81.

—— (1998) 'Coxian Historicism as an Alternative Perspective in International Studies', *Alternatives*, 23(1): 63–92.

Moran, J. (1998) 'The Dynamics of Class Politics and National Economies in Globalisation: The Marginalisation of the Unacceptable', *Capital & Class*, 66 (Autumn): 53–83.

Moravcsik, A. (1991) 'Negotiating the Single European Act', in R. O. Keohane and Stanley Hoffman (eds) *The New European Community: Decision-Making and Institutional Change* (Boulder, CO: Westview Press).

—— (1993) 'Preferences and Power in the European Community: A Liberal Intergovernmentalist Approach', *Journal of Common Market Studies*, 31(4): 473–524.

—— (1995) 'Liberal Intergovernmentalism and Integration: A Rejoinder', *Journal of Common Market Studies*, 33(4): 611–28.

—— (1998) *The Choice for Europe: Social Purpose and State Power from Messina to Maastricht* (Ithaca, NY: Cornell University Press).

Morera, E. (1990) *Gramsci's Historicism: A Realist Interpretation* (London: Routledge).

Morton, A. D. (1999) 'On Gramsci', *Politics*, 19(1): 1–8.

—— (2000) 'Mexico in the Global Political Economy: Contesting the Construction of Hegemony' (Unpublished PhD thesis, University of Wales, Aberystwyth).

Mouffe, C. (ed.) (1979) *Gramsci and Marxist Theory* (London: Routledge & Kegan Paul).

Murphy, C. N. (1994) *International Organisation and Industrial Change* (Cambridge: Polity Press).

—— (1998) 'Understanding IR: Understanding Gramsci', *Review of International Studies*, 24(3): 417–25.

—— (1999) 'Inequality, Turmoil and Democracy: Global Political-economic Visions at the End of the Century', *New Political Economy*, 4(2): 289–304.

—— and R. Tooze (eds) (1991) *The New International Political Economy* (Boulder, CO: Lynne Rienner).

Mutimer, D. (1989) '1992 and the Political Integration of Europe: Neofunctionalism Reconsidered', *Journal of European Integration*, 13(1): 75–101.

Neuhold, H. (1992) 'Die dauernde Neutralität Österreichs in einem sich wandelnden internationalen System', in H. Neuhold and P. Luif (eds) *Das Aussenpolitische Bewusstsein Der Österreicher: Aktuelle internationale Probleme im Spiegel der Meinungsforschung* (Vienna: Braumüller).

Nield, K. and J. Seed (1981) 'Waiting for Gramsci', *Social History*, 6(2): 209–27.

Niessen, J. and F. Mochel (1999) *EU External Relations and International Migration* (Brussels: Migration Policy Group).

Nimni, E. (1994) *Marxism and Nationalism: Theoretical Origins of a Political Crisis* (London: Pluto, first published 1991).

NNN (1993) *Berretningen 19. Ordinære Landsmøte 1993* (Oslo: Norsk Nœrings- og Nytelsesmiddelarbiderforbund).

Nugent, N. (1999) *The Government and Politics of the European Union*, 4th edn (London: Macmillan – now Palgrave).

NUO (Noryes Offentliya Utradminyer) (1992) *En Nasjonal Strategi for Økt Sysselsetting i 1990-aarene* (Oslo: Statens Forvaltningstjeneste).

Obradovic, D. (1996) 'Policy Legitimacy and the European Union', *Journal of Common Market Studies*, 34(2): 191–221.

OECD (1996a) *Towards Multilateral Investment Rules* (Paris: OECD).
—— (1996b) *Multilateral Agreement on Investment: State of Play as of July 1996* (Paris: OECD).
—— (1999) *OECD Economic Surveys: Norway* (Paris: OECD).
SOPEMI (Système d'obervation permanente des migratias, internationales) (1996) *Trends in International Migration* (Paris: OECD).
—— (1998) *Trends in International Migration* (Paris: OECD).
—— (1999) *Trends in International Migration* (Paris: OECD).
ÖGB (1988) *Europa Memorandum (Dezember)* (Vienna: ÖGB).
—— (1991) 'ÖGB-Präsident Fritz Verzetnitsch: 'Enttäuscht vom EG-Gipfel', ÖGB-Pressedienst (12.12.1991)', in G. Kunnert (1992) *Spurensicherung auf dem österreichischen Weg nach Brüssel* (Vienna: Verlag der Österreichischen Staatsdruckerei).
ÖGB-Rednerdienst (1988) *'EG-EFTA: Österreichs Rolle in Europa'*, No. 3 (August).
Overbeek, H. (1990) *Global Capitalism and National Decline: The Thatcher Decade in Perspective* (London: Routledge).
—— (ed.) (1993) *Restructuring Hegemony in the Global Political Economy: The Rise of Transnational Liberalism in the 1980s* (London: Routledge).
—— (1998) 'Global Restructuring and Neo-liberal Labour-Market Regulation in Europe', *International Journal of Political Economy*, 28(1): 54–99.
—— (1999) 'The Budapest Process: Internationalisation of Migration Controls', mimeo, Paper Prepared for the 40th Annual Conference of the International Studies Association, 16–20 February (Washington, DC).
—— and K. van der Pijl (1993) 'Restructuring Capital and Restructuring Hegemony: Neo-liberalism and the Unmaking of the Post-War Order', in H. Overbeek (ed.) *Restructuring Hegemony in the Global Political Economy: The Rise of Transnational Liberalism in the 1980s* (London: Routledge).
Pakulski, J. and M. Waters (1996) *The Death of Class* (London: Sage).
Panitch, L. (1994) 'Globalisation and the State', in R. Miliband and L. Panitch (eds) *The Socialist Register 1994: Between Globalism and Nationalism* (London: Merlin Press).
Payne, A. (1996) 'The United States and its Enterprise for the Americas', in A. Gamble and A. Payne (eds) *Regionalism and World Order* (London: Macmillan – now Palgrave).
—— (1998) 'The New Political Economy of Area Studies', *Millennium*, 27(2): 253–73.
—— (2000) 'Rethinking United States-Caribbean Relations: Towards a New Mode of Trans-Territorial Governance', *Review of International Studies*, 26(1): 69–82.
Pearce, J. and J. Sutton (1986) *Protection and Industrial Policy in Europe* (London: Routledge).
Pellerin, H. (1999) 'The Cart Before the Horse? The Coordination of Migration Policies in the Americas and the Neo-liberal Economic Project of Integration', *Review of International Political Economy*, 6(4): 468–93.
Petras, J. (1991) 'The Retreat of the Intellectuals', *Socialism and Democracy*, 12: 43–81.
Pichl, C. (1989) 'Internationale Investitionen: Verflechtung der österreichischen Wirtschaft', *WIFO Monatsberichte*, 62(3): 161–75.
Pierson, P. (1998) 'Social Policy and European Integration', in A. Moravcsik (ed.) *Centralisation or Fragmentation? Europe Facing the Challenges of Deepening, Diversity and Democracy* (New York: Council on Foreign Relations).

van der Pijl, K. (1984) *The Making of an Atlantic Ruling Class* (London: Verso).
—— (1997a) 'Atlantic Rivalries and the Collapse of the USSR', in S. Gill (ed.) *Globalisation, Democratisation and Multilateralism* (London: Macmillan – now Palgrave).
van der Pijl, K. (1997b) 'Transnational Class Formation and State Forms', in Stephen Gill and J. H. Mittelman (eds) *Innovation and Transformation in International Studies* (Cambridge: Cambridge University Press).
—— (1998) *Transnational Classes and International Relations* (London: Routledge).
—— (1999) 'America Over Europe: Atlantic Unity and Rivalry From Gorbachev to Kosovo', mimeo, Paper prepared for the 24th Annual British International Studies Association Conference, 20–22 December (UMIST/Manchester).
Polanyi, K. (1957) *The Great Transformation: The Political and Economic Origins of Our Time* (Boston, MA: Beacon).
Poulantzas, N. (1974) *Les classes sociales dans le capitalisme aujourd'hui* (Paris: Le Seuil).
Puchala, D. (1972) 'Of Blind Men, Elephants and International Integration', *Journal of Common Market Studies*, 10(3): 267–84.
Putnam, R. D. (1988) 'Diplomacy and Domestic Politics: The Logic of Two-Level Games', *International Organisation*, 42(3): 427–60.
Radice, H. (1999) 'Taking Globalisation Seriously', in L. Panitch and C. Leys (eds) *The Socialist Register 1999: Global Capitalism versus Democracy* (London: Merlin Press).
RCM (1999) *Joint Communiqué*, 4th Regional Conference on Migration, January (San Salvador).
Rengger, N. and M. Hoffman (1996) 'Modernity, Postmodernism and International Relations', in J. Doherty, E. Graham and M. Malek (eds) *Postmodernism and the Social Sciences* (London: Macmillan – now Palgrave).
Rhodes, M. (1992) 'The Future of the "Social Dimension": Labour Market Regulation in Post-1992 Europe', *Journal of Common Market Studies*, 30(1): 23–51.
—— (1995) 'A Regulatory Conundrum: Industrial Relations and the Social Dimension', in S. Leibfried and P. Pierson (eds) *European Social Policy: Between Fragmentation and Integration* (Washington, DC: The Brookings Institute).
—— (1997) 'Globalisation, Labour Markets and Welfare States: A Future of "Competitive Corporatism"?', *EUI Working Papers*, Robert Schuman Centre 97(36).
—— (1998) 'Globalisation, Labour Markets, and Welfare States: A Future of "Competitive Corporatism"?', in M. Rhodes and Y. Mény (eds) *The Future of European Welfare: A New Social Contract?* (London: Macmillan – now Palgrave).
—— and B. van Apeldoorn (1997) 'Capitalism versus Capitalism in Western Europe', in M. Rhodes, P. Heywood and V. Wright (eds) *Developments in West European Politics* (New York: St Martin's Press).
Richardson, J. J. (ed.) (1996) *European Union: Power and Policy-Making* (London: Routledge).
Robinson, W. I. (1996) *Promoting Polyarchy: Globalisation, U.S. Intervention and Hegemony* (Cambridge: Cambridge University Press).
Rosamond, B. (1995) 'Mapping the European Condition: The Theory of Integration and the Integration of Theory', *European Journal of International Relations*, 1(3): 391–408.

Ross, G. (1995) *Jacques Delors and European Integration* (Cambridge: Polity Press).

Ruggie J. G. (1982) 'International Regimes, Transactions and Change: Embedded Liberalism in the Postwar Economic Order', *International Organisation*, 36(2): 379–416.

Ruggie J. G. (1993) 'Territoriality and Beyond: Problematising Modernity in International Relations', *International Organisation*, 47(1): 139–74.

Rupert, M. (1995) *Producing Hegemony: The Politics of Mass Production and American Global Power* (Cambridge: Cambridge University Press).

—— (1998) '(Re-)Engaging Gramsci: A Response to Germain and Kenny', *Review of International Studies*, 24(3): 427–34.

Ryner, M. (1998) 'Maastricht Convergence in the Social and Christian Democratic Heartland', *International Journal of Political Economy*, 28(2): 85–123.

—— (1999) 'Neoliberal Globalisation and the Crisis of Swedish Social Democracy', *Economic and Industrial Democracy*, 20(1): 39–79.

Sabatier, P. A. (1998) 'The Advocacy Coalition Framework: Revisions and Relevance for Europe', *Journal of European Public Policy*, 5(1), 98–130.

Said, E. W. (1978/1995) *Orientalism* (Harmondsworth: Penguin).

—— (1983a) 'Opponents, Audiences, Constituencies and Community', in W. J. T Mitchell (ed.) *The Politics of Interpretation* (Chicago, IL: University of Chicago Press).

—— (1983b) *The World, the Text and the Critic* (London: Faber & Faber).

—— (1985) 'Orientalism Reconsidered', *Race & Class*, 27(2): 1–15.

—— (1990) 'American Intellectuals and Middle East Politics', in B. Robbins (ed.) *Intellectuals, Aesthetics, Politics, Academics* (Minneapolis, MN: University of Minnesota Press).

—— (1993) *Culture and Imperialism* (London: Vintage).

—— (1994) *Representations of the Intellectual: The 1993 Reith Lectures* (London: Vintage).

—— (1997) *Covering Islam: How the Media and the Experts Determine How We See the Rest of the World* (London: Vintage).

Samary, C. (1995) *Yugoslavia Dismembered* (New York: Monthly Review Press).

Sampol (1993) *Sam.pol. konferansen 1993: 'Migration: The Politics of Contemporary Population Movements'* (Bergen/Norway: University of Bergen).

Sandholtz, W. (1993) 'Choosing Union: Monetary Politics and Maastricht', *International Organisation*, 47(1): 1–39.

—— and A. Stone Sweet (eds) (1998) *European Integration and Supranational Governance* (Oxford: Oxford University Press).

—— and J. Zysman (1989) '1992: Recasting the European Bargain', *World Politics*, 17(1): 95–128.

Sassen, S. (1996) *Transnational Economies and National Migration Policies* (Amsterdam: Institute for Migration and Ethnic Studies).

Sassoon, D. (1996) *One Hundred Years of Socialism: The West European Left in the Twentieth Century* (New York: The New Press).

Sbragia, A. M. (ed.) (1992) *Euro-Politics: Institutions and Policymaking in the "New" European Community* (Washington, DC: The Brookings Institute).

Schaller, C. (1994) 'Die innenpolitische EG-Diskussion seit den 80er Jahren', in A. Pelinka, C. Schaller and P. Luif (eds) *Ausweg EG? Innenpolitische Motive einer aussenpolitischen Umorientierung* (Vienna, Cologne/Graz: Böhlau Verlag).

Scharpf, F. W. (1999) *Regieren in Europa: Effektiv und demokratisch?* (Frankfurt, New York: Campus).

Schulten, T. (1996) *'European Works Councils'* – *New Forms of European Labour Relations Regulation?'*, Working Paper, No. 14 (Marburg: Forschungsgruppe Europäische Gemeinschaften).

—— and R. Bispinck (eds) (1999) *Tarifpolitik unter dem EURO: Perspektiven einer europäischen Koordinierung: das Beispiel Metallindustrie* (Hamburg: VSA-Verlag).

van Selm-Thorburn, J. (1998) 'Asylum in the Amsterdam Treaty: A Harmonious Future?', *Journal of Ethnic and Migration Studies*, 24(4): 627–38.

Showstack Sassoon, A. (1987) *Gramsci's Politics*, 2nd edn (Minneapolis: University of Minnesota Press).

—— (1990) 'Gramsci's Subversion of the Language of Politics', *Rethinking Marxism*, 3(1): 14–25.

—— (1995) 'Family, Civil Society, and the State: The Actuality of Gramsci's Notion of *"Società Civile"'*, *Dialektik*, 3: 67–82.

Siegel, D. (1992) 'Die Bedeutung österreichischer multinationaler Konzerne für die Internationalisierung', in W. Clement (ed.) *Neue Entwicklungen – neue Formen – neue Herausforderungen. Internationalisierung Band VI* (Vienna: Signum Verlag).

Simai, M. (1998a) 'Transnational Corporations in Central and Eastern Europe and in the Former Soviet Union: A Return or a New Beginning?', in R. Kozul-Wright and R. Rowthorn (eds) *Transnational Corporations and the Global Economy* (London: Macmillan – now Palgrave).

—— (1998b) 'Experiences with Foreign Direct Investment in Eastern Europe', *Eastern European Economics*, 36(3): 28–48.

Simmons, B. A. (1999) 'The Internationalisation of Capital' in H. Kitschelt *et al.* (eds) *Continuity and Change in Contemporary Capitalism* (Cambridge: Cambridge University Press).

Sklair, L. (1997) 'Social Movements for Global Capitalism: The Transnational Capitalist Class in Action', *Review of International Political Economy*, 4(3): 514–38.

Smith, H. (1996) 'The Silence of the Academics: International Social Theory, Historical Materialism and Political Values', *Review of International Studies*, 22(2): 191–212.

Smith, S. (1995) 'The Canadian–Italian School of International Relations', *Mershon International Studies Review*, 39(1): 162–6.

—— (1996) 'Positivism and Beyond', in S. Smith, K. Booth and M. Zalewski (eds) *International Theory: Positivism and Beyond* (Cambridge: Cambridge University Press).

SSB (1998) *Statistisk Aarbok* (Oslo: Statistisk Sentralbyraa).

—— (1999a) *Najonalregnskapet* (Oslo: Statistisk Sentralbyraa).

—— (1999b) *Statistisk Aarbok* (Oslo: Statistisk Sentralbyraa).

Stevis, D. and T. Boswell (1998) 'International Labour Politics under the North American Agreement for Labour Cooperation: Comparisons to the European Union', mimeo, Paper Prepared for the International Studies Association Convention, 17–21 March (Minneapolis).

Stienstra, D. (1994) *Women's Movements and International Organisations* (London: Macmillan – now Palgrave).

Strange, S. (1984) 'What About International Relations?', in S. Strange (ed.) *Paths to International Political Economy* (London: George, Allen & Unwin).

—— (1994) *States And Markets*, 2nd edn (London: Pinter).

—— *The Retreat of the State: The Diffusion of Power in the World Economy* (Cambridge: Cambridge University Press).

Streeck, W. (1995a) 'From Market-Making to State Building? Reflections on the Political Economy of European Social Policy', in S. Leibfried and P. Pierson (eds) *European Social Policy: Between Fragmentation and Integration* (Washington, DC: The Brookings Institute).

Streeck, W. (1995b) 'Neo-voluntarism: A New European Social Policy Regime?', *European Law Journal*, 1(1): 31–59.

—— (1998) *The Internationalisation of Industrial Relations in Europe: Prospects and Problems*. MPIFG Working Paper 98/2 (Cologne).

—— and P. Schmitter (1991) 'From National Corporatism to Transnational Pluralism: Organised Interests in the Single European Market', *Politics and Society*, 19(2): 133–64.

Sun, Jeanne-May and J. Pelkmans (1995) 'Regulatory Competition in the Single Market', *Journal of Common Market Studies*, 33(1): 67–89.

Swedenborg, B. (1979) *The Multinational Operations of Swedish Firms: An Analysis of Determinants and Effects* (Stockholm: Industriens Utredningsinstitut).

Swenson, P. (1991a) 'Bringing Capital Back In, or Social Democracy Reconsidered: Employer Power, Cross-Class Alliances and Centralisation of Industrial Relations in Denmark and Sweden', *World Politics*, 43(4): 513–44.

—— (1991b) 'Labor and the Limits of the Welfare State: The Politics of Intraclass Conflict and Cross-Class Alliances in Sweden and West Germany', *Comparative Politics*, 23(4): 379–99.

Tálos, E. (1996) 'Corporatism – The Austrian Model', in V. Lauber (ed.) *Contemporary Austrian Politics* (Boulder, CO: Westview Press).

Tanzi, V. (2000) 'Globalisation and the Future of Social Protection', IMF Working Paper, WP/00/12.

TCO (1993) *A Trade Union Policy for Europe* (Stockholm: TCO).

—— (1994) *TCO's Assessment of the EU Agreement* (Stockholm: TCO).

Teague, P. (1999) *Economic Citizenship in the European Union: Employment Relations in the New Europe* (London: Routledge).

The Swedish Institute (1994) *Labour Relations in Sweden: Fact Sheets on Sweden (FS 3 t Oha)* (Stockholm: The Swedish Institute).

Thompson, J. E. (1992) 'Explaining the Regulation of Transnational Practices: A State-Building Approach', in J. N. Rosenau and E.-O. Czempiel (eds) *Governance without Government: Order and Change in World Politics* (Cambridge: Cambridge University Press).

Thränhardt, D. (ed.) (1992) *Europe, A New Immigration Continent: Policies and Politics in Comparative Perspective* (Münster: Lit Verlag).

Tranholm-Mikkelsen, J. (1991) 'Neo-functionalism: Obstinate or Obsolete? A Reappraisal in the Light of the New Dynamism of the EC', *Millennium*, 20(1): 1–22.

Traxler, F. (1991) Gewerkschaften und Unternehmerverbände in Österreichs politischem System', in H. Dachs *et al.* (eds) *Handbuch des Politischen Systems Österreichs* (Vienna: Manz).

Tsoukalis, L. (1997) 'Economic and Monetary Union: The Primacy of High Politics', in H. Wallace and W. Wallace (eds) *Policy-Making in the European Union*, 3rd edn (Oxford: Oxford University Press).

UNCTAD (1992) *World Investment Report 1992: Transnational Corporations as Engines of Growth* (Geneva: UN).

—— (1997) *World Investment Report 1997: Transnational Corporations, Market Structure and Competition Policy* (Geneva: UN).

—— (1998) *World Investment Report 1998: Trends and Determinants* (Geneva: UN).

UNDP (1996) *Human Development Report 1996* (Oxford: Oxford University Press).

US Department of State (1984) 'Secretary Shultz: Building Confidence in Europe' (Washington, 17 January).

Van Tulder, R. and G. Junne (1988) *European Multinationals in Core Technologies* (New York: Wiley).

Venturini, P. (1989) *Ein europäischer Sozialraum für 1992* (Brussels and Luxemburg: Amt für amtliche Veröffentlichungen der Europäischen Gemeinschaften).

Vico, G. (1744/1984) *The New Science of Giambattista Vico*, trs. from the 3rd edn with the addition of 'Practic of the New Science', by T. Goddard Bergin and M. Harold Fisch (Ithaca, NY: Cornell University Press).

Vogler, H. (1991) 'Zukunft der Sozialpartnerschaft im Binnenmarkt aus der Sicht der Arbeitnehmer', in H. Kienzl (ed.) *Österreichs Wirtschafts- und Währungspolitik auf dem Weg nach Europa. Festschrift für Maria Schaumayer* (Vienna: Österreichische Nationalbank).

Wallace, H. and A. R. Young (1997) 'The Single Market: A New Approach to Policy', in H. Wallace and W. Wallace (eds) *Policy-Making in the European Union*, 3rd edn (Oxford: Oxford University Press).

Waltz, K. N. (1979) *Theory of International Politics* (Reading, MA: Addison-Wesley).

Whitworth, S. (1994) *Feminism and International Relations: Towards a Political Economy of Gender in Interstate and Non-Governmental Institutions* (London: Macmillan – now Palgrave).

Williams, R. (1977) *Marxism and Literature* (Oxford: Oxford University Press).

Wincott, D. (1995) 'Institutional Interaction and European Integration: Towards an Everyday Critique of Liberal Intergovernmentalism', *Journal of Common Market Studies*, 33(4): 597–609.

Wisnewski, G., W. Landgraeber and E. Sieker (1993) *Das RAF-Phantom: Wozu Politik und Wirtschaft Terroristen brauchen* (Munich: Knaur).

Wolf, F. O. and Dräger, K. (1999) 'Beschäftigungsglamour', *Blätter für Deutsche und Internationale Politik*, 44(7): 782–6.

Woods, N. (1995) 'Economic Ideas and International Relations: Beyond Rational Neglect', *International Studies Quarterly*, 39(2): 161–80.

Woodward, S. L. (1995) *Balkan Tragedy: Chaos and Dissolution After the Cold War* (Washington, DC: The Brookings Institute).

World Bank (1997), *World Bank Development Report: The State in a Changing World* (Washington, DC: World Bank).

Wright, E. Olin (1996) 'The Continuing Relevance of Class Analysis – Comments', *Theory and Society*, 25: 693–716.

van der Wurff, R. (1993) 'Neo-Liberalism in Germany? The "Wende" in Perspective', in H. Overbeek (ed.) *Restructuring Hegemony in the Global Political Economy: The Rise of Transnational Neo-Liberalism in the 1980s* (London: Routledge).

Wyatt-Walter, A. (1998) 'Globalisation, Corporate Identity and European Technology Policy', in W. D. Coleman and G. R. D. Underhill (eds) *Regionalism and Global Economic Integration: Europe, Asia and the Americas* (London: Routledge).

Zalewski, M. (1996) '"All these theories yet the bodies keep piling up": Theory, Theorists, Theorising', in S. Smith, K. Booth and M. Zalewski (eds) *International Theory: Positivism and Beyond* (Cambridge: Cambridge University Press).

Zimmerman, W. (1981) 'Soviet-East European Relations in the 1980s and the Changing International System', in M. Bornstein, Z. Gitelman and W. Zimmerman (eds) *East–West Relations and the Future of Eastern Europe: Politics and Economics* (London: Allen & Unwin).

Zolberg, A. R. (1993) 'Are the Industrial Countries under Siege?', in L. Luciani (ed.) *Migration Policies in Europe and the United States* (The Hague: Kluwer).

Zourek, H. (1989) 'Der EG-Beitritt aus der Sicht der Arbeitnehmervertretungen', in H. Glatz and H. Moser (eds) *Herausforderung Binnenmarkt: Kopfüber in die EG?* (Vienna: Service).

Index